The Last Journals of David Livingstone

in Central Africa, from 1865 to His Death, Volume II (of 2), 1869-1873
Continued By A Narrative Of His Last Moments And Sufferings,
Obtained From His Faithful Servants Chuma And Susi

David Livingstone
Editor: Horace Waller

Contents

CHAPTER I. 7
CHAPTER II. 32
CHAPTER III. 53
CHAPTER IV. 73
CHAPTER V. 94
CHAPTER VI. 116
CHAPTER VII. 138
CHAPTER VIII. 165
CHAPTER IX. 182
CHAPTER X. 196
CHAPTER XI. 218
CHAPTER XII. 240
CHAPTER XIII. 256

THE LAST JOURNALS OF DAVID LIVINGSTONE

IN CENTRAL AFRICA, FROM 1865 TO HIS DEATH

VOLUME II (OF 2), 1869-1873 CONTINUED BY A

NARRATIVE OF HIS LAST MOMENTS AND SUFFERINGS,

OBTAINED FROM HIS FAITHFUL SERVANTS CHUMA

AND SUSI

BY

David Livingstone

Editor: Horace Waller

CHAPTER I.

Bad beginning of the new year. Dangerous illness. Kindness of Arabs. Complete helplessness. Arrive at Tanganyika. The Doctor is conveyed in canoes. Kasanga Islet. Cochin-China fowls. Beaches Ujiji. Receives some stores. Plundering hands. Slow recovery. Writes despatches. Refusal of Arabs to take letters. Thani bin Suellim. A den of slavers. Puzzling current in Lake Tanganyika. Letters sent off at last. Contemplates visiting the Manyuema. Arab depredations. Starts for new explorations in Manyuema, 12th July, 1869. Voyage on the Lake. Kabogo East. Crosses Tanganyika. Evil effects of last illness. Elephant hunter's superstition. Dugumbe. The Lualaba reaches the Manyuema. Sons of Moenekuss. Sokos first heard of. Manyuema customs. Illness.

[The new year opened badly enough, and from letters he wrote subsequently concerning the illness which now attacked him, we gather that it left evils behind, from which he never quite recovered. The following entries were made after he regained sufficient strength, but we see how short they necessarily were, and what labour it was to make the jottings which relate to his progress towards the western shore of Lake Tanganyika. He was not able at any time during this seizure to continue the minute maps of the country in his pocket-books, which for the first time fail here.]

1st January, 1869. --I have been wet times without number, but the wetting of yesterday was once too often: I felt very ill, but fearing that the Lofuko might flood, I resolved to cross it. Cold up to the waist, which made me worse, but I went on for 2-1/2 hours E.

3rd January, 1869. --I marched one hour, but found I was too ill to go further. Moving is always good in fever; now I had a pain in the chest, and rust of iron sputa:

my lungs, my strongest part, were thus affected. We crossed a rill and built sheds, but I lost count of the days of the week and month after this. Very ill all over.

About 7th January, 1869. --Cannot walk: Pneumonia of right lung, and I cough all day and all night: sputa rust of iron and bloody: distressing weakness. Ideas flow through the mind with great rapidity and vividness, in groups of twos and threes: if I look at any piece of wood, the bark seems covered over with figures and faces of men, and they remain, though I look away and turn to the same spot again. I saw myself lying dead in the way to Ujiji, and all the letters I expected there useless. When I think of my children and friends, the lines ring through my head perpetually:

> *"I shall look into your faces,*
> *And listen to what you say,*
> *And be often very near you*
> *When you think I'm far away."*

Mohamad Bogharib came up, and I have got a cupper, who cupped my chest.

8th and 9th January, 1869. --Mohamad Bogharib offered to carry me. I am so weak I can scarcely speak. We are in Marungu proper now--a pretty but steeply-undulating country. This is the first time in my life I have been carried in illness, but I cannot raise myself to the sitting posture. No food except a little gruel. Great distress in coughing all night long; feet swelled and sore. I am carried four hours each day on a kitanda or frame, like a cot; carried eight hours one day. Then sleep in a deep ravine. Next day six hours, over volcanic tufa; very rough. We seem near the brim of Tanganyika. Sixteen days of illness. May be 23rd of January; it is 5th of lunar month. Country very undulating; it is perpetually up and down. Soil red, and rich knolls of every size and form. Trees few. Erythrinas abound; so do elephants. Carried eight hours yesterday to a chief's village. Small sharp thorns hurt the men's feet, and so does the roughness of the ground. Though there is so much slope, water does not run quickly off Marungu. A compact mountain-range flanks the undulating country through which we passed, and may stop the water flowing. Mohamad Bogharib is very kind to me in my extreme weakness; but carriage is painful; head down and feet up alternates with feet down and head up; jolted up and down and sideways--changing shoulders involves a toss from one side to the other of the kitanda. The sun is vertical, blistering any part of the skin exposed, and I try to shelter my face and head as well as I can with a bunch of leaves, but it is dreadfully fatiguing in my weakness.

I had a severe relapse after a very hot day. Mohamad gave me medicines; one was a sharp purgative, the others intended for the cure of the cough.

14th February, 1869. --Arrived at Tanganyika. Parra is the name of the land at the confluence of the River Lofuko: Syde bin Habib had two or three large canoes at this place, our beads were nearly done, so I sent to Syde to say that all the Arabs had served me except himself. Thani bin Suellim by his letter was anxious to send a canoe as soon as I reached the Lake, and the only service I wanted of Syde was to inform Thani, by one of his canoes, that I was here very ill, and if I did not get to Ujiji to get proper food and medicine I should die. Thani would send a canoe as soon as he knew of my arrival I was sure: he replied that he too would serve me: and sent some flour and two fowls: he would come in two days and see what he could do as to canoes.

15th February, 1869. --The cough and chest pain diminished, and I feel thankful; my body is greatly emaciated. Syde came to-day, and is favourable to sending me up to Ujiji. Thanks to the Great Father in Heaven.

24th February, 1869. --We had remarkably little rain these two months.

25th February, 1869. --I extracted twenty **Funyes**, an insect like a maggot, whose eggs had been inserted on my having been put into an old house infested by them; as they enlarge they stir about and impart a stinging sensation; if disturbed, the head is drawn in a little. When a poultice is put on they seem obliged to come out possibly from want of air: they can be pressed out, but the large pimple in which they live is painful; they were chiefly in my limbs.

26th February, 1869. --Embark, and sleep at Katonga after seven hours' paddling.

27th February, 1869. --Went 1-3/4 hour to Bondo or Thembwe to buy food. Shore very rough, like shores near Caprera, but here all is covered with vegetation. We were to cross to Kabogo, a large mass of mountains on the eastern side, but the wind was too high.

28th February, 1869. --Syde sent food back to his slaves.

2nd March, 1869. --Waves still high, so we got off only on ***3rd*** at 1h. 30m. A.M. 6-1/2 hours, and came to M. Bogharib, who cooked bountifully.

6th March, 1869. --5 P.M. Off to Toloka Bay--three hours; left at 6 A.M., and came, in four hours, to Uguha, which is on the west side of Tanganyika.

7th March, 1869. --Left at 6 P.M., and went on till two canoes ran on rocks in the way to Kasanga islet. Rounded a point of land, and made for Kasanga with a storm in our teeth; fourteen hours in all. We were received by a young Arab Muscat, who dined us sumptuously at noon: there are seventeen islets in the Kasanga group.

8th March, 1869. --On Kasanga islet. Cochin-China fowls[1] and Muscovy ducks appear, and plenty of a small milkless breed of goats. Tanganyika has many deep bays running in four or five miles; they are choked up with aquatic vegetation, through which canoes can scarcely be propelled. When the bay has a small rivulet at its head, the water in the bay is decidedly brackish, though the rivulet be fresh, it made the Zanzibar people remark on the Lake water, "It is like that we get near the sea-shore--a little salt;" but as soon as we get out of the shut-in bay or lagoon into the Lake proper the water is quite sweet, and shows that a current flows through the middle of the Lake lengthways.

Patience was never more needed than now: I am near Ujiji, but the slaves who paddle are tired, and no wonder; they keep up a roaring song all through their work, night and day. I expect to get medicine, food, and milk at Ujiji, but dawdle and do nothing. I have a good appetite, and sleep well; these are the favourable symptoms; but am dreadfully thin, bowels irregular, and I have no medicine. Sputa increases; hope to hold out to Ujiji. Cough worse. Hope to go to-morrow.

9th March, 1869. --The Whydah birds have at present light breasts and dark necks. Zahor is the name of our young Arab host.

11th March, 1869. --Go over to Kibize islet, 1-1/2 hour from Kasanga. Great care is taken not to encounter foul weather; we go a little way, then wait for fair

---

1 On showing Chuma and Susi some immense Cochin-China fowls at a poultry show, they said that they were not larger than those which they saw when with Dr. Livingstone on these islands. Muscovy ducks abound throughout Central Africa.--ED.

wind in crossing to east side of Lake.

12th March, 1869. --People of Kibize dress like those in Rua, with cloth made of the Muabe or wild-date leaves; the same is used in Madagascar for the "lamba."[2] Their hair is collected up to the top of the head.

From Kibize islet to Kabogo River on east side of Lake ten hours; sleep there. Syde slipped past us at night, but we made up to him in four hours next morning.

13th March, 1869. --At Rombole; we sleep, then on.

[At last he reached the great Arab settlement at Ujiji, on the eastern shore of Tanganyika. It was his first visit, but he had arranged that supplies should be forwarded thither by caravans bound inland from Zanzibar. Most unfortunately his goods were made away with in all directions--not only on this, but on several other occasions. The disappointment to a man shattered in health, and craving for letters and stores, must have been severe indeed.]

14th March, 1869. --Go past Malagarasi River, and reach Ujiji in 3-1/2 hours. Found Haji Thani's agent in charge of my remaining goods. Medicines, wine, and cheese had been left at Unyanyembe, thirteen days east of this. Milk not to be had, as the cows had not calved, but a present of Assam tea from Mr. Black, the Inspector of the Peninsular and Oriental Company's affairs, had come from Calcutta, besides my own coffee and a little sugar. I bought butter; two large pots are sold for two fathoms of blue calico, and four-year-old flour, with which we made bread. I found great benefit from the tea and coffee, and still more from flannel to the skin.

15th March, 1869. --Took account of all the goods left by the plunderer; sixty-two out of eighty pieces of cloth (each of twenty-four yards) were stolen, and most of my best beads. The road to Unyembe[3] is blocked up by a Mazitu or Watuta war, so I must wait till the Governor there gets an opportunity to send them. The Musa sent with the buffaloes is a genuine specimen of the ill-conditioned, English-hating Arab. I was accosted on arriving by, "You must give me five dollars a month for all my time;" this though he had brought nothing--the buffaloes all died--and did nothing but receive stolen goods. I tried to make use of him to go a mile every second day for milk, but he shammed sickness so often on that day I had to get

---

2 The natural dress of the Malagash.
3 The same as Unyanyembe, the half-way settlement on the great caravan road from the coast to the interior.

another to go; then he made a regular practice of coming into my house, watching what my two attendants were doing, and going about the village with distorted statements against them.

I clothed him, but he tried to make bad blood between the respectable Arab who supplied me with milk and myself, telling him that I abused him, and then he would come back, saying that he abused me! I can account for his conduct only by attributing it to that which we call ill-conditioned: I had to expel him from the house.

I repaired a house to keep out the rain, and on the **23rd** moved into it. I gave our Kasanga host a cloth and blanket; he is ill of pneumonia of both lungs.

28th March, 1869.--Flannel to the skin and tea very beneficial in the cure of my disease; my cough has ceased, and I walk half a mile. I am writing letters for home.

8th April, 1869.--Visited Moene Mokaia, who sent me two fowls and rice; gave him two cloths. He added a sheep.

13th April, 1869.--Employed Suleyman to write notes to Governor of Unyembe, Syde bin Salem Burashid, to make inquiries about the theft of my goods, as I meant to apply to Syed Majid, and wished to speak truly about his man Musa bin Salum, the chief depredator.

Wrote also to Thani for boat and crew to go down Tanganyika.

Syde bin Habib refused to allow his men to carry my letters to the coast; as he suspected that I would write about his doings in Rua.

27th April, 1869.--Syde had three canoes smashed in coming up past Thembwe; the wind and waves drove them on the rocks, and two were totally destroyed: they are heavy unmanageable craft, and at the mercy of any storm if they cannot get into a shut bay, behind the reeds and aquatic vegetation. One of the wrecks is said to have been worth 200 dollars (40 *l*).

The season called Masika commenced this month with the usual rolling thunder, and more rain than in the month preceding.

I have been busy writing letters home, and finished forty-two, which in some measure will make up for my long silence. The Ujijians are unwilling to carry my letters, because, they say, Seyed Majid will order the bearer to return with others:

he may say, "You know where he is, go back to him," but I suspect they fear my exposure of their ways more than anything else[4].

16th May, 1869. --Thani bin Suellim sent me a note yesterday to say that he would be here in two days, or say three; he seems the most active of the Ujijians, and I trust will help me to get a canoe and men.

The malachite at Katanga is loosened by fire, then dug out of four hills: four manehs of the ore yield one maneh of copper, but those who cultivate the soil get more wealth than those who mine the copper.

[No change of purpose was allowed to grow out of sickness and disappointment. Here and there, as in the words written on the next day, we find Livingstone again with his back turned to the coast and gazing towards the land of the Manyuema and the great rivers reported there.]

17th May, 1869. --Syde bin Habib arrived to-day with his cargo of copper and slaves. I have to change house again, and wish I were away, now that I am getting stronger. Attendants arrive from Parra or Mparra.

[The old slave-dealer, whom he met at Casembe's, and who seems to have been set at liberty through Livingstone's instrumentality, arrives at Ujiji at last.]

18th May, 1869. --Mohamad bin Saleh arrived to-day. He left this when comparatively young, and is now well advanced in years.

The Bakatala at Lualaba West killed Salem bin Habib. **Mem.** --Keep clear of them. Makwamba is one of the chiefs of the rock-dwellers, Ngulu is another, and Masika-Kitobwe on to Baluba. Sef attached Kilolo N'tambwe.

19th May, 1869. --The emancipation of our West-Indian slaves was the work of but a small number of the people of England--the philanthropists and all the more advanced thinkers of the age. Numerically they were a very small minority of the population, and powerful only from the superior abilities of the leading men, and from having the right, the true, and just on their side. Of the rest of the population an immense number were the indifferent, who had no sympathies to spare for any beyond their own fireside circles. In the course of time sensation writers came up on the surface of society, and by way of originality they condemned almost every measure and person of the past. "Emancipation was a mistake;" and these fast

---

4 These letters must have been destroyed purposely by the Arabs, for they never arrived at Zanzibar.--ED.

writers drew along with them a large body, who would fain be slaveholders themselves. We must never lose sight of the fact that though the majority perhaps are on the side of freedom, large numbers of Englishmen are not slaveholders only because the law forbids the practice. In this proclivity we see a great part of the reason of the frantic sympathy of thousands with the rebels in the great Black war in America. It is true that we do sympathize with brave men, though we may not approve of the objects for which they fight. We admired Stonewall Jackson as a modern type of Cromwell's Ironsides; and we praised Lee for his generalship, which, after all, was chiefly conspicuous by the absence of commanding abilities in his opponents, but, unquestionably, there existed besides an eager desire that slaveocracy might prosper, and the Negro go to the wall. The would-be slaveholders showed their leanings unmistakably in reference to the Jamaica outbreak; and many a would-be Colonel Hobbs, in lack of revolvers, dipped his pen in gall and railed against all Niggers who could not be made slaves. We wonder what they thought of their hero, when informed that, for very shame at what he had done and written, he had rushed unbidden out of the world.

26th May, 1869.--Thani bin Suellim came from Unyanyembe on the 20th. He is a slave who has risen to freedom and influence; he has a disagreeable outward squint of the right eye, teeth protruding from the averted lips, is light-coloured, and of the nervous type of African. He brought two light boxes from Unyembe, and charged six fathoms for one and eight fathoms for the other, though the carriage of both had been paid for at Zanzibar. When I paid him he tried to steal, and succeeded with one cloth by slipping it into the hands of a slave. I gave him two cloths and a double blanket as a present. He discovered afterwards what he knew before, that all had been injured by the wet on the way here, and sent two back openly, which all saw to be an insult. He asked a little coffee, and I gave a plateful; and he even sent again for more coffee after I had seen reason to resent his sending back my present. I replied, "He won't send coffee back, for I shall give him none." In revenge he sends round to warn all the Ujijians against taking my letters to the coast; this is in accordance with their previous conduct, for, like the Kilwa people on the road to Nyassa, they have refused to carry my correspondence.

This is a den of the worst kind of slave-traders; those whom I met in Urungu and Itawa were gentlemen slavers: the Ujiji slavers, like the Kilwa and Portuguese, are the vilest of the vile. It is not a trade, but a system of consecutive murders; they go to plunder and kidnap, and every trading trip is nothing but a foray. Moene Mokaia, the headman of this place, sent canoes through to Nzige, and his people, feeling their prowess among men ignorant of guns, made a regular assault but were repulsed, and the whole, twenty in number, were killed. Moene Mokaia is now negotiating with Syde bin Habib to go and revenge this, for so much ivory, and all he can get besides. Syde, by trying to revenge the death of Salem bin Habib, his brother, on the Bakatala, has blocked up one part of the country against me, and will probably block Nzige, for I cannot get a message sent to Chowambe by anyone, and may have to go to Karagwe on foot, and then from Rumanyika down to this water.

[In reference to the above we may add that there is a vocabulary of Masai words at the end of a memorandum-book. Livingstone compiled this with the idea that it would prove useful on his way towards the coast, should he eventually pass through the Masai country. No doubt some of the Arabs or their slaves knew the language, and assisted him at his work.]

29th May, 1869. --Many people went off to Unyembe, and their houses were untenanted; I wished one, as I was in a lean-to of Zahor's, but the two headmen tried to secure the rent for themselves, and were defeated by Mohamad bin Saleh. I took my packet of letters to Thani, and gave two cloths and four bunches of beads to the man who was to take them to Unyanyembe; an hour afterwards, letters, cloths, and beads were returned: Thani said he was afraid of English letters; he did not know what was inside. I had sewed them up in a piece of canvas, that was suspicious, and he would call all the great men of Ujiji and ask them if it would be safe to take them; if they assented he would call for the letters, if not he would not send them. I told Mohamad bin Saleh, and he said to Thani that he and I were men of the Government, and orders had come from Syed Majid to treat me with all respect: was this conduct respectful? Thani then sent for the packet, but whether it will reach Zanzibar I am doubtful. I gave the rent to the owner of the house and went into it on 31st May. They are nearly all miserable Suaheli at Ujiji, and have neither the manners nor the sense of Arabs.

[We see in the next few lines how satisfied Livingstone was concerning the current in the Lake: he almost wishes to call Tanganyika *a river*. Here then is a problem left for the future explorer to determine. Although the Doctor proved by experiments during his lengthy stay at Ujiji that the set is towards the north, his two men get over the difficulty thus: "If you blow upon the surface of a basin of water on one side, you will cause the water at last to revolve round and round; so with Tanganyika, the prevailing winds produce a similar circulation.". They feel certain there is no outlet, because at one time or another they virtually completed the survey of the coast line and listened to native testimony besides. How the phenomenon of sweet water is to be accounted for we do not pretend to say. The reader will see further on that Livingstone grapples with the difficulty which this Lake affords, and propounds an exceedingly clever theory.]

Lines of Green Scum

Tanganyika has encroached on the Ujiji side upwards of a mile, and the bank, which was in the memory of men now living, garden ground, is covered with about two fathoms of water: in this Tanganyika resembles most other rivers in this country, as the Upper Zambesi for instance, which in the Barotse country has been wearing eastwards for the last thirty years: this Lake, or river, has worn eastwards too.

1st June, 1869. --I am thankful to feel getting strong again, and wish to go down Tanganyika, but cannot get men: two months must elapse ere we can face the long grass and superabundant water in the way to Manyuema.

The green scum which forms on still water in this country is of vegetable origin--confervae. When the rains fall they swell the lagoons, and the scum is swept into the Lake; here it is borne along by the current from south to north, and arranged in long lines, which bend from side to side as the water flows, but always N.N.W. or N.N.E., and not driven, as here, by the winds, as plants floating above the level of the water would be.

7th June, 1869. --It is remarkable that all the Ujiji Arabs who have any opinion on the subject, believe that all the water in the north, and all the water in the south, too, flows into Tanganyika, but where it then goes they have no conjecture. They assert, as a matter of fact, that Tanganyika, Usige water, and Loanda, are one and the same piece of river.

Thani, on being applied to for men and a canoe to take me down this line of drainage, consented, but let me know that his people would go no further than Uvira, and then return. He subsequently said Usige, but I wished to know what I was to do when left at the very point where I should be most in need. He replied, in his silly way, "My people are afraid; they won't go further; get country people," &c. Moeneghere sent men to Loanda to force a passage through, but his people were repulsed and twenty killed.

Three men came yesterday from Mokamba, the greatest chief in Usige, with four tusks as a present to his friend Moeneghere, and asking for canoes to be sent down to the end of Urundi country to bring butter and other things, which the three men could not bring: this seems an opening, for Mokamba being Moeneghere's friend I shall prefer paying Moeneghere for a canoe to being dependent on

Thani's skulkers. If the way beyond Mokamba is blocked up by the fatal skirmish referred to, I can go from Mokamba to Rumanyika, three or four or more days distant, and get guides from him to lead me back to the main river beyond Loanda, and by this plan only three days of the stream will be passed over unvisited. Thani would evidently like to receive the payment, but without securing to me the object for which I pay. He is a poor thing, a slaveling: Syed Majid, Sheikh Suleiman, and Koroje, have all written to him, urging an assisting deportment in vain: I never see him but he begs something, and gives nothing, I suppose he expects me to beg from him. I shall be guided by Moeneghere.

I cannot find anyone who knows where the outflow of the unvisited Lake S.W. of this goes; some think that it goes to the Western Ocean, or, I should say, the Congo. Mohamad Bogharib goes in a month to Manyuema, but if matters turn out as I wish, I may explore this Tanganyika line first. One who has been in Manyuema three times, and was of the first party that ever went there, says that the Manyuema are not cannibals, but a tribe west of them eats some parts of the bodies of those slain in war. Some people south of Moenekuss[5], chief of Manyuema, build strong clay houses.

22nd June, 1869. --After listening to a great deal of talk I have come to the conclusion that I had better not go with Moeneghere's people to Mokamba. I see that it is to be a mulcting, as in Speke's case: I am to give largely, though I am not thereby assured of getting down the river. They say, "You must give much, because you are a great man: Mokamba will say so"--though Mokamba knows nothing about me! It is uncertain whether I can get down through by Loanda, and great risk would be run in going to those who cut off the party of Moeneghere, so I have come to the conclusion that it will be better for me to go to Manyuema about a fortnight hence, and, if possible, trace down the western arm of the Nile to the north--if this arm is indeed that of the Nile, and not of the Congo. Nobody here knows anything about it, or, indeed, about the eastern or Tanganyika line either; they all confess that they have but one question in their minds in going anywhere, they ask for ivory and for nothing else, and each trip ends as a foray. Moeneghere's last trip ended disastrously, twenty-six of his men being cut off; in extenuation he says that

5   It is curious that this name occurs amongst the Zulu tribes south
of the Zambesi, and, as it has no vowel at the end, appears to be of
altogether foreign origin.--ED.

it was not his war but Mokamba's: he wished to be allowed to go down through Loanda, and as the people in front of Mokamba and Usige own his supremacy, he said, "Send your force with mine and let us open the way," so they went on land and were killed. An attempt was made to induce Syde bin Habib to clear the way, and be paid in ivory, but Syde likes to battle with those who will soon run away and leave the spoil to him.

The Manyuema are said to be friendly where they have not been attacked by Arabs: a great chief is reported as living on a large river flowing northwards, I hope to make my way to him, and I feel exhilarated at the thought of getting among people not spoiled by contact with Arab traders. I would not hesitate to run the risk of getting through Loanda, the continuation of Usige beyond Mokamba's, had blood not been shed so very recently there; but it would at present be a great danger, and to explore some sixty miles of the Tanganyika line only. If I return hither from Manyuema my goods and fresh men from Zanzibar will have arrived, and I shall be better able to judge as to the course to be pursued after that. Mokamba is about twenty, miles beyond Uvira; the scene of Moeneghere's defeat, is ten miles beyond Mokamba; so the unexplored part cannot be over sixty miles, say thirty if we take Baker's estimate of the southing of his water to be near the truth.

Salem or Palamotto told me that he was sent for by a headman near to this to fight his brother for him: he went and demanded prepayment; then the brother sent him three tusks to refrain: Salem took them and came home. The Africans have had hard measures meted out to them in the world's history!

28th June, 1869. --The current in Tanganyika is well marked when the lighter-coloured water of a river flows in and does not at once mix--the Luishe at Ujiji is a good example, and it shows by large light greenish patches on the surface a current of nearly a mile an hour north. It begins to flow about February, and continues running north till November or December. Evaporation on 300 miles of the south is then at its strongest, and water begins to flow gently south till arrested by the flood of the great rains there, which takes place in February and March. There is, it seems, a reflux for about three months in each year, flow and reflow being the effect of the rains and evaporation on a lacustrine river of some three hundred miles in length lying south of the equator. The flow northwards I have myself observed, that again southwards rests on native testimony, and it was elicited from the Arabs by pointing out the northern current: they attributed the southern current to the effect of the wind, which they say then blows south. Being cooled by the rains, it comes south into the hot valley of this great Riverein Lake, or lacustrine river.

In going to Moenekuss, the paramount chief of the Manyuema, forty days are required. The headmen of trading parties remain with this chief (who is said by all to be a very good man), and send their people out in all directions to trade. Moenemogaia says that in going due north from Moenekuss they come to a large river, the Robumba, which flows into and is the Luama, and that this again joins the Lualaba, which retains its name after flowing with the Lufira and Lofu into the still unvisited Lake S.S.W. of this: it goes thence due north, probably into Mr. Baker's part of the eastern branch of the Nile. When I have gone as far north along Lualaba as I can this year, I shall be able to judge as to the course I ought to take after receiving my goods and men from Zanzibar, and may the Highest direct me, so that I may finish creditably the work I have undertaken. I propose to start for Manyuema on the 3rd July.

The dagala or nsipe, a small fish caught in great numbers in every flowing water, and very like whitebait, is said to emit its eggs by the mouth, and these immediately burst and the young fish manages for itself. The dagala never becomes larger than two or three inches in length. Some, putrefied, are bitter, as if the bile were in them in a good quantity. I have eaten them in Lunda of a pungent bitter taste, probably arising from the food on which the fish feeds. Men say that they have seen the eggs kept in the sides of the mouth till ready to go off as independent fishes. The nghede-dege, a species of perch, and another, the ndusi, are said to do the same. The Arabs imagine that fish in general fall from the skies, but they except the shark, because they can see the young when it is cut open.

10th July, 1869.--After a great deal of delay and trouble about a canoe, we got one from Habee for ten dotis or forty yards of calico, and a doti or four yards to each of nine paddlers to bring the vessel back. Thani and Zahor blamed me for not taking their canoes for nothing; but they took good care not to give them, but made vague offers, which meant, "We want much higher pay for our dhows than Arabs generally get:" they showed such an intention to fleece me that I was glad to get out of their power, and save the few goods I had. I went a few miles, when two strangers I had allowed to embark (from being under obligations to their masters), worked against each other: so I had to let one land, and but for his master would have dismissed the other: I had to send an apology to the landed man's master for politeness' sake.

[It is necessary to say a few words here, so unostentatiously does Livingstone introduce this new series of explorations to the reader. The Manyuema country, for which he set out on the 12th of July, 1869, was hitherto unknown. As we follow him we shall see that in almost every respect both the face of the country and the people differ from other regions lying nearer to the East Coast. It appears that the Arabs had an inkling of the vast quantities of ivory which might be procured there, and Livingstone went into the new field with the foremost of those hordes of Ujijian traders who, in all probability, will eventually destroy tribe after tribe by slave-trading and pillage, as they have done in so many other regions.]

Off at 6 A.M., and passed the mouth of the Luishe, in Kibwe Bay; 3-1/2 hours took us to Rombola or Lombola, where all the building wood of Ujiji is cut.

12th July, 1869. --Left at 1.30 A.M., and pulled 7-1/2 hours to the left bank of the Malagarasi River. We cannot go by day, because about 11 A.M. a south-west wind commences to blow, which the heavy canoes cannot face; it often begins earlier or later, according to the phases of the moon. An east wind blows from sunrise till 10 or 11 A.M., and the south-west begins. The Malagarasi is of considerable size at its confluence, and has a large islet covered with eschinomena, or pith hat material, growing in its way.

Were it not for the current Tanganyika would be covered with green scum now rolling away in miles of length and breadth to the north; it would also be salt like its shut-in bays. The water has now fallen two feet perpendicularly. It took us twelve hours to ascend to the Malagarasi River from Ujiji, and only seven to go down that distance. Prodigious quantities of confervae pass us day and night in slow majestic flow. It is called Shuare. But for the current Tanganyika would be covered with "Tikatika" too, like Victoria Nyanza.

13th July, 1869. --Off at 3.15 A.M., and in five hours reached Kabogo Eiver; from this point the crossing is always accomplished: it is about thirty miles broad. Tried to get off at 6 P.M., but after two miles the south wind blew, and as it is a dangerous wind and the usual one in storms, the men insisted on coming back, for the wind, having free scope along the entire southern length of Tanganyika, raises waves perilous to their heavy craft; after this the clouds cleared all away, and the wind died off too; the full moon shone brightly, and this is usually accompanied by calm weather here. Storms occur at new moon most frequently.

14th July, 1869. --Sounded in dark water opposite the high fountain Kabogo, 326 fathoms, but my line broke in coming up, and we did not see the armed end of the sounding lead with sand or mud on it: this is 1965 feet.

People awaking in fright utter most unearthly yells, and they are joined in them by all who sleep near. The first imagines himself seized by a wild beast, the rest roar because they hear him doing it: this indicates the extreme of helpless terror.

15th July, 1869. --After pulling all night we arrived at some islands and cooked breakfast, then we went on to Kasenge islet on their south, and came up to Mohamad Bogharib, who had come from Tongwe, and intended to go to Manyuema. We cross over to the mainland, that is, to the western shore of the Lake, about 300 yards off, to begin our journey on the 21st. Lunars on 20th. Delay to prepare food for journey. Lunars again 22nd.

A strong wind from the East to-day. A current sweeps round this islet Kisenge from N.E. to S.E., and carries trees and duckweed at more than a mile an hour in spite of the breeze blowing across it to the West. The wind blowing along the Lake either way raises up water, and in a calm it returns, off the shore. Sometimes it causes the current to go southwards. Tanganyika narrows at Uvira or Vira, and goes out of sight among the mountains there; then it appears as a waterfall into the Lake of Quando seen by Banyamwezi.

23rd July, 1869. --I gave a cloth to be kept for Kasanga, the chief of Kasenge, who has gone to fight with the people of Goma.

1st August, 1869. --Mohamad killed a kid as a sort of sacrifice, and they pray to Hadrajee before eating it. The cookery is of their very best, and I always get a share; I tell them that I like the cookery, but not the prayers, and it is taken in good part.

2nd August, 1869. --We embarked from the islet and got over to the mainland, and slept in a hooked-thorn copse, with a species of black pepper plant, which we found near the top of Mount Zomba, in the Manganja country[6], in our vicinity; it shows humidity of climate.

---

6 In 1859.

3rd August, 1869.--Marched 3-1/4 hours south, along Tanganyika, in a very undulating country; very fatiguing in my weakness. Passed many screw-palms, and slept at Lobamba village.

4th August, 1869.--A relative of Kasanga engaged to act as our guide, so we remained waiting for him, and employed a Banyamwezi smith to make copper balls with some bars of that metal presented by Syde bin Habib. A lamb wasstolen, and all declared that the deed must have been done by Banyamwezi. "At Guha people never steal," and I believe this is true.

7th August, 1869.--The guide having arrived, we marched 2-1/4 hours west and crossed the River Logumba, about forty yards broad and knee deep, with a rapid current between deep cut banks; it rises in the western Kabogo range, and flows about S.W. into Tanganyika. Much dura or **Holcus sorghum** is cultivated on the rich alluvial soil on its banks by the Guha people.

8th August, 1869.--West through open forest; very undulating, and the path full of angular fragments of quartz. We see mountains in the distance.

9th-10th August, 1869.--Westwards to Makhato's village, and met a company of natives beating a drum as they came near; this is the peace signal; if war is meant the attack is quiet and stealthy. There are plenty of Masuko trees laden with fruit, but unripe. It is cold at night, but dry, and the people sleep with only a fence at their heads, but I have a shed built at every camp as a protection for the loads, and sleep in it.

Any ascent, though gentle, makes me blow since the attack of pneumonia; if it is inclined to an angle of 45 deg., 100 or 150 yards make me stop to pant in distress.

11th August, 1869.--Came to a village of Ba Rua, surrounded by hills of some 200 feet above the plain; trees sparse.

12th-13th August, 1869.--At villages of Mekheto. Guha people. Remain to buy and prepare food, and because many are sick.

16th August, 1869.--West and by north through much forest reach Kalalibebe; buffalo killed.

17th August, 1869.--To a high mountain, Golu or Gulu, and sleep at its base.

18th August, 1869.--Cross two rills flowing into River Mgoluye. Kagoya and

Moishe flow into Lobumba.

19th August, 1869.--To the River Lobumba, forty-five yards Avide, thigh deep, and rapid current. Logumba and Lobumba are both from Kabogo Mounts: one goes into Tanganyika, and the other, or Lobumba, into and is the Luamo: prawns are found in this river. The country east of the Lobumba is called Lobanda, that west of it, Kitwa.

21st August, 1869.--Went on to the River Loungwa, which has worn for itself a rut in new red sandstone twenty feet deep, and only three or four feet wide at the lips.

25th August, 1869.--We rest because all are tired; travelling at this season is excessively fatiguing. It is very hot at even 10 A.M., and 2 1/2 or 3 hours tires the strongest--carriers especially so: during the rains five hours would not have fatigued so much as three do now. We are now on the same level as Tanganyika. The dense mass of black smoke rising from the burning grass and reeds on the Lobumba, or Robumba, obscures the sun, and very sensibly lowers the temperature of the sultriest day; it looks like the smoke in Martin's pictures. The Manyuema arrows here are very small, and made of strong grass stalks, but poisoned, the large ones, for elephants and buffaloes, are poisoned also.

31st August, 1869.--Course N.W. among Palmyras and Hyphene Palms, and many villages swarming with people. Crossed Kibila, a hot fountain about 120 deg., to sleep at Kolokolo River, five yards wide, and knee deep: midway we passed the River Kanzazala. On asking the name of a mountain on our right I got three names for it--Kaloba, Chingedi, and Kihomba, a fair specimen of the superabundance of names in this country!

1st September, 1869.--West in flat forest, then cross Kishila River, and go on to Kunde's villages. The Katamba is a fine rivulet. Kunde is an old man without dignity or honour: he came to beg, but offered nothing.

2nd September, 1869.--We remained at Katamba to hunt buffaloes and rest, as I am still weak. A young elephant was killed, and I got the heart: the Arabs do not eat it, but that part is nice if well cooked.

A Lunda slave, for whom I interceded to be freed of the yoke, ran away, and as he is near the Barna, his countrymen, he will be hidden. He told his plan to our guide, and asked to accompany him back to Tanganyika, but he is eager to deliver him up for a reward: all are eager to press each other down in the mire into which they are already sunk.

5th September, 1869. --Kunde's people refused the tusks of an elephant killed by our hunter, asserting that they had killed it themselves with a hoe: they have no honour here, as some have elsewhere.

7th September, 1869. --W. and N.W., through forest and immense fields of cassava, some three years old, with roots as thick as a stout man's leg.

8th September, 1869. --Across five rivers and through many villages. The country is covered with ferns and gingers, and miles and miles of cassava. On to village of Karun-gamagao.

9th September, 1869. --Rest again to shoot meat, as elephants and buffaloes are very abundant: the Suaheli think that adultery is an obstacle to success in killing this animal: no harm can happen to him who is faithful to his wife, and has the proper charms inserted under the skin of his forearms.

10th September, 1869. --North and north-west, over four rivers, and. past the village of Makala, to near that of Pyana-mosinde.

12th September, 1869. --We had wandered, and now came back to our path on hilly ground. The days are sultry and smoking. We came to some villages of Pyana-mosinde; the population prodigiously large. A sword was left at the camp, and at once picked up; though the man was traced to a village it was refused, till he accidentally cut his foot with it, and became afraid that worse would follow, elsewhere it would have been given up at once: Pyana-mosinde came out and talked very sensibly.

13th September, 1869. --Along towards the Moloni or Mononi; cross seven rills. The people seized three slaves who lagged behind, but hearing a gun fired at guinea-fowls let them go. Route N.

14th September, 1869. --Up and down hills perpetually. We went down into some deep dells, filled with gigantic trees, and I measured one twenty feet in circumference, and sixty or seventy feet high to the first branches; others seemed fit to be ship's spars. Large lichens covered many and numerous new plants appeared on the ground.

15th September, 1869. --Got clear of the mountains after 1-1/2 hour, and then the vast valley of Mamba opened out before us; very beautiful, and much of it cleared of trees. Met Dugumbe carrying 18,000 lbs. of ivory, purchased in this new field very cheaply, because no traders had ever gone into the country beyond Bambarre, or Moenekuss's district before. We were now in the large bend of the Lualaba, which is here much larger than at Mpweto's, near Moero Lake. River Kesingwe.

16th September, 1869. --To Kasangangazi's. We now came to the first palm-oil trees (***Elais Guineensis***) in our way since we left Tanganyika. They had evidently been planted at villages. Light-grey parrots, with red tails, also became common, whose name, Kuss or Koos, gives the chief his name, Moenekuss ("Lord of the Parrot"); but the Manyuema pronunciation is Monanjoose. Much reedy grass, fully half an inch in diameter in the stalk on our route, and over the top of the range Moloni, which we ascended: the valleys are impassable.

17th September, 1869. --Remain to buy food at Kasanga's, and rest the carriers. The country is full of pahn-oil palms, and very beautiful. Our people are all afraid to go out of sight of the camp for necessary purposes, lest the Manyuema should kill them. Here was the barrier to traders going north, for the very people among whom we now are, murdered anyone carrying a tusk, till last year, when Moene-mokaia, or Katomba, got into friendship with Moenekuss, who protected his people, and always behaved in a generous sensible manner. Dilongo, now a chief here, came to visit us: his elder brother died, and he was elected; he does not wash in consequence, and is very dirty.

Two buffaloes were killed yesterday. The people have their bodies tattooed with new and full moons, stars, crocodiles, and Egyptian gardens.

19th September, 1869. --We crossed several rivulets three yards to twelve yards, and calf deep. The mountain where we camped is called Sangomelambe.

20th September, 1869. --Up to a broad range of high mountains of light grey granite; there are deep dells on the top filled with gigantic trees, and having running rills in them. Some trees appear with enormous roots, buttresses in fact like mangroves in the coast swamps, six feet high at the trunk and flattened from side to side to about three inches in diameter. There are many villages dotted over the slopes which we climbed; one had been destroyed, and revealed the hard clay walls and square forms of Manyuema houses. Our path lay partly along a ridge, with a deep valley on each side: one on the left had a valley filled with primeval forests, into which elephants when wounded escape completely. The forest was a dense mass, without a bit of ground to be seen except a patch on the S.W., the bottom of this great valley was 2000 feet below us, then ranges of mountains with villages on their bases rose as far as they could reach. On our right there was another deep but narrow gorge, and mountains much higher than on our ridge close adjacent. Our ridge looked like a glacier, and it wound from side to side, and took us to the edge of deep precipices, first on the right, then on the left, till down below we came to the villages of Chief Monandenda. The houses here are all well filled with firewood on shelves, and each has a bed on a raised platform in an inner room.

The paths are very skilfully placed on the tops of the ridges of hills, and all gullies are avoided. If the highest level were not in general made the ground for passing through the country the distances would at least be doubled, and the fatigue greatly increased. The paths seem to have been used for ages: they are worn deep on the heights; and in hollows a little mound rises on each side, formed by the feet tossing a little soil on one side.

21st September, 1869. --Cross five or six rivulets, and as many villages, some burned and deserted, or inhabited. Very many people come running to see the strangers. Gigantic trees all about the villages. Arrive at Bambarre or Moenekuss.

About eighty hours of actual travelling, say at 2' per hour = say 160' or 140'. Westing from 3rd August to 21st September. My strength increased as I persevered. From Tanganyika west bank say =

```
29 deg. 30' east - 140' = 2 deg. 20,'
 2 20     -------    27 deg. 10' Long.
```

Chief village of Moenekuss.
Observations show a little lower altitude than Tanganyika.

22nd September, 1869. --Moenekuss died lately, and left his two sons to fill his place. Moenembagg is the elder of the two, and the most sensible, and the spokesman on all important occasions, but his younger brother, Moenemgoi, is the chief, the centre of authority. They showed symptoms of suspicion, and Mohamad performed the ceremony of mixing blood, which is simply making a small incision on the forearm of each person, and then mixing the bloods, and making declarations of friendship. Moenembagg said, "Your people must not steal, we never do," which is true: blood in a small quantity was then conveyed from one to the other by a fig-leaf. "No stealing of fowls or of men," said the chief: "Catch the thief and bring him to me, one who steals a person is a pig," said Mohamad. Stealing, however, began on our side, a slave purloining a fowl, so they had good reason to enjoin honesty on us! They think that we have come to kill them: we light on them as if from another world: no letters come to tell who we are, or what we want. We cannot conceive their state of isolation and helplessness, with nothing to trust to but their charms and idols--both being bits of wood. I got a large beetle hung up before an idol in the idol house of a deserted and burned village; the guardian was there, but the village destroyed.

I presented the two brothers with two table cloths, four bunches of beads, and one string of neck-beads; they were well satisfied.

A wood here when burned emits a horrid faecal smell, and one would think the camp polluted if one fire was made of it. I had a house built for me because the village huts are inconvenient, low in roof, and low doorways; the men build them, and help to cultivate the soil, but the women have to keep them well filled with firewood and supplied with water. They carry the wood, and almost everything else in large baskets, hung to the shoulders, like the Edinburgh fishwives. A man made a long loud prayer to Mulungu last night after dark for rain.

The sons of Moenekuss have but little of their father's power, but they try to behave to strangers as he did. All our people are in terror of the Manyema, or Manyuema, man-eating fame: a woman's child had crept into a quiet corner of the hut to eat a banana--she could not find him, and at once concluded that the Manyuema had kidnapped him to eat him, and with a yell she ran through the camp and screamed at the top of her shrill voice, "Oh, the Manyuema have stolen my child to make meat of him! Oh, my child eaten--oh, oh!"

26th-28th September, 1869. --A Lunda slave-girl was sent off to be sold for a tusk, but the Manyuema don't want slaves, as we were told in Lunda, for they are generally thieves, and otherwise bad characters. It is now clouded over and preparing for rain, when sun comes overhead. Small-pox comes every three or four years, and kills many of the people. A soko alive was believed to be a good charm for rain; so one was caught, and the captor had the ends of two fingers and toes bitten off. The soko or gorillah always tries to bite off these parts, and has been known to overpower a young man and leave him without the ends of fingers and toes. I saw the nest of one: it is a poor contrivance; no more architectural skill shown than in the nest of our Cushat dove.

29th September, 1869. --I visited a hot fountain, an hour west of our camp, which has five eyes, temperature 150 deg., slightly saline taste, and steam issues constantly. It is called Kasugwe Colambu. Earthquakes are well known, and to the Manyuema they seem to come from the east to west; pots rattle and fowls cackle on these occasions.

2nd October, 1869. --A rhinoceros was shot, and party sent off to the River Luamo to buy ivory.

5th October, 1869. --An elephant was killed, and the entire population went off to get meat, which was given freely at first, but after it was known how eagerly the Manyuema sought it, six or eight goats were demanded for a carcase and given.

9th October, 1869. --The rite of circumcision is general among all the Manyuema; it is performed on the young. If a headman's son is to be operated on, it is tried on a slave first; certain times of the year are unpropitious, as during a drought for instance; but having by this experiment ascertained the proper time, they go into the forest, beat drums, and feast as elsewhere: contrary to all African custom they are not ashamed to speak about the rite, even before women.

Two very fine young men came to visit me to-day. After putting several preparatory inquiries as to where our country lay, &c., they asked whether people died with us, and where they went to after death. "Who kills them?" "Have you no charm (Buanga) against death?" It is not necessary to answer such questions save in a land never visited by strangers. Both had the "organs of intelligence" largely developed. I told them that we prayed to the Great Father, "Mulungu," and He hears us all; they thought this to be natural.

14th October, 1869. --An elephant killed was of the small variety, and only 5 feet 8 inches high at the withers. The forefoot was in circumference 3 feet 9 inches, which doubled gives 7 feet 6 inches; this shows a deviation from the usual rule "twice round the forefoot = the height of the animal." Heart 1-1/2 foot long, tusks 6 feet 8 inches in length.

15th October, 1869.--Fever better, and thankful. Very cold and rainy.

18th October, 1869.--Our Hassani returned from Moene Kirumbo's; then one of Dugumbe's party (also called Hassani) seized ten goats and ten slaves before leaving, though great kindness had been shown: this is genuine Suaheli or Nigger-Moslem tactics--four of his people were killed in revenge.

A whole regiment of Soldier ants in my hut were put into a panic by a detachment of Driver ants called Sirufu. The Chungu or black soldiers rushed out with their eggs and young, putting them down and running for more. A dozen Sirafu pitched on one Chungu and killed him. The Chungu made new quarters for themselves. When the white ants cast off their colony of winged emigrants a canopy is erected like an umbrella over the ant-hill. As soon as the ants fly against the roof they tumble down in a shower and their wings instantly become detached from their bodies. They are then helpless, and are swept up in baskets to be fried, when they make a very palatable food.

24th-25th October, 1869.--Making copper rings, as these are highly prized by Manyuema. Mohamad's Tembe fell. It had been begun on an unlucky day, the 26th of the moon; and on another occasion on the same day, he had fifty slaves swept away by a sudden flood of a dry river in the Obena country: they are great observers of lucky and unlucky days.

A strong wind from the East to-day

CHAPTER II.

Prepares to explore River Lualaba. Beauty of the Manyuema country. Irritation at conduct of Arabs. Dugumbe's ravages. Hordes of traders arrive. Severe fever. Elephant trap. Sickness in camp. A good Samaritan. Reaches Mamohela and is prostrated. Beneficial effects of Nyumbo plant. Long illness. An elephant of three tusks. All men desert except Susi, Chuma, and Gardner. Starts with these to Lualaba. Arab assassinated by outraged Manyuema. Returns baffled to Mamohela. Long and dreadful suffering from ulcerated feet. Questionable cannibalism. Hears of four river sources close together. Resume of discoveries. Contemporary explorers. The soko. Description of its habits. Dr. Livingstone feels himself failing. Intrigues of deserters.

1st November, 1869. --Being now well rested, I resolved to go west to Lualaba and buy a canoe for its exploration. Our course was west and south-west, through a country surpassingly beautiful, mountainous, and villages perched on the talus of each great mass for the sake of quick drainage. The streets often run east and west, in order that the bright blazing sun may lick up the moisture quickly from off them. The dwelling houses are generally in line, with public meeting houses at each end, opposite the middle of the street, the roofs are low, but well thatched with a leaf resembling the banana leaf, but more tough; it seems from its fruit to be a species of Euphorbia. The leaf-stack has a notch made in it of two or three inches lengthways, and this hooks on to the rafters, which are often of the leaf-stalks of palms, split up so as to be thin; the water runs quickly off this roof, and the walls, which are of well-beaten clay, are screened from the weather. Inside, the dwellings are clean and comfortable, and before the Arabs came bugs were unknown--as I have before observed, one may know where these people have come by the presence or absence of these nasty vermin: the human tick, which infests all Arab and Suaheli houses, is to the Manyuema unknown.

In some cases, where the south-east rains are abundant, the Manyuema place the back side of the houses to this quarter, and prolong the low roof down, so that the rain does not reach the walls. These clay walls stand for ages, and men often return to the villages they left in infancy and build again the portions that many rains have washed away. The country generally is of clayey soil, and suitable for building. Each housewife has from twenty-five to thirty earthen pots slung to the ceiling by very neat cord-swinging tressels; and often as many neatly made baskets hung up in the same fashion, and much firewood.

5th November, 1869. --In going we crossed the River Luela, of twenty yards in width, five times, in a dense dripping forest. The men of one village always refused to accompany us to the next set of hamlets, "They were at war, and afraid of being killed and eaten." They often came five or six miles through the forests that separate the districts, but when we drew near to the cleared spaces cultivated by their enemies they parted civilly, and invited us to come the same way back, and they would sell us all the food we required.

The Manyuema country is all surpassingly beautiful. Palms crown the highest heights of the mountains, and their gracefully bended fronds wave beautifully in the wind; and the forests, usually about five miles broad, between groups of villages, are indescribable. Climbers of cable size in great numbers are hung among the gigantic trees, many unknown wild fruits abound, some the size of a child's head, and strange birds and monkeys are everywhere. The soil is excessively rich, and the people, although isolated by old feuds that are never settled, cultivate largely. They have selected a kind of maize that bends its fruit-stalk round into a hook, and hedges some eighteen feet high are made by inserting poles, which sprout like Robinson Crusoe's hedge, and never decay. Lines of climbing plants are tied so as to go along from pole to pole, and the maize cobs are suspended to these by their own hooked fruit-stalk. As the corn cob is forming, the hook is turned round, so that the fruit-leaves of it hang down and form a thatch for the grain beneath, or inside it. This upright granary forms a solid-looking, wall round the villages, and the people are not stingy, but take down maize and hand it to the men freely.

The women are very naked. They bring loads of provisions to sell, through the rain, and are eager traders for beads. Plantains, cassava, and maize, are the chief food. The first rains had now begun, and the white ants took the hint to swarm and colonize.

6th, 7th, and 8th November, 1869.--We came to many large villages, and were variously treated; one headman presented me with a parrot, and on my declining it, gave it to one of my people; some ordered us off, but were coaxed to allow us to remain over night. They have no restraint; some came and pushed off the door of my hut with a stick while I was resting, as we should do with a wild-beast cage.

Though reasonably willing to gratify curiosity, it becomes tiresome to be the victim of unlimited staring by the ugly, as well as by the good-looking. I can bear the women, but ugly males are uninteresting, and it is as much as I can stand when a crowd will follow me wherever I move. They have heard of Dugumbe Hassani's deeds, and are evidently suspicious of our intentions: they say, "If you have food at home, why come so far and spend your beads to buy it here?" If it is replied, on the strength of some of Mohamad's people being present, "We want to buy ivory too;" not knowing its value they think that this is a mere subterfuge to plunder them. Much palm-wine to-day at different parts made them incapable of reasoning further; they seemed inclined to fight, but after a great deal of talk we departed without collision.

9th November, 1869.--We came to villages where all were civil, but afterwards arrived where there were other palm-trees and palm-toddy, and people low and disagreeable in consequence. The mountains all around are grand, and tree-covered. I saw a man with two great great toes: the double toe is usually a little one.

11th November, 1869.--We had heard that the Manyuema were eager to buy slaves, but that meant females only to make wives of them: they prefer goats to men. Mohamad had bought slaves in Lunda in order to get ivory from these Manyuema, but inquiry here and elsewhere brought it out plainly that they would rather let the ivory lie unused or rot than invest in male slaves, who are generally criminals--at least in Lunda. I advised my friend to desist from buying slaves who would all "eat off their own heads," but he knew better than to buy copper, and on our return he acknowledged that I was right.

15th November, 1869.--We came into a country where Dugumbe's slaves had maltreated the people greatly, and they looked on us as of the same tribe, and we had much trouble in consequence. The country is swarming with villages. Hassani of Dugumbe got the chief into debt, and then robbed him of ten men and ten goats to clear off the debt: The Dutch did the same in the south of Africa.

17th November, 1869. --Copious rains brought us to a halt at Muana Balange's, on the banks of the Luamo River. Moerekurambo had died lately, and his substitute took seven goats to the chiefs on the other side in order to induce them to come in a strong party and attack us for Hassani's affair.

20th to 25th November, 1869. --We were now only about ten miles from the confluence of the Luamo and Lualaba, but all the people had been plundered, and some killed by the slaves of Dugumbe. The Luamo is here some 200 yards broad and deep; the chiefs everywhere were begged to refuse us a passage. The women were particularly outspoken in asserting our identity with the cruel strangers, and when one lady was asked in the midst of her vociferation just to look if I were of the same colour with Dugumbe, she replied with a bitter little laugh, "Then you must be his father!"

It was of no use to try to buy a canoe, for all were our enemies. It was now the rainy season, and I had to move with great caution. The worst our enemies did, after trying to get up a war in vain, was to collect as we went by in force fully armed with their large spears and huge wooden shields, and show us out of their districts. All are kind except those who have been abused by the Arab slaves. While waiting at Luamo a man, whom we sent over to buy food, got into a panic and fled he knew not whither; all concluded that he had been murdered, but some Manyuema whom we had never seen found him, fed him, and brought him home unscathed: I was very glad that no collision had taken place. We returned to Bambarre 19th December, 1869.

20th December, 1869. --While we were away a large horde of Ujijians came to Bambarre, all eager to reach the cheap ivory, of which a rumour had spread far and wide; they numbered 500 guns, and invited Mohamad to go with them, but he preferred waiting for my return from the west. We now resolved to go due north; he to buy ivory, and I to reach another part of the Lualaba and buy a canoe.

Wherever the dense primeval forest has been cleared off by man, gigantic grasses usurp the clearances. None of the sylvan vegetation can stand the annual grass-burnings except a species of Bauhinia, and occasionally a large tree which sends out new wood below the burned places. The parrots build thereon, and the men make a stair up 150 feet by tying climbing plants (called Binayoba) around, at about four feet distance, as steps: near the confluence of the Luamo, men build huts on this same species of tree for safety against the arrows of their enemies.

21st December, 1869. --The strong thick grass of the clearances dries down to the roots at the surface of the soil, and fire does it no harm. Though a few of the great old burly giants brave the fires, none of the climbers do: they disappear, but the plants themselves are brought out of the forests and ranged along the plantations like wire fences to keep wild beasts off; the poles of these vegetable wire hedges often take root, as also those in stages for maize.

22nd, 23rd, and 24th December, 1869. --Mohamad presented a goat to be eaten on our Christmas. I got large copper bracelets made of my copper by Manyuema smiths, for they are considered very valuable, and have driven iron bracelets quite out of fashion.

25th December, 1869. --We start immediately after Christmas: I must try with all my might to finish my exploration before next Christmas.

26th December, 1869. --I get fever severely, and was down all day, but we march, as I have always found that moving is the best remedy for fever: I have, however, no medicine whatever. We passed over the neck of Mount Kinyima, north-west of Moenekuss, through very slippery forest, and encamped on the banks of the Lulwa Rivulet.

28th December, 1869. --Away to Monangoi's village, near the Luamo River, here 150 or more yards wide and deep. A man passed us, bearing a human finger wrapped in a leaf; it was to be used as a charm, and belonged to a man killed in revenge: the Arabs all took this as clear evidence of cannibalism: I hesitated, however, to believe it.

29th, 30th, and 31st December, 1869. --Heavy rains. The Luamo is called the Luasse above this. We crossed in canoes.

1st January, 1870. --May the Almighty help me to finish, the work in hand, and retire through the Basango before the year is out. Thanks for all last year's loving kindness.

Our course was due north, with the Luasse flowing in a gently undulating green country on our right, and rounded mountains in Mbongo's country on our left.

2nd January, 1870. --Rested a day at Mbongo's, as the people were honest.

3rd January, 1870. --Reached a village at the edge of a great forest, where the people were excited and uproarious, but not ill-bred, they ran alongside the path with us shouting and making energetic remarks to each other about us. A newly-married couple stood in a village where we stopped to inquire the way, with arms around each other very lovingly, and no one joked or poked fun at them. We marched five hours through forest and crossed three rivulets and much stagnant water which the sun by the few rays he darts in cannot evaporate. We passed several huge traps for elephants: they are constructed thus--a log of heavy wood, about 20 feet long, has a hole at one end for a climbing plant to pass through and suspend it, at the lower end a mortice is cut out of the side, and a wooden lance about 2 inches broad by 1-1/2 thick, and about 4 feet long, is inserted firmly in the mortice; a latch down on the ground, when touched by the animal's foot, lets the beam run down on to his body, and the great weight of the wood drives in the lance and kills the animal. I saw one lance which had accidentally fallen, and it had gone into the stiff clay soil two feet.

4th January, 1870. --- The villagers we passed were civil, but like noisy children, all talked and gazed. When surrounded by 300 or 400, some who have not been accustomed to the ways of wild men think that a fight is imminent; but, poor things, no attack is thought of, if it does not begin on our side. Many of Mohamad's people were dreadfully afraid of being killed and eaten; one man out in search of ivory seemed to have lost sight of his companions, for they saw him running with all his might to a forest with no path in it; he was searched for for several days, and was given up as a murdered man, a victim of the cannibal Manyuema! On the seventh day after he lost his head, he was led into camp by a headman, who not only found him wandering but fed and lodged and restored him to his people.

[With reference to the above we may add that nothing can exceed the terror in which cannibal nations are held by other African tribes. It was common on the River Shire to hear Manganja and Ajawa people speak of tribes far away to the north who eat human bodies, and on every occasion the fact was related with the utmost horror and disgust.]

The women here plait the hair into the form of a basket behind; it is first rolled into a very long coil, then wound round something till it is about 8 or 10 inches long, projecting from the back of the head.

5th, 6th, and 7th January, 1870. --Wettings by rain and grass overhanging our paths, with bad water, brought on choleraic symptoms; and opium from Mohamad had no effect in stopping it: he, too, had rheumatism. On suspecting the water as the cause, I had all I used boiled, and this was effectual, but I was greatly reduced in flesh, and so were many of our party.

We proceeded nearly due north, through wilderness and many villages and running rills; the paths are often left to be choked up by the overbearing vegetation, and then the course of the rill is adopted as the only clear passage; it has also this advantage, it prevents footmarks being followed by enemies: in fact the object is always to make approaches to human dwellings as difficult as possible, even the hedges around villages sprout out and grow a living fence, and this is covered by a great mass of a species of calabash with its broad leaves, so that nothing appears of the fence outside.

11th January, 1870. --The people are civil, but uproarious from the excitement of having never seen strangers before; all visitors from a distance came with their large wooden shields; many of the men are handsome and tall but the women are plainer than at Bambarre.

12th January, 1870. --Cross the Lolinde, 35 yards and knee deep, flowing to join Luamo far down: dark water. (***13th.***) Through the hills Chimunemune; we see many albinos and partial lepers and syphilis is prevalent. It is too trying to travel during the rains.

14th January, 1870. --The Muabe palm had taken possession of a broad valley, and the leaf-stalks, as thick as a strong man's arm and 20 feet long, had fallen off and blocked up all passage except by one path made and mixed up by the feet of buffaloes and elephants. In places like this the leg goes into elephants' holes up to the thigh and it is grievous; three hours of this slough tired the strongest: a brown stream ran through the centre, waist deep, and washed off a little of the adhesive mud. Our path now lay through a river covered with tikatika, a living vegetable bridge made by a species of glossy leafed grass which felts itself into a mat capable of bearing a man's weight, but it bends in a foot or fifteen inches every step; a stick six feet long could not reach the bottom in certain holes we passed. The lotus, or sacred lily, which grows in nearly all the shallow waters of this country, sometimes spreads its broad leaves over the bridge so as to lead careless observers to think that it is the bridge builder, but the grass mentioned is the real agent. Here it is called Kintefwetefwe; on Victoria Nyanza Titatika.

15th January, 1870. --Choleraic purging again came on till all the water used was boiled, but I was laid up by sheer weakness near the hill Chanza.

20th and 21st January. 1870. --Weakness and illness goes on because we get wet so often; the whole party suffers, and they say that they will never come here again. The Manyango Rivulet has fine sweet water, but the whole country is smothered with luxuriant vegetation.

27th, 29th, and 30th January, 1870. --Rest from sickness in camp. The country is indescribable from rank jungle of grass, but the rounded hills are still pretty; an elephant alone can pass through it--these are his head-quarters. The stalks are from half an inch to an inch and a half in diameter, reeds clog the feet, and the leaves rub sorely on the face and eyes: the view is generally shut in by this megatherium grass, except when we come to a slope down to a valley or the bed of a rill.

We came to a village among fine gardens of maize, bananas, ground-nuts, and cassava, but the villagers said, "Go on to next village;" and this meant, "We don't want you here." The main body of Mohamad's people was about three miles before us, but I was so weak I sat down in the next hamlet and asked for a hut to rest in. A woman with leprous hands gave me hers, a nice clean one, and very heavy rain came on: of her own accord she prepared dumplings of green maize, pounded and boiled; which are sweet, for she said that she saw I was hungry. It was excessive weakness from purging, and seeing that I did not eat for fear of the leprosy, she kindly pressed me: "Eat, you are weak only from hunger; this will strengthen you." I put it out of her sight, and blessed her motherly heart.

I had ere this come to the conclusion that I ought not to risk myself further in the rains in my present weakness, for it may result in something worse, as in Marungu and Liemba.

The horde mentioned as having passed Bambarre was now somewhere in our vicinity, and it was impossible to ascertain from the Manyuema where the Lualaba lay.

In going north on 1st February we came to some of this horde belonging to

Katomba or Moene-mokaia, who stated that the leader was anxious for advice as to crossing Lualaba and future movements. He supposed that this river was seven days in front of him, and twelve days in front of us. It is a puzzle from its north-westing and low level: it is possibly Petherick's Bahr Ghazal. Could get no latitude.

2nd February, 1870. --I propose to cross it, and buy an exploring canoe, because I am recovering my strength; but we now climb over the bold hills Bininango, and turn south-west towards Katomba to take counsel: he knows more than anyone else about the country, and his people being now scattered everywhere seeking ivory, I do not relish their company.

3rd February, 1870. --Caught in a drenching rain, which made me fain to sit, exhausted as I was, under an umbrella for an hour trying to keep the trunk dry. As I sat in the rain a little tree-frog, about half an inch long, leaped on to a grassy leaf, and began a tune as loud as that of many birds, and very sweet; it was surprising to hear so much music out of so small a musician. I drank some rain-water as I felt faint--in the paths it is now calf deep. I crossed a hundred yards of slush waist deep in mid channel, and full of holes made by elephants' feet, the path hedged in by reedy grass, often intertwined and very tripping. I stripped off my clothes on reaching my hut in a village, and a fire during night nearly dried them. At the same time I rubbed my legs with palm oil, and in the morning had a delicious breakfast of sour goat's milk and porridge.

5th February, 1870. --The drenching told on me sorely, and it was repeated after we had crossed the good-sized rivulets Mulunkula and many villages, and I lay on an enormous boulder under a Muabe palm, and slept during the worst of the pelting. I was seven days southing to Mamohela, Katomba's camp, and quite knocked up and exhausted. I went into winter quarters on 7th February, 1870.

7th February, 1870. --This was the camp of the headman of the ivory horde now away for ivory. Katomba, as Moene-mokaia is called, was now all kindness. We were away from his Ujijian associates, and he seemed to follow his natural bent without fear of the other slave-traders, who all hate to see me as a spy on their proceedings. Rest, shelter, and boiling all the water I used, and above all the new species of potato called Nyumbo, much famed among the natives as restorative, soon put me all to rights. Katomba supplied me liberally with nyumbo; and, but for a slightly medicinal taste, which is got rid of by boiling in two waters, this vegetable would be equal to English potatoes.

11th February, 1870.--First of all it was proposed to go off to the Lualaba in the north-west, in order to procure **Holcus sorghum** or dura flour, that being, in Arab opinion, nearly equal to wheat, or as they say "heating," while the maize flour we were obliged to use was cold or cooling.

13th February, 1870.--I was too ill to go through mud waist deep, so I allowed Mohamad (who was suffering much) to go away alone in search of ivory. As stated above, shelter and nyumbo proved beneficial.

22nd February, 1870.--Falls between Vira and Baker's Water seen by Wanyamwezi. This confirms my conjecture on finding Lualaba at a lower level than Tanganyika. Bin Habib went to fight the Batusi, but they were too strong, and he turned.

1st March, 1870.--Visited my Arab friends in their camp for the first time to-day. This is Kasessa's country, and the camp is situated between two strong rivulets, while Mamohela is the native name, Mount Bombola stands two miles from it north, and Mount Bolunkela is north-east the same distance. Wood, water, and grass, the requisites of a camp abound, and the Manyuema bring large supplies of food every day; forty large baskets of maize for a goat; fowls and bananas and nyumbo very cheap.

25th March, 1870.--Iron bracelets are the common medium of exchange, and coarse beads and cowries: for a copper bracelet three large fowls are given, and three and a half baskets of maize; one basket three feet high is a woman's load, and they are very strong.

The Wachiogone are a scattered tribe among the Maarabo or Suaheli, but they retain their distinct identity as a people.

The Mamba fish has breasts with milk, and utters a cry; its flesh is very white, it is not the crocodile which goes by the same name, but is probably the Dugong or Peixe Mulher of the Portuguese(?). Full-grown leeches come on the surface in this wet country.

Some of Katomba's men returned with forty-three tusks. An animal with short horns and of a reddish colour is in the north; it is not known to the Arabs(?).

Joseph, an Arab from Oman, says that the Simoom is worse in Sham (Yemen?) than in Oman: it blows for three or four hours. Butter eaten largely is the remedy against its ill effects, and this is also smeared on the body: in Oman a wetted cloth is put over the head, body, and legs, while this wind blows.

1st May, 1870. --An elephant was killed which had three tusks; all of good size[7].

Rains continued; and mud and mire from the clayey soil of Manyuema were too awful to be attempted.

24th May, 1870. --I sent to Bambarre for the cloth and beads I left there. A party of Thani's people came south and said that they had killed forty Manyuema, and lost four of theirown number; nine villages were burned, and all this about a single string of beads which a man tried to steal!

June, 1870. --Mohamad bin Nassur and Akila's men brought 116 tusks from the north, where the people are said to be all good and obliging: Akila's chief man had a large deep ulcer on the foot from the mud. When we had the people here, Kassessa gave ten goats and one tusk to hire them to avenge a feud in which his elder brother was killed, and they went; the spoils secured were 31 captives, 60 goats, and about 40 Manyuema killed: one slave of the attacking party was killed, and two badly wounded. Thani's man, Yahood, who was leader in the other case of 40 killed, boasted before me of the deed. I said, "You were sent here not to murder, but to trade;" he replied, "We are sent to murder." Bin Nassur said, "The English are always killing people;" I replied, "Yes, but only slavers who do the deeds that were done yesterday."

Various other tribes sent large presents to the Arabs to avert assaults, and tusks too were offered.

The rains had continued into June, and fifty-eight inches fell.

26th June, 1870. --Now my people failed me; so, with only three attendants, Susi, Chuma, and Gardner, I started off to the north-west for the Lualaba. The numbers of running rivulets to be crossed were surprising, and at each, for some forty yards, the path had been worked by the feet of passengers into adhesive mud: we crossed fourteen in one day--some thigh deep; most of them run into the Liya, which we crossed, and it flows to the Lualaba. We passed through many villages, for the paths all lead through human dwellings. Many people presented bananas,

---

7 Susi and Chuma say that the third tusk grew out from the base of
the trunk, that is, midway between the other two.--ED.

and seemed surprised when I made a small return gift; one man ran after me with a sugar-cane; I paid for lodgings too: here the Arabs never do.

28th June, 1870. --The driver ants were in millions in some part of the way; on this side of the continent they seem less fierce than I have found them in the west.

29th June, 1870. --At one village musicians with calabashes, having holes in them, flute-fashion, tried to please me by their vigorous acting, and by beating drums in time.

30th June, 1870. --We passed through the nine villages burned for a single string of beads, and slept in the village of Malola.

July, 1870. --While I was sleeping quietly here, some trading Arabs camped at Nasangwa's, and at dead of night one was pinned to the earth by a spear; no doubt this was in revenge for relations slain in the forty mentioned: the survivors now wished to run a muck in all directions against the Manyuema.

When I came up I proposed to ask the chief if he knew the assassin, and he replied that he was not sure of him, for he could only conjecture who it was; but death to all Manyuemas glared from the eyes of half-castes and slaves. Fortunately, before this affair was settled in their way, I met Mohamad Bogharib coming back from Kasonga's, and he joined in enforcing peace: the traders went off, but let my three people know, what I knew long before, that they hated having a spy in me on their deeds. I told some of them who were civil tongued that ivory obtained by bloodshed was unclean evil--"unlucky" as they say: my advice to them was, "Don't shed human blood, my friends; it has guilt not to be wiped off by water." Off they went; and afterwards the bloodthirsty party got only one tusk and a half, while another party, which avoided shooting men, got fifty-four tusks!

From Mohamad's people I learned that the Lualaba was not in the N.W. course I had pursued, for in fact it flows W.S.W. in another great bend, and they had gone far to the north without seeing it, but the country was exceedingly difficult from forest and water. As I had already seen, trees fallen across the path formed a breast-high wall which had to be climbed over: flooded rivers, breast and neck deep, had to be crossed, the mud was awful, and nothing but villages eight or ten miles apart.

In the clearances around these villages alone could the sun be seen. For the first time in my life my feet failed me, and now having but three attendants it would have been unwise to go further in that direction. Instead of healing quietly as heretofore, when torn by hard travel, irritable-eating ulcers fastened on both feet; and I limped back to Bambarre on 22nd.

The accounts of Ramadan (who was desired by me to take notes as he went in the forest) were discouraging, and made me glad I did not go. At one part, where the tortuous river was flooded, they were five hours in the water, and a man in a small canoe went before them sounding for places not too deep for them, breast and chin deep, and Hassani fell and hurt himself sorely in a hole. The people have goats and sheep, and love them as they do children.

[Fairly baffled by the difficulties in his way, and sorely troubled by the demoralised state of his men, who appear not to have been proof against the contaminating presence of the Arabs, the Doctor turns back at this point.]

6th July, 1870. --Back to Mamohela, and welcomed by the Arabs, who all approved of my turning back. Katomba presented abundant provisions for all the way to Bambarre. Before we reached this, Mohamad made a forced march, and Moenemokaia's people came out drunk: the Arabs assaulted them, and they ran off.

23rd July, 1870. --The sores on my feet now laid me up as irritable-eating ulcers. If the foot were put to the ground, a discharge of bloody ichor flowed, and the same discharge happened every night with considerable pain, that prevented sleep: the wailing of the slaves tortured with these sores is one of the night sounds of a slave-camp: they eat through everything--muscle, tendon, and bone, and often lame permanently if they do not kill the poor things. Medicines have very little effect on such wounds: their periodicity seems to say that they are allied to fever. The Arabs make a salve of bees'-wax and sulphate of copper, and this applied hot, and held on by a bandage affords support, but the necessity of letting the ichor escape renders it a painful remedy: I had three ulcers, and no medicine. The native plan of support by means of a stiff leaf or bit of calabash was too irritating, and so they continued to eat in and enlarge in spite of everything: the vicinity was hot, and the pain increased with the size of the wound.

2nd August, 1870. --An eclipse at midnight: the Moslems called loudly on Moses. Very cold.

On *17th August, 1870,* Monanyembe, the chief who was punished by Mohamad Bogharib, lately came bringing two goats; one he gave to Mohamad, the other to Moenekuss' son, acknowledging that he had killed his elder brother: he had killed eleven persons over at Linamo in our absence, in addition to those killed in villages on our S.E. when we were away. It transpired that Kandahara, brother of old Moenekuss, whose village is near this, killed three women and a child, and that a trading man came over from Kasangangaye, and was murdered too, for no reason but to eat his body. Mohamad ordered old Kandahara to bring ten goats and take them over to Kasangangaye to pay for the murdered man. When they tell of each other's deeds they disclose a horrid state of bloodthirsty callousness. The people over a hill N.N.E. of this killed a person out hoeing; if a cultivator is alone, he is almost sure of being slain. Some said that people in the vicinity, or hyaenas, stole the buried dead; but Posho's wife died, and in Wanyamesi fashion was thrown out of camp unburied. Mohamad threatened an attack if Manyuema did not cease exhuming the dead; it was effectual, neither men nor hyaenas touched her, though exposed now for seven days.

The head of Moenekuss is said to be preserved in a pot in his house, and all public matters are gravely communicated to it, as if his spirit dwelt therein: his body was eaten, the flesh was removed from the head and eaten too; his father's head is said to be kept also: the foregoing refers to Bambarre alone. In other districts graves show that sepulture is customary, but here no grave appears: some admit the existence of the practice here; others deny it. In the Metamba country adjacent to the Lualaba, a quarrel with a wife often ends in the husband killing her and eating her heart, mixed up in a huge mess of goat's flesh: this has the charm character. Fingers are taken as charms in other parts, but in Bambarre alone is the depraved taste the motive for cannibalism.

Bambarre, 18th August, 1870. --I learn from Josut and Moenepembe, who have been to Katanga and beyond, that there is a Lake N.N.W. of the copper mines, and twelve days distant; it is called Chibungo, and is said to be large. Seven days west of Katanga flows another Lualaba, the dividing line between Rua and Lunda or Londa; it is very large, and as the Lufira flows into Chibungo, it is probable that the Lualaba West and the Lufira form the Lake. Lualaba West and Lufira rise by fountains south of Katanga, three or four days off. Luambai and Lunga fountains are only about ten miles distant from Lualaba West and Lufira fountains: a mound rises between them, the most remarkable in Africa. Were this spot in Armenia it would serve exactly the description of the garden of Eden in Genesis, with its four rivers, the Gihon, Pison, Hiddekel, and Euphrates; as it is, it possibly gave occasion to the story told to Herodotus by the Secretary of Minerva in the City of Sais, about two hills with conical tops, Crophi and Mophi. "Midway between them," said he, "are the fountains of the Nile, fountains which it is impossible to fathom: half the water runs northward into Egypt; half to the south towards Ethiopia."

Four fountains rising so near to each other would readily be supposed to have one source, and half the water flowing into the Nile and the other half to the Zambesi, required but little imagination to originate, seeing the actual visitor would not feel bound to say how the division was effected. He could only know the fact of waters rising at one spot, and separating to flow north and south. The conical tops to the mound look like invention, as also do the names.

A slave, bought on Lualaba East, came from Lualaba West in about twelve days: these two Lualabas may form the loop depicted by Ptolemy, and upper and lower Tanganyika be a third arm of the Nile.

Patience is all I can exercise: these irritable ulcers hedge me in now, as did my attendants in June, but all will be for the best, for it is in Providence and not in me.

The watershed is between 700 and 800 miles long from west to east, or say from 22 deg. or 23 deg. to 34 deg. or 35 deg. East longitude. Parts of it are enormous sponges; in other parts innumerable rills unite into rivulets, which again form rivers--Lufira, for instance, has nine rivulets, and Lekulwe other nine. The convex surface of the rose of a garden watering-can is a tolerably apt similitude, as the rills do not spring off the face of it, and it is 700 miles across the circle; but in the numbers of rills coming out at different heights on the slope, there is a faint resemblance, and I can at present think of no other example.

I am a little thankful to old Nile for so hiding his head that all "theoretical discoverers" are left out in the cold. With all real explorers I have a hearty sympathy, and I have some regret at being obliged, in a manner compelled, to speak somewhat disparagingly of the opinions formed by my predecessors. The work of Speke and Grant is part of the history of this region, and since the discovery of the sources of the Nile was asserted so positively, it seems necessary to explain, not offensively, I hope, wherein their mistake lay, in making a somewhat similar claim. My opinions may yet be shown to be mistaken too, but at present I cannot conceive how. When Speke discovered Victoria Nyanza in 1858, he at once concluded that therein lay the sources of the Nile. His work after that was simply following a foregone conclusion, and as soon as he and Grant looked towards the Victoria Nyanza, they turned their backs on the Nile fountains; so every step of their splendid achievement of following the river down took them further and further away from the Caput Nili. When it was perceived that the little river that leaves the Nyanza, though they called it the White Nile, would not account for that great river, they might have gone west and found headwaters (as the Lualaba) to which it can bear no comparison. Taking their White Nile at 80 or 90 yards, or say 100 yards broad, the Lualaba, far south of the latitude of its point of departure, shows an average breadth of from 4000 to 6000 yards, and always deep.

Considering that more than sixteen hundred years have elapsed since Ptolemy put down the results of early explorers, and emperors, kings, philosophers--all the great men of antiquity in short longed to know the fountains whence flowed the famous river, and longed in vain--exploration does not seem to have been very becoming to the other sex either. Madame Tinne came further up the river than the centurions sent by Nero Caesar, and showed such indomitable pluck as to reflect honour on her race. I know nothing about her save what has appeared in the public papers, but taking her exploration along with what was done by Mrs. Baker, no long time could have elapsed before the laurels for the modern re-discovery of the sources of the Nile should have been plucked by the ladies. In 1841 the Egyptian Expedition under D'Arnauld and Sabatier reached lat. 4 deg. 42': this was a great advance into the interior as compared with Linant in 1827, 13 deg. 30' N., and even on the explorations of Jomard(?); but it turned when nearly a thousand miles from the sources.

[The subjoined account of the soko--which is in all probability an entirely new species of chimpanzee, and *not* the gorilla, is exceedingly interesting, and no doubt Livingstone had plenty of stories from which to select. Neither Susi nor Chuma can identify the soko of Manyuema with the gorilla, as we have it stuffed in the British Museum. They think, however, that the soko is quite as large and as strong as the gorilla, judging by the specimens shown to them, although they could have decided with greater certainty, if the natives had not invariably brought in the dead sokos disembowelled; as they point out, and as we imagine from Dr. Livingstone's description, the carcase would then appear much less bulky. Livingstone gives an animated sketch of a soko hunt.]

24th August, 1870. --Four gorillas or sokos were killed yesterday: an extensive grass-burning forced them out of their usual haunt, and coming on the plain they were speared. They often go erect, but place the hand on the head, as if to steady the body. When seen thus, the soko is an ungainly beast. The most sentimental young lady would not call him a "dear," but a bandy-legged, pot-bellied, low-looking villain, without a particle of the gentleman in him. Other animals, especially the antelopes, are graceful, and it is pleasant to see them, either at rest or in motion: the natives also are well made, lithe and comely to behold, but the soko, if large, would do well to stand for a picture of the Devil.

He takes away my appetite by his disgusting bestiality of appearance. His light-yellow face shows off his ugly whiskers, and faint apology for a beard; the forehead villainously low, with high ears, is well in the back-ground of the great dog-mouth; the teeth are slightly human, but the canines show the beast by their large development. The hands, or rather the fingers, are like those of the natives. The flesh of the feet is yellow, and the eagerness with which the Manyuema devour it leaves the impression that eating sokos was the first stage by which they arrived at being cannibals; they say the flesh is delicious. The soko is represented by some to be extremely knowing, successfully stalking men and women while at their work, kidnapping children, and running up trees with them--he seems to be amused by the sight of the young native in his arms, but comes down when tempted by a bunch of bananas, and as he lifts that, drops the child: the young soko in such a case would cling closely to the armpit of the elder. One man was cutting out honey from a tree, and naked, when a soko suddenly appeared and caught him, then let him go: another man was hunting, and missed in his attempt to stab a soko: it seized the spear and broke it, then grappled with the man, who called to his companions, "Soko has caught me," the soko bit off the ends of his fingers and escaped unharmed. Both men are now alive at Bambarre.

The soko is so cunning, and has such sharp eyes, that no one can stalk him in front without being seen, hence, when shot, it is always in the back; when surrounded by men and nets, he is generally speared in the back too, otherwise he is not a very formidable beast: he is nothing, as compared in power of damaging his assailant, to a leopard or lion, but is more like a man unarmed, for it does not occur to him to use his canine teeth, which are long and formidable. Numbers of them come down in the forest, within a hundred yards of our camp, and would be unknown but for giving tongue like fox-hounds: this is their nearest approach to speech. A man hoeing was stalked by a soko, and seized; he roared out, but the soko giggled and grinned, and left him as if he had done it in play. A child caught up by a soko is often abused by being pinched and scratched, and let fall.

The soko kills the leopard occasionally, by seizing both paws, and biting them so as to disable them, he then goes up a tree, groans over his wounds, and sometimes recovers, while the leopard dies: at other times, both soko and leopard die. The lion kills him at once, and sometimes tears his limbs off, but does not eat him. The soko eats no flesh--small bananas are his dainties, but not maize. His food consists of wild fruits, which abound: one, Stafene, or Manyuema Mamwa, is like large sweet sop but indifferent in taste and flesh. The soko brings forth at times twins. A very large soko was seen by Mohamad's hunters sitting picking his nails; they tried to stalk him, but he vanished. Some Manyuema think that their buried dead rise as sokos, and one was killed with holes in his ears, as if he had been a man. He is very strong and fears guns but not spears: he never catches women.

Sokos collect together, and make a drumming noise, some say with hollow trees, then burst forth into loud yells which are well imitated by the natives' embryotic music. If a man has no spear the soko goes away satisfied, but if wounded he seizes the wrist, lops off the fingers, and spits them out, slaps the cheeks of his victim, and bites without breaking the skin: he draws out a spear (but never uses it), and takes some leaves and stuffs them into his wound to staunch the blood; he does not wish an encounter with an armed man. He sees women do him no harm, and never molests them; a man without a spear is nearly safe from him. They beat hollow trees as drums with hands, and then scream as music to it; when men hear them, they go to the sokos; but sokos never go to men with hostility. Manyuema say, "Soko is a man, and nothing bad in him."

They live in communities of about ten, each having his own female; an intruder from another camp is beaten off with their fists and loud yells. If one tries to seize the female of another, he is caught on the ground, and all unite in boxing and biting the offender. A male often carries a child, especially if they are passing from one patch of forest to another over a grassy space; he then gives it to the mother.

I now spoke with my friend Mohamad, and he offered to go with me to see Lualaba from Luamo, but I explained that merely to see and measure its depth would not do, I must see whither it went. This would require a number of his people in lieu of my deserters, and to take them away from his ivory trade, which at present is like gold digging, I must make amends, and I offered him 2000 rupees, and a gun worth 700 rupees, R. 2700 in all, or 270 *l.* He agreed, and should he enable me to finish up my work in one trip down Lualaba, and round to Lualaba West, it would be a great favour.

[How severely he felt the effects of the terrible illnesses of the last two years may be imagined by some few words here, and it must ever be regretted that the conviction which he speaks of was not acted up to.]

The severe pneumonia in Marunga, the choleraic complaint in Manyuema, and now irritable ulcers warn me to retire while life lasts. Mohamad's people went north, and east, and west, from Kasonga's: sixteen marches north, ten ditto west, and four ditto E. and S.E. The average march was 6-1/2 hours, say 12' about 200' N. and W., lat. of Kasongo, say 4 deg. south. They may have reached 1 deg., 2 deg. S. They were now in the Balegge country, and turned. It was all dense forest, they never saw the sun except when at a village, and then the villages were too far apart. The people were very fond of sheep, which they call ngombe, or ox, and tusks are never used. They went off to where an elephant had formerly been killed, and brought the tusks rotted and eaten or gnawed by "Dere" (?)--a Rodent, probably the ***Aulocaudatus Swindermanus***. Three large rivers were crossed, breast and chin deep; in one they were five hours, and a man in a small canoe went ahead sounding for water capable of being waded. Much water and mud in the forest. This report makes me thankful I did not go, for I should have seen nothing, and been worn out by fatigue and mud. They tell me that the River Metunda had black water, and took two hours to cross it, breast deep. They crossed about forty smaller rivers over the River Mohunga, breast deep. The River of Mbite also is large. All along Lualaba and Metumbe the sheep have hairy dew-laps, no wool, Tartar breed (?), small thin tails.

A broad belt of meadow-land, with no trees, lies along Lualaba, beyond that it is all dense forest, and trees so large, that one lying across the path is breast high:

clearances exist only around the villages. The people are very expert smiths and weavers of the "Lamba," and make fine large spears, knives, and needles. Marketplaces, called "Tokos," are numerous all along Lualaba; to these the Barua of the other bank come daily in large canoes, bringing grass-cloth, salt, flour, cassava, fowls, goats, pigs, and slaves. The women are beautiful, with straight noses, and well-clothed; when the men of the districts are at war, the women take their goods to market as if at peace and are never molested: all are very keen traders, buying one thing with another, and changing back again, and any profit made is one of the enjoyments of life.

I knew that my deserters hoped to be fed by Mohamad Bogharib when we left the camp at Mamohela, but he told them that he would not have them; this took them aback, but they went and lifted his ivory for him, and when a parley was thus brought about, talked him over, saying that they would go to me, and do all I desired: they never came, but, as no one else would take them, I gave them three loads to go to Bambarre; there they told Mohamad that I would not give them beads, and they did not like to steal; they were now trying to get his food by lies. I invited them three times to come and take beads, but having supplies of food from the camp women, they hoped to get the upper hand with me, and take what they liked by refusing to carry or work. Mohamad spoke long to them, but speaking mildly makes them imagine that the spokesman is afraid of them. They kept away from my work and would fain join Mohamad's, but he won't have them. I gave beads to all but the ringleaders. Their conduct looks as if a quarrel had taken place between us, but no such excuse have they.

I am powerless, as they have left me, and think that they may do as they like, and the "Manyuema are bad" is the song. Their badness consists in being dreadfully afraid of guns, and the Arabs can do just as they like with them and their goods. If spears alone were used the Manyuema would be considered brave, for they fear no one, though he has many spears. They tell us truly "that were it not for our guns not one of us would return to our own country." Moene-mokaia killed two Arab agents, and took their guns; this success led to their asserting, in answer to the remonstrances of the women, "We shall take their goats, guns, and women from them." The chief, in reporting the matter to Moenemger(?) at Luamo, said, "The Englishman told my people to go away as he did not like fighting, but my men were filled with 'malofu,' or palm-toddy, and refused to their own hurt." Elsewhere they made regular preparation to have a fight with Dugumbe's people, just to see who was strongest--they with their spears and wooden shields, and the Arabs with what in derision they called tobacco-pipes (guns). They killed eight or nine Arabs.

No traders seem ever to have come in before this. Banna brought copper and skins for tusks, and the Babisa and Baguha coarse beads. The Bavira are now enraged at seeing Ujijians pass into their ivory field, and no wonder; they took the tusks which cost them a few strings of beads, and received weight for weight in beads, thick brass wire, and loads of calico.

CHAPTER III.

Footsteps of Moses. Geology of Manyuema land. "A drop of comfort." Continued sufferings. A stationary explorer. Consequences of trusting to theory. Nomenclature of Rivers and Lakes. Plunder and murder is Ujijian trading. Comes out of hut for first time after eighty days' illness. Arab cure for ulcerated sores. Rumour of letters. The loss of medicines a great trial now. The broken-hearted chief. Return of Arab ivory traders. Future plans. Thankfulness for Mr. Edward Young's Search Expedition. The Hornbilled Phoenix. Tedious delays. The bargain for the boy. Sends letters to Zanzibar. Exasperation of Manyuema against Arabs. The "Sassassa bird." The disease "Safura."

Bambarre, *25th August, 1870.* --One of my waking dreams is that the legendary tales about Moses coming up into Inner Ethiopia with Merr his foster-mother, and founding a city which he called in her honour "Meroe," may have a substratum of fact. He was evidently a man of transcendent genius, and we learn from the speech of St. Stephen that "he was learned in all the wisdom of the Egyptians, and was mighty in words and in deeds." His deeds must have been well known in Egypt, for "he supposed that his brethren would have understood how that God by His hand would deliver them, but they understood not." His supposition could not be founded on his success in smiting a single Egyptian; he was too great a man to be elated by a single act of prowess, but his success on a large scale in Ethiopia afforded reasonable grounds for believing that his brethren would be proud of their countryman, and disposed to follow his leadership, but they were slaves. The notice taken of the matter by Pharaoh showed that he was eyed by the great as a dangerous, if not powerful, man. He "dwelt" in Midian for some time before his gallant bearing towards the shepherds by the well, commended him to the priest or prince of the country. An uninteresting wife, and the want of intercourse with kindred spirits during the long forty years' solitude of a herdsman's life, seem to have acted injuriously on his spirits, and it was not till he had with Aaron struck terror into the Egyptian mind, that the "man Moses" again became "very great in the eyes of Pharaoh and his servants." The Ethiopian woman whom he married could scarcely be the daughter of Renel or Jethro, for Midian was descended from Keturah, Abraham's concubine, and they were never considered Cushite or Ethiopian. If he left his wife in Egypt she would now be some fifty or sixty years old, and all the more likely to be despised by the proud prophetess Miriam as a daughter of Ham.

I dream of discovering some monumental relics of Meroe, and if anything confirmatory of sacred history does remain, I pray to be guided thereunto. If the sacred chronology would thereby be confirmed, I would not grudge the toil and hardships, hunger and pain, I have endured--the irritable ulcers would only be discipline.

Above the fine yellow clay schist of Manyuema the banks of Tanganyika reveal 50 feet of shingle mixed with red earth; above this at some parts great boulders lie; after this 60 feet of fine clay schist, then 5 strata of gravel underneath, with a foot stratum of schist between them. The first seam of gravel is about 2 feet, the second 4 feet, and the lowest of all about 30 feet thick. The fine schist was formed in still water, but the shingle must have been produced in stormy troubled seas if not carried hither and thither by ice and at different epochs.

This Manyuema country is unhealthy, not so much from fever as from debility of the whole system, induced by damp, cold, and indigestion: this general weakness is ascribed by some to maize being the common food, it shows itself in weakness of bowels and choleraic purging. This may be owing to bad water, of which there is no scarcity, but it is so impregnated with dead vegetable matter as to have the colour of tea. Irritable ulcers fasten on any part abraded by accident, and it seems to be a spreading fungus, for the matter settling on any part near becomes a fresh centre of propagation. The vicinity of the ulcer is very tender, and it eats in frightfully if not allowed rest. Many slaves die of it, and its periodical discharges of bloody ichor makes me suspect it to be a development of fever. I have found lunar caustic useful: a plaister of wax, and a little finely-ground sulphate of copper is used by the Arabs, and so is cocoa-nut oil and butter. These ulcers are excessively intractable, there is no healing them before they eat into the bone, especially on the shins.

Rheumatism is also common, and it cuts the natives off. The traders fear these diseases, and come to a stand if attacked, in order to use rest in the cure. "Taema," or Tape-worm, is frequently met with, and no remedy is known among the Arabs and natives for it.

[Searching in his closely-written pocket-books we find many little mementoes of his travels; such, for instance, as two or three tsetse flies pressed between the leaves of one book; some bees, some leaves and moths in another, but, hidden away in the pocket of the note-book which Livingstone used during the longest and most painful illness he ever underwent lies a small scrap of printed paper which tells a tale in its own simple way. On one side there is written in his well-known hand:--]

"Turn over and see a drop of comfort found when suffering from irritable eating ulcers on the feet in Manyuema, August, 1870."

[On the reverse we see that the scrap was evidently snipped off a list of books advertised at the end of some volume which, with the tea and other things sent to Ujiji, had reached him before setting out on this perilous journey. The "drop of comfort" is as follows:--]

"A NARRATIVE OF AN EXPEDITION TO THE ZAMBESI AND ITS TRIBU TARIES,

"And the discovery of Lakes Shirwa and Nyassa.
"***Fifth Thousand. With Map and Illustrations***. 8vo. 21s.

"'Few achievements in our day have made a greater impression than that of the adventurous missionary who unaided crossed the Continent of Equatorial Africa. His unassuming simplicity, his varied intelligence, his indomitable pluck, his steady religious purpose, form a combination of qualities rarely found in one man. By common consent, Dr. Livingstone has come to be regarded as one of the most remarkable travellers of his own or of any other age.'-- ***British Quarterly Review*** ."

[The kindly pen of the reviewer served a good turn when there was "no medicine" but the following:--]

I was at last advised to try malachite, rubbed down with water on a stone, and applied with a feather: this is the only thing that has any beneficial effect.

9th September, 1870. --A Londa slave stole ten goats from the Manyuema; he was bound, but broke loose, and killed two goats yesterday. He was given to the Manyuema. The Balonda evidently sold their criminals only. He was shorn of his ears and would have been killed, but Monangoi said: "Don't let the blood of a freeman touch our soil."

26th September, 1870. --I am able now to report the ulcers healing. For eighty days I have been completely laid up by them, and it will be long ere the lost substance will be replaced. They kill many slaves; and an epidemic came to us which carried off thirty in our small camp[8].

[We come to a very important note under the next date. It may be necessary to remind the reader that when Livingstone left the neighbourhood of Lake Nyassa and bent his steps northwards, he believed that the "Chambeze" River, which the natives reported to be ahead of him, was in reality the Zambezi, for he held in his hand a map manufactured at home, and so conveniently manipulated as to clear up a great difficulty by simply inserting "New Zambezi" in the place of the Chambeze. As we now see, Livingstone handed back this addled geographical egg to its progenitor, who, we regret to say, has not only smashed it in wrath, but has treated us

---

8 A precisely similar epidemic broke out at the settlement at Magomero, in which fifty-four of the slaves liberated by Dr. Livingstone and Bishop Mackenzie died. This disease is by far the most fatal scourge the natives suffer from, not even excepting small-pox. It is common throughout Tropical Africa. We believe that some important facts have recently been brought to light regarding it, and we can only trust sincerely that the true nature of the disorder will be known in time, so that it may be successfully treated: at present change of air and high feeding on a meat diet are the best remedies we know.--ED.

to so much of its savour in a pamphlet written against the deceased explorer, that few will care to turn over its leaves.

However, the African traveller has a warning held up before him which may be briefly summed up in a caution to be on the look out for constant repetitions in one form or another of the same name. Endless confusion has arisen from Nyassas and Nyanzas, from Chiroas and Kiroas and Shirwas, to say nothing of Zambesis and Ohambezes. The natives are just as prone to perpetuate Zambezi or Lufira in Africa as we are to multiply our Avons and Ouses in England.]

4th October, 1870. --A trading party from Ujiji reports an epidemic raging between the coast and Ujiji, and very fatal. Syde bin Habib and Dugumbe are coming, and they have letters and perhaps people for me, so I remain, though the irritable ulcers are well-nigh healed. I fear that my packet for the coast may have fared badly, for the Lewale has kept Musa Kamaal by him, so that no evidence against himself or the dishonest man Musa bin Saloom should be given: my box and guns, with despatches, I fear will never be sent. Zahor, to whom I gave calico to pay carriers, has been sent off to Lobemba.

Mohamad sowed rice yesterday, and has to send his people (who were unsuccessful among the Balegga) away to the Metambe, where they got ivory before.

I cannot understand very well what a "Theoretical Discoverer" is. If anyone got up and declared in a public meeting that he was the theoretical discoverer of the philosopher's stone, or of perpetual motion for watches, should we not mark him as a little wrong in the head? So of the Nile sources. The Portuguese crossed the Chambeze some seventy years before I did, but to them it was a branch of the Zambezi and nothing more. Cooley put it down as the New Zambesi, and made it run backwards, up-hill, between 3000 and 4000 feet! I was misled by the similarity of names and a map, to think it the eastern branch of the Zambezi. I was told that it formed a large water in the south-west, this I readily believed to be the Liambai, in the Barotse Valley, and it took me eighteen months of toil to come back again to the Chambeze in Lake Bangweolo, and work out the error into which I was led-- twenty-two months elapsed ere I got back to the point whence I set out to explore Chambeze, Bangweolo, Luapula, Moero, and Lualaba. I spent two full years at this work, and the Chief Casembe was the first to throw light on the subject by saying, "It is the same water here as in the Chambeze, the same in Moero and Lualaba, and one piece of water is just like another. Will you draw out calico from it that you wish to see it? As your chief desired you to see Bangweolo, go to it, and if in going north you see a travelling party, join it; if not, come back to me, and I will send you safely by my path along Moero."

The central Lualaba I would fain call the Lake River Webb; the western, the Lake River Young. The Lufira and Lualaba West form a Lake, the native name of which, "Chibungo," must give way to Lake Lincoln. I wish to name the fountain of the Liambai or Upper Zambesi, Palmerston Fountain, and adding that of Sir Bartle Frere to the fountain of Lufira, three names of men who have done more to abolish slavery and the slave-trade than any of their contemporaries.

[Through the courtesy of the Earl of Derby we are able to insert a paragraph here which occurs in a despatch written to Her Majesty's Foreign Office by Dr. Livingstone a few weeks before his death. He treats more fully in it upon the different names that he gave to the most important rivers and lakes which he discovered, and we see how he cherished to the last the fond memory of old well-tried friendships, and the great examples of men like President Lincoln and Lord Palmerston.]

"I have tried to honour the name of the good Lord Palmerston, in fond remembrance of his long and unwearied labour for the abolition of the Slave Trade; and I venture to place the name of the good and noble Lincoln on the Lake, in gratitude to him who gave freedom to 4,000,000 of slaves. These two great men are no longer among us; but it pleases me, here in the wilds, to place, as it were, my poor little garland of love on their tombs. Sir Bartle Frere having accomplished the grand work of abolishing slavery in Scindiah, Upper India, deserves the gratitude of every lover of human kind.

"Private friendship guided me in the selection of other names where distinctive epithets were urgently needed. 'Paraffin' Young, one of my teachers in chemistry, raised himself to be a merchant prince by his science and art, and has shed pure white light in many lowly cottages, and in some rich palaces. Leaving him and chemistry, I went away to try and bless others. I, too, have shed light of another kind, and am fain to believe that I have performed a small part in the grand revolution which our Maker has been for ages carrying on, by multitudes of conscious, and many unconscious agents, all over the world. Young's friendship never faltered.

"Oswell and Webb were fellow-travellers, and mighty hunters. Too much engrossed myself with mission-work to hunt, except for the children's larder, when going to visit distant tribes, I relished the sight of fair stand-up fights by my friends with the large denizens of the forest, and admired the true Nimrod class for their great courage, truthfulness, and honour. Being a warm lover of natural history, the entire butcher tribe, bent only on making 'a bag,' without regard to animal suffering, have not a single kindly word from me. An Ambonda man, named Mokantju, told Oswell and me in 1851 that the Liambai and Kafue rose as one fountain and then separated, but after a long course came together again in the Zambezi above Zumbo."

8th October, 1870.--Mbarawa and party came yesterday from Katomba at Mamohela. He reports that Jangeonge (?) with Moeneokela's men had been killing people of the Metamba or forest, and four of his people were slain. He intended fighting, hence his desire to get rid of me when I went north: he got one and a half tusks, but little ivory, but Katomba's party got fifty tusks; Abdullah had got two tusks, and had also been fighting, and Katomba had sent a fighting party down to Lolinde; plunder and murder is Ujijian trading. Mbarawa got his ivory on the Lindi, or as he says, "Urindi," which has black water, and is very large: an arrow could not be shot across its stream, 400 or 500 yards wide, it had to be crossed by canoes, and goes into Lualaba. It is curious that all think it necessary to say to me, "The Manyuema are bad, very bad;" the Balegga will be let alone, because they can fight, and we shall hear nothing of their badness.

10th October, 1870.--I came out of my hut to-day, after being confined to it since the 22nd July, or eighty days, by irritable ulcers on the feet. The last twenty days I suffered from fever, which reduced my strength, taking away my voice, and purging me. My appetite was good, but the third mouthful of any food caused nausea and vomiting--purging took place and profuse sweating; it was choleraic, and how many Manyuema died of it we could not ascertain. While this epidemic raged here, we heard of cholera terribly severe on the way to the coast. I am thankful to feel myself well.

Only one ulcer is open, the size of a split pea: malachite was the remedy most useful, but the beginning of the rains may have helped the cure, as it does to others; copper rubbed down is used when malachite cannot be had. We expect Syde bin Habib soon: he will take to the river, and I hope so shall I. The native traders reached people who had horns of oxen, got from the left bank of the Lualaba. Katomba's people got most ivory, namely, fifty tusks; the others only four. The Metamba or forest is of immense extent, and there is room for much ivory to be picked up at five or seven bracelets of copper per tusk, if the slaves sent will only be merciful. The nine villages destroyed, and 100 men killed, by Katomba's slaves at Nasangwa's, were all about a string of beads fastened to a powder horn, which a Manyuema man tried in vain to steal!

Katomba gets twenty-five of the fifty tusks brought by his people. We expect letters, and perhaps men by Syde bin Habib. No news from the coast had come to Ujiji, save a rumour that some one was building a large house at Bagamoio, but whether French or English no one can say: possibly the erection of a huge establishment on the mainland may be a way of laboriously proving that it is more healthy than the island. It will take a long time to prove by stone and lime that the higher lands, 200 miles inland, are better still, both for longevity and work[9]. I am in agony for news from home; all I feel sure of now is that my friends will all wish me to complete my task. I join in the wish now, as better than doing it in vain afterwards.

The Manyuema hoeing is little better than scraping the soil, and cutting through the roots of grass and weeds, by a horizontal motion of the hoe or knife; they leave the roots of maize, ground-nuts, sweet potatoes, and dura, to find their way into the rich soft soil, and well they succeed, so there is no need for deep ploughing: the ground-nuts and cassava hold their own against grass for years, and bananas, if cleared of weeds, yield abundantly. Mohamad sowed rice just outside the camp without any advantage being secured by the vicinity of a rivulet, and it yielded forone measure of seed one hundred and twenty measures of increase. This season he plants along the rivulet called "Bonde," and on the damp soil.

The rain-water does not percolate far, for the clay retains it about two feet beneath the surface: this is a cause of unhealthiness to man. Fowls and goats have been

---

9 Dr. Livingstone never ceased to impress upon Europeans the utter necessity of living on the high table-lands of the interior, rather than on the sea-board or the banks of the great arterial rivers. Men may escape death in an unhealthy place, but the system is enfeebled and energy reduced to the lowest ebb. Under such circumstances life becomes a misery, and important results can hardly be looked for when one's vitality is preoccupied in wrestling with the unhealthiness of the situation, day and night.--ED.

cut off this year in large numbers by an epidemic.

The visits of the Ujijian traders must be felt by the Manyuema to be a severe infliction, for the huts are appropriated, and no leave asked: firewood, pots, baskets, and food are used without scruple, and anything that pleases is taken away; usually the women flee into the forest, and return to find the whole place a litter of broken food. I tried to pay the owners of the huts in which I slept, but often in vain, for they hid in the forest, and feared to come near. It was common for old men to come forward to me with a present of bananas as I passed, uttering with trembling accents, "Bolongo, Bolongo!" ("Friendship, Friendship!"), and if I stopped to make a little return present, others ran for plantains or palm-toddy. The Arabs' men ate up what they demanded, without one word of thanks, and turned round to me and said, "They are bad, don't give them anything." "Why, what badness is there in giving food?" I replied. "Oh! they like you, but hate us." One man gave me an iron ring, and all seemed inclined to be friendly, yet they are undoubtedly bloodthirsty to other Manyuema, and kill each other.

I am told that journeying inland the safe way to avoid tsetse in going to Merere's is to go to Mdonge, Makinde, Zungomero, Masapi, Irundu, Nyangore, then turn north to the Nyannugams, and thence to Nyembe, and so on south to Merere's. A woman chief lies in the straight way to Merere, but no cattle live in the land. Another insect lights on the animals, and when licked off bites the tongue, or breeds, and is fatal as well as tsetse: it is larger in size. Tipo Tipo and Syde bin Ali come to Nyembe, thence to Nsama's, cross Lualaba at Mpweto's, follow left bank of that river till they cross the next Lualaba, and so into Lunda of Matiamvo. Much ivory may be obtained by this course, and it shows enterprise. Syde bin Habib and Dugumbe will open up the Lualaba this year, and I am hoping to enter the West Lualaba, or Young's River, and if possible go up to Katanga. The Lord be my guide and helper. I feel the want of medicine strongly, almost as much as the want of men.

16th October, 1870. --Moenemgoi, the chief, came to tell me that Monamyembo had sent five goats to Lohombo to get a charm to kill him. "Would the English and Kolokolo (Mohamad) allow him to be killed while they were here?" I said that it was a false report, but he believes it firmly: Monamyembo sent his son to assure us that he was slandered, but thus quarrels and bloodshed feuds arise!

The great want of the Manyuema is national life, of this they have none: each headman is independent of every other. Of industry they have no lack, and the villagers are orderly towards each other, but they go no further. If a man of another district ventures among them, it is at his peril; he is not regarded with more favour as a Manyuema than one of a herd of buffaloes is by the rest: and he is almost sure to be killed.

Moenekuss had more wisdom than his countrymen: his eldest son went over to Monamyembo (one of his subjects) and was there murdered by five spear wounds. The old chief went and asked who had slain his son. All professed ignorance, whilst some suggested "perhaps the Bahombo did it," so he went off to them, but they also denied it and laid it at the door of Monamdenda, from whom he got the same reply when he arrived at his place--no one knew, and so the old man died. This, though he was heartbroken, was called witchcraft by Monamyembo. Eleven people were murdered, and after this cruel man was punished he sent a goat with the confession that he had killed Moenekuss' son. This son had some of the father's wisdom: the others he never could get to act like men of sense.

19th October, 1870. --Bambarre. The ringleading deserters sent Chuma to say that they were going with the people of Mohamad (who left to-day), to the Metamba, but I said that I had nought to say to them. They would go now to the Metamba, whom, on deserting, they said they so much feared, and they think nothing of having left me to go with only three attendants, and get my feet torn to pieces in mud and sand. They probably meant to go back to the women at Mamohela, who fed them in the absence of their husbands. They were told by Mohamad that they must not follow his people, and he gave orders to bind them, and send them back if they did. They think that no punishment will reach them whatever they do: they are freemen, and need not work or do anything but beg. "English," they call themselves, and the Arabs fear them, though the eagerness with which they engaged in slave-hunting showed them to be genuine niggers.

20th October, 1870. --The first heavy rain of this season fell yesterday afternoon. It is observable that the permanent halt to which the Manyuema have come is not affected by the appearance of superior men among them: they are stationary, and improvement is unknown. Moenekuss paid smiths to teach his sons, and they learned to work in copper and iron, but he never could get them to imitate his own generous and obliging deportment to others; he had to reprove them perpetually for mean shortsightedness, and when he died he virtually left no successor, for his sons are both narrowminded, mean, shortsighted creatures, without dignity or honour. All they can say of their forefathers is that they came from Lualaba up Luamo, then to Luelo, and thence here. The name seems to mean "forest people"--*Manyuema*.

The party under Hassani crossed the Logumba at Kanyingere's, and went N. and N.N.E. They found the country becoming more and more mountainous, till at last, approaching Morere, it was perpetually up and down. They slept at a village on the top, and could send for water to the bottom only once, it took so much time to descend and ascend. The rivers all flowed into Kerere or Lower Tanganyika. There is a hot fountain whose water could not be touched nor stones stood upon. The Balegga were very unfriendly, and collected in thousands. "We come to buy ivory," said Hassani, "and if there is none we go away." "Nay," shouted they, "you come to die here!" and then they shot with arrows; when musket-balls were returned they fled, and would not come to receive the captives.

25th October, 1870. --Bambarre. In this journey I have endeavoured to follow with unswerving fidelity the line of duty. My course has been an even one, turning neither to the right hand nor to the left, though my route has been tortuous enough. All the hardship, hunger, and toil were met with the full conviction that I was right in persevering to make a complete work of the exploration of the sources of the Nile. Mine has been a calm, hopeful endeavour to do the work that has been given me to do, whether I succeed or whether I fail. The prospect of death in pursuing what I knew to be right did not make me veer to one side or the other. I had a strong presentiment during the first three years that I should never live through the enterprise, but it weakened as I came near to the end of the journey, and an eager desire to discover any evidence of the great Moses having visited these parts bound me, spell-bound me, I may say, for if I could bring to light anything to confirm the Sacred Oracles, I should not grudge one whit all the labour expended. I have to go down the Central Lualaba or Webb's Lake River, then up the Western or Young's Lake River to Katanga head waters and then retire. I pray that it may be to my native home.

Syde bin Habib, Dugumbe, Juma Merikano, Abdullah Masendi are coming in with 700 muskets, and an immense store of beads, copper, &c. They will cross Lualaba and trade west of it: I wait for them because they may have letters for me.

28th October, 1870.--Moenemokata, who has travelled further than most Arabs, said to me, "If a man goes with a good-natured, civil tongue, he may pass through the worst people in Africa unharmed:" this is true, but time also is required: one must not run through a country, but give the people time to become acquainted with you, and let their first fears subside.

29th October, 1870.--The Manyuema buy their wives from each other; a pretty girl brings ten goats. I saw one brought home to-day; she came jauntily with but one attendant, and her husband walking behind. They stop five days, then go back and remain other five days at home: then the husband fetches her again. Many are pretty, and have perfect forms and limbs.

31st October, 1870.--Monangoi, of Luamo, married to the sister of Moenekuss, came some time ago to beg that Kanyingere might be attacked by Mohamad's people: no fault has he, "but he is bad." Monangoi, the chief here, offered two tusks to effect the same thing; on refusal, he sends the tusks to Katomba, and may get his countryman spoiled by him. "He is bad," is all they can allege as a reason. Meantime this chief here caught a slave who escaped, a prisoner from Moene-mokia's, and sold him or her to Moene-mokia for thirty spears and some knives; when asked about this captive, he said, "She died:" it was simply theft, but he does not consider himself bad.

2nd November, 1870.--The plain without trees that flanks the Lualaba on the right bank, called Mbuga, is densely peopled, and the inhabitants are all civil and friendly. From fifty to sixty large canoes come over from the left bank daily to hold markets; these people too "are good," but the dwellers in the Metamba or dense forest are treacherous and murder a single person without scruple: the dead body is easily concealed, while on the plain all would become aware of it.

I long with intense desire to move on and finish my work, I have also an excessive wish to find anything that may exist proving the visit of the great Moses and the ancient kingdom of Tirhaka, but I pray give me just what pleases Thee my Lord, and make me submissive to Thy will in all things.

I received information about Mr. Young's search trip up the Shire and Nyassa only in February 1870, and now take the first opportunity of offering hearty thanks in a despatch to Her Majesty's Government, and all concerned in kindly inquiring after my fate.

Musa and his companions were fair average specimens for heartlessness and falsehood of the lower classes of Mohamadans in East Africa. When we were on the Shire we used to swing the ship into mid-stream every night, in order to let the air which was put in motion by the water, pass from end to end. Musa's brother-in-law stepped into the water one morning, in order to swim off for a boat, and was seized by a crocodile, the poor fellow held up his hand imploringly, but Musa and the rest allowed him to perish. On my denouncing his heartlessness, Musa-replied, "Well, no one tell him go in there." When at Senna a slave woman was seized by a crocodile: four Makololo rushed in unbidden, and rescued her, though they knew nothing about her: from long intercourse with both Johanna men and Makololo I take these incidents as typical of the two races. Those of mixed blood possess the vices of both races, and the virtues of neither.

A gentleman of superior abilities[10] has devoted life and fortune to elevate the Johanna men, but fears that they are "an unimprovable race."

The Sultan of Zanzibar, who knows his people better than any stranger, cannot entrust any branch of his revenue to even the better class of his subjects, but places all his customs, income, and money affairs, in the hands of Banians from India, and his father did before him.

When the Mohamadan gentlemen of Zanzibar are asked "why their sovereign places all his pecuniary affairs and fortune in the hands of aliens?" they frankly avow that if he allowed any Arab to farm his customs, he would receive nothing but a crop of lies.

Burton had to dismiss most of his people at Ujiji for dishonesty: Speke's followers deserted at the first approach of danger. Musa fled in terror on hearing a false report from a half-caste Arab about the Mazitu, 150 miles distant, though I promised to go due west, and not turn to the north till far past the beat of that tribe. The few liberated slaves with whom I went on had the misfortune to be Mohamadan slaves in boyhood, but did fairly till we came into close contact with Moslems again. A black Arab was released from a twelve years' bondage by Casembe, through my own influence and that of the Sultan's letter: we travelled together for a time, and he sold the favours of his female slaves to my people for goods which he perfectly well knew were stolen from me. He received my four deserters, and when I had

---

10   Mr. John Sunley, of Pomone, Johanna, an island in the Comoro group.

gone off to Lake Bangweolo with only four attendants, the rest wished to follow, but he dissuaded them by saying that I had gone into a country where there was war: he was the direct cause of all my difficulties with these liberated slaves, but judged by the East African Moslem standard, as he ought to be, and not by ours, he isa very good man, and I did not think it prudent to come to a rupture with the old blackguard.

"Laba" means in the Manyuema dialect "medicine;" a charm, "boganga:" this would make Lualaba mean the River of Medicine or charms. Hassani thought that it meant "great," because it seemed to mean flowing greatly or grandly.

Casembe caught all the slaves that escaped from Mohamad, and placed them in charge of Fungafunga; so there is little hope for fugitive slaves so long as Casembe lives: this act is to the Arabs very good: he is very sensible, and upright besides.

3rd November, 1870.--Got a Kondohondo, the large double-billed Hornbill (the ***Buceros cristata***), Kakomira, of the Shire, and the Sassassa of Bambarre. It is good eating, and has fat of an orange tinge, like that of the zebra; I keep the bill to make a spoon of it.

An ambassador at Stamboul or Constantinople was shown a hornbill spoon, and asked if it were really the bill of the Phoenix. He replied that he did not know, but he had a friend in London who knew all these sort of things, so the Turkish ambassador in London brought the spoon to Professor Owen. He observed something in the divergences of the fibres of the horn which he knew before, and went off into the Museum of the College of Surgeons, and brought a preserved specimen of this very bird. "God is great--God is great," said the Turk, "this is the Phoenix of which we have heard so often." I heard the Professor tell this at a dinner of the London Hunterian Society in 1857.

There is no great chief in Manyuema or Balegga; all are petty headmen, each of whom considers himself a chief: it is the ethnic state, with no cohesion between the different portions of the tribe. Murder cannot be punished except by a war, in which many fall, and the feud is made worse, and transmitted to their descendants.

The heathen philosophers were content with mere guesses at the future of the soul. The elder prophets were content with the Divine support in life and in death. The later prophets advance further, as Isaiah: "Thy dead men shall live, together with my dead body shall they arise. Awake, and sing, ye that dwell in the dust: for thy dew is as the dew of herbs. The earth also shall cast out her dead." This, taken with the sublime spectacle of Hades in the fourteenth chapter, seems a forecast of the future, but Jesus instructed Mary and her sister and Lazarus; and Martha without hesitation spoke of the resurrection at the last day as a familiar doctrine, far in advance of the Mosaic law in which she had been reared.

The Arabs tell me that Monyungo, a chief, was sent for five years among the Watuta to learn their language and ways, and he sent his two sons and a daughter to Zanzibar to school. He kills many of his people, and says they are so bad that if not killed they would murder strangers. Once they were unruly, when he ordered some of them to give their huts to Mohamad; on refusing, he put fire to them, and they soon called out, "Let them alone; we will retire." He dresses like an Arab, and has ten loaded guns at his sitting-place, four pistols, two swords, several spears, and two bundles of the Batuta spears: he laments that his father filed his teeth when he was young. The name of his very numerous people is Bawungu, country Urungu: his other names are Ironga, Mohamu.

The Basango, on the other hand, consider their chief as a deity, and fear to say aught wrong, lest he should hear them: they fear both before him and when out of sight.

The father of Merere never drank pombe or beer, and assigned as a reason that a great man who had charge of people's lives should never become intoxicated so as to do evil. Bange he never smoked, but in council smelled at a bunch of it, in order to make his people believe that it had a great effect on him. Merere drinks pombe freely, but never uses bange: he alone kills sheep; he is a lover of mutton and beef, but neither goats nor fowls are touched by him.

9th November, 1870. --I sent to Lohombo for dura, and planted some Nyumbo. I long excessively to be away and finish my work by the two Lacustrine rivers, Lualaba of Webb and Young, but wait only for Syde and Dugumbe, who may have letters, and as I do not intend to return hither, but go through Karagwe homewards, I should miss them altogether. I groan and am in bitterness at the delay, but thus it is: I pray for help to do what is right, but sorely am I perplexed, and grieved and mourn: I cannot give up making a complete work of the exploration.

10th November, 1870. --A party of Katomba's men arrived on their way to Ujiji for carriers, they report that a foray was made S.W. of Mamohela to recover four guns, which were captured from Katomba; three were recovered, and ten of the Arab party slain. The people of Manyuema fought very fiercely with arrows, and not till many were killed and others mutilated would they give up the guns; they probably expected this foray, and intended to fight till the last. They had not gone in search of ivory while this was enacting, consequently Mohamad's men have got the start of them completely, by going along Lualaba to Kasongo's, and then along the western verge of the Metamba or forest to Loinde or Rindi River. The last men sent took to fighting instead of trading, and returned empty; the experience gained thus, and at the south-west, will probably lead them to conclude that the Manyuema are not to be shot down without reasonable cause. They have sown rice and maize at Mamohela, but cannot trade now where they got so much ivory before. Five men were killed at Rindi or Loinde, and one escaped: the reason of this outbreak by men who have been so peaceable is not divulged, but anyone seeing the wholesale plunder to which the houses and gardens were subject can easily guess the rest. Mamohela's camp had several times been set on fire at night by the tribes which suffered assault, but did not effect all that was intended. The Arabs say that the Manyuema now understand that every gunshot does not kill; the next thing they will learn will be to grapple in close quarters in the forest, where their spears will outmatch the guns in the hands of slaves, it will follow, too, that no one will be able to pass through this country; this is the usual course of Suaheli trading; it is murder and plunder, and each slave as he rises in his owner's favour is eager to show himself a mighty man of valour, by cold-blooded killing of his countrymen: if they can kill a fellow-nigger, their pride boils up. The conscience is not enlightened enough to cause uneasiness, and Islam gives less than the light of nature.

I am grievously tired of living here. Mohamad is as kind as he can be, but to sit idle or give up before I finish my work are both intolerable; I cannot bear either, yet I am forced to remain by want of people.

11th November, 1870.--I wrote to Mohamad bin Saleh at Ujiji for letters and medicines to be sent in a box of China tea, which is half empty: if he cannot get carriers for the long box itself, then he is to send these, the articles of which I stand in greatest need.

The relatives of a boy captured at Monanyembe brought three goats to redeem him: he is sick and emaciated; one goat was rejected. The boy shed tears when he saw his grandmother, and the father too, when his goat was rejected. "So I returned, and considered all the oppressions that are done under the sun: and behold the tears of such as were oppressed, and they had no comforter; and on the side of their oppressors there was power; but they had no comforter."--Eccles. iv. 1. The relations were told either to bring the goat, or let the boy die; this was hard-hearted. At Mamohela ten goats are demanded for a captive, and given too; here three are demanded. "He that is higher than the highest regardeth, and there be higher than they. Marvel not at the matter."

I did not write to the coast, for I suspect that the Lewale Syde bin Salem Buraschid destroys my letters in order to quash the affair of robbery by his man Saloom, he kept the other thief, Kamaels, by him for the same purpose. Mohamad writes to Bin Saleh to say that I am here and well; that I sent a large packet of letters in June 1869, with money, and received neither an answer, nor my box from Unyanyembe, and this is to be communicated to the Consul by a friend at Zanzibar. If I wrote, it would only be to be burned; this is as far as I can see at present: the friend who will communicate with the Consul is Mohamad bin Abdullah the Wuzeer, Seyd Suleiman is the Lewale of the Governor of Zanzibar, Suleiman bin Ali or **Sheikh** Suleiman the Secretary.

The Mamohela horde is becoming terrified, for every party going to trade has lost three or four men, and in the last foray they saw that the Manyuema can fight, for they killed ten men: they will soon refuse to go among those whom they have forced to become enemies.

One of the Bazula invited a man to go with him to buy ivory; he went with him, and on getting into the Zulas country the stranger was asked by the guide if his gun killed men, and how it did it: whilst he was explaining the matter he was stabbed to death. No one knows the reason of this, but the man probably lost some of his relations elsewhere: this is called murder without cause. When Syde and Dugumbe come, I hope to get men and a canoe to finish my work among those who have not been abused by Ujijians, and still retain their natural kindness of disposition; none of the people are ferocious without cause; and the sore experience which they gain from slaves with guns in their hands usually ends in sullen hatred of all strangers.

The education of the world is a terrible one, and it has come down with relentless rigour on Africa from the most remote times! What the African will become after this awfully hard lesson is learned, is among the future developments of Providence. When He, who is higher than the highest, accomplishes His purposes, this will be a wonderful country, and again something like what it was of old, when Zerah and Tirhaka flourished, and were great.

The soil of Manyuema is clayey and remarkably fertile, the maize sown in it rushes up to seed, and everything is in rank profusion if only it be kept clear of weeds, but the Bambarre people are indifferent cultivators, planting maize, bananas and plantains, and ground-nuts only--no dura, a little cassava, no pennisetum, meleza, pumpkins, melons, or nyumbo, though they all flourish in other districts: a few sweet potatoes appear, but elsewhere all these native grains and roots are abundant and cheap. No one would choose this as a residence, except for the sake of Moenekuss. Oil is very dear, while at Lualaba a gallon may be got for a single string of beads, and beans, ground-nuts, cassava, maize, plantains in rank profusion. The Balegga, like the Bambarre people, trust chiefly to plantains and ground-nuts; to play with parrots is their great amusement.

13th November, 1870.--The men sent over to Lohombo, about thirty miles off, got two and a half loads of dura for a small goat, but the people were unwilling to trade. "If we encourage Arabs to trade, they will come and kill us with their guns," so they said, and it is true: the slaves are overbearing, and when this is resented, then slaughter ensues. I got some sweet plantains and a little oil, which is useful in cooking, and with salt, passes for butter on bread, but all were unwilling to trade. Monangoi was over near Lohombo, and heard of a large trading party coming, and not far off; this may be Syde and Dugumbe, but reports are often false. When Katomba's men were on the late foray, they were completely overpowered, and compelled by the Manyuema to lay down their guns and powder-horns, on pain of being instantly despatched by bow-shot: they were mostly slaves, who could only draw the trigger and make a noise. Katomba had to rouse out all the Arabs who could shoot, and when they came they killed many, and gained the lost day; the Manyuema did not kill anyone who laid down his gun and powder-horn. This is the beginning of an end which was easily perceived when it became not a trading, but a foray of a murdering horde of savages.

The foray above mentioned was undertaken by Katomba for twenty goats from Kassessa!--ten men lost for twenty goats, but they will think twice before they try another foray.

A small bird follows the "Sassassa" or ***Buceros cristata***. It screams and pecks at his tail till he discharges the contents of his bowels, and then leaves him; it is called "play" by the natives, and by the Suaheli "Utane" or "Msaha"--fun or wit; he follows other birds in the same merciless way, screaming and pecking to produce purging; Manyuema call this bird "Mambambwa." The buffalo bird warns its big friend of danger, by calling "Chachacha," and the rhinoceros bird cries out, "Tye, tye, tye, tye," for the same purpose. The Manyuema call the buffalo bird "Mojela," and the Suaheli, "Chassa." A climbing plant in Africa is known as "Ntulungope," which mixed with flour of dura kills mice; they swarm in our camp and destroy everything, but Ntulungope is not near this.

The Arabs tell me that one dollar a day is ample for provisions for a large family at Zanzibar; the food consists of wheat, rice, flesh of goats or ox, fowls, bananas, milk, butter, sugar, eggs, mangoes, and potatoes. Ambergris is boiled in milk and sugar, and used by the Hindoos as a means of increasing blood in their systems; a small quantity is a dose; it is found along the shore of the sea at Barawa or Brava, and at Madagascar, as if the sperm whale got rid of it while alive. Lamoo or Amu is wealthy, and well supplied with everything, as grapes, peaches, wheat, cattle, camels, &c. The trade is chiefly with Madagascar: the houses are richly furnished with furniture, dishes from India, &c. At Garaganza there are hundreds of Arab traders, there too all fruits abound, and the climate is healthy, from its elevation. Why cannot we missionaries imitate these Arabs in living on heights?

24th November, 1870.--Herpes is common at the plantations in Zanzibar, but the close crowding of the houses in the town they think prevents it; the lips and mouth are affected, and constipation sets in for three days, all this is cured by going over to the mainland. Affections of the lungs are healed by residence at Bariwa or Brava, and also on the mainland. The Tafori of Halfani took my letters from Ujiji, but who the person employed is I do not know.

29th November, 1870. -- ***Safura*** is the name of the disease of clay or earth eating, at Zanzibar; it often affects slaves, and the clay is said to have a pleasant odour to the eaters, but it is not confined to slaves, nor do slaves eat in order to kill themselves; it is a diseased appetite, and rich men who have plenty to eat are often subject to it. The feet swell, flesh is lost, and the face looks haggard; the patient can scarcely walk for shortness of breath and weakness, and he continues eating till he dies. Here many slaves are now diseased with safura; the clay built in walls is preferred, and Manyuema women when pregnant often eat it. The cure is effected by drastic purges composed as follows: old vinegar of cocoa-trees is put into a large basin, and old slag red-hot cast into it, then "Moneye," asafoetida, half a rupee in weight, copperas, sulph. ditto: a small glass of this, fasting morning and evening, produces vomiting and purging of black dejections, this is continued for seven days; no meat is to be eaten, but only old rice or dura and water; a fowl in course of time: no fish, butter, eggs, or beef for two years on pain of death. Mohamad's father had skill in the cure, and the above is his prescription. Safura is thus a disease *per se*; it is common in Manyuema, and makes me in a measure content to wait for my medicines; from the description, inspissated bile seems to be the agent of blocking up the gall-duct and duodenum and the clay or earth may be nature trying to clear it away: the clay appears unchanged in the stools, and in large quantity. A Banyamwezi carrier, who bore an enormous load of copper, is now by safura scarcely able to walk; he took it at Lualaba where food is abundant, and he is contented with his lot. Squeeze a finger-nail, and if no blood appears beneath it, safura is the cause of the bloodlessness.

CHAPTER IV.

Degraded state of the Manyuema. Want of writing materials. Lion's fat a specific against tsetse. The Neggeri. Jottings about Merere. Various sizes of tusks. An epidemic. The strangest disease of all! The New Year. Detention at Bambarre. Goitre. News of the cholera. Arrival of coast caravan. The parrot's-feather challenge. Murder of James. Men arrive as servants. They refuse to go north. Parts at last with malcontents. Receives letters from Dr. Kirk and the Sultan. Doubts as to the Congo or Nile. Katomba presents a young soko. Forest scenery. Discrimination of the Manyuema. They "want to eat a white one." Horrible bloodshed by Ujiji traders. Heartsore and sick of blood. Approach Nyangwe. Reaches the Lualaba.

6th December, 1870. --Oh, for Dugumbe or Syde to come! but this delay may be all for the best. The parrots all seize their food, and hold it with the left hand, the lion, too, is left-handed; he strikes with the left, so are all animals left-handed save man.

I noticed a very pretty woman come past this quite jauntily about a month ago, on marriage with Monasimba. Ten goats were given; her friends came and asked another goat, which being refused, she was enticed away, became sick of rheumatic fever two days afterwards, and died yesterday. Not a syllable of regret for the beautiful young creature does one hear, but for the goats: "Oh, our ten goats!"--they cannot grieve too much--"Our ten goats--oh! oh!"

Basanga wail over those who die in bed, but not over those who die in battle: the cattle are a salve for all sores. Another man was killed within half a mile of this: they quarrelled, and there is virtually no chief. The man was stabbed, the village burned, and the people all fled: they are truly a bloody people!

A man died near this, Monasimba went to his wife, and after washing he may appear among men. If no widow can be obtained, he must sit naked behind his house till some one happens to die, all the clothes he wore are thrown away. They are the lowest of the low, and especially in bloodiness: the man who killed a woman without cause goes free, he offered his grandmother to be killed in his stead, and after a great deal of talk nothing was done to him!

8th December, 1870.--Suleiman-bin-Juma lived on the mainland, Mosessame, opposite Zanzibar: it is impossible to deny his power of foresight, except by rejecting all evidence, for he frequently foretold the deaths of great men among Arabs, and he was pre-eminently a good man, upright and sincere: "Thirti," none like him now for goodness and skill. He said that two middle-sized white men, with straight noses and flowing hair down to the girdle behind, came at times, and told him things to come. He died twelve years ago, and left no successor; he foretold his own decease three days beforehand by cholera. "Heresi," a ball of hair rolled in the stomach of a lion, is a grand charm to the animal and to Arabs. Mohamad has one.

10th December, 1870.--I am sorely let and hindered in this Manyuema. Rain every day, and often at night; I could not travel now, even if I had men, but I could make some progress; this is the sorest delay I ever had. I look above for help and mercy.

[The wearied man tried to while away the time by gaining little scraps of information from the Arabs and the natives, but we cannot fail to see what a serious stress was all the time put upon his constitution under these circumstances; the reader will pardon the disjointed nature of his narrative, written as it was under the greatest disadvantage.]

Lion's fat is regarded as a sure preventive of tsetse or bungo. This was noted before, but I add now that it is smeared on the ox's tail, and preserves hundreds of the Banyamwesi cattle in safety while going to the coast; it is also used to keep pigs and hippopotami away from gardens: the smell is probably the efficacious part in "Heresi," as they call it.

12th December, 1870.--It may be all for the best that I am so hindered, and compelled to inactivity.

An advance to Lohombo was the furthest point of traders for many a day, for the slaves returning with ivory were speared mercilessly by Manyuema, because they did not know guns could kill, and their spears could. Katomba coming to Moenekuss was a great feat three or four years ago; then Dugumbe went on to Lualaba, and fought his way, so I may be restrained now in mercy till men come.

The Neggeri, an African animal, attacks the tenderest parts of man and beast, cuts them off, and retires contented: buffaloes are often castrated by him. Men who know it, squat down, and kill him with knife or gun. The Zibu or mbuide flies at the tendon Achilles; it is most likely the Ratel.

The Fisi ea bahari, probably the seal, is abundant in the seas, but the ratel or badger probably furnished the skins for the Tabernacle: bees escape from his urine, and he eats their honey in safety; lions and all other animals fear his attacks of the heel.

The Babemba mix a handful (about twenty-five to a measure) of castor-oil seeds with the dura and meleza they grind, and usage makes them like it, the nauseous taste is not perceptible in porridge; the oil is needed where so much farinaceous or starchy matter exists, and the bowels are regulated by the mixture: experience has taught them the need of a fatty ingredient.

[Dr. Livingstone seems to have been anxious to procure all the information possible from the Arabs respecting the powerful chief Merere, who is reported to live on the borders of the Salt Water Lake, which lies between Lake Tanganyika and the East Coast. It would seem as if Merere held the most available road for travellers passing to the south-west from Zanzibar, and although the Doctor did not go through his country, he felt an interest no doubt in ascertaining as much as he could for the benefit of others.]

Goambari is a prisoner at Merere's, guarded by a thousand or more men, to prevent him intriguing with Monyungo, who is known as bloodthirsty. In the third generation Charura's descendants numbered sixty able-bodied spearmen, Garahenga or Kimamure killed many of them. Charura had six white attendants with him, but all died before he did, and on becoming chief he got all his predecessor's wives. Merere is the son of a woman of the royal stock, and of a common man, hence he is a shade or two darker than Charura's descendants, who are very light coloured, and have straight noses. They shave the head, and straight hair is all cut off; they drink much milk, warm, from the teats of the cows, and think that it is strengthening by its heat.

December 23rd, 1870.--Bambarre people suffer hunger now because they will not plant cassava; this trading party eats all the maize, and sends to a distance for more, and the Manyuema buy from them with malofu, or palm-toddy. Rice is all coming into ear, but the Manyuema planted none: maize is ripening, and mice are a pest. A strong man among the Manyuema does what he pleases, and no chief interferes: for instance, a man's wife for ten goats was given off to a Mene man, and his child, now grown, is given away, too; he comes to Mohamad for redress! Two elephants killed were very large, but have only small tusks: they come from the south in the rains. All animals, as elephants, buffaloes, and zebras, are very large in the Basango country; tusks are full in the hollows, and weigh very heavy, and animals are fat and good in flesh: eleven goats are the exchange for the flesh of an elephant.

[The following details respecting ivory cannot fail to be interesting here: they are very kindly furnished by Mr. F.D. Blyth, whose long experience enables him to speak with authority upon the subject. He says, England imports about 550 tons of ivory annually,--of this 280 tons pass away to other countries, whilst the remainder is used by our manufacturers, of whom the Sheffield cutlers alone require about 170 tons. The whole annual importation is derived from the following countries, and in the quantities given below, as near as one can approach to actual figures:

Bombay and Zanzibar export	160 tons.
Alexandria and Malta	180 "
West Coast of Africa	140 "
Cape of Good Hope	50 "
Mozambique	20 "

The Bombay merchants collect ivory from all the southern countries of Asia, and the East Coast of Africa, and after selecting that which is most suited to the wants of the Indian and Chinese markets, ship the remainder to Europe.

From Alexandria and Malta we receive ivory collected from Northern and Central Africa, from Egypt, and the countries through which the Nile flows.

Immediately after the Franco-German war the value of ivory increased considerably; and when we look at the prices realized on large Zanzibar tusks at the public sales, we can well understand the motive power which drove the Arab ivory hunters further and further into the country from which the chief supply was derived when Dr. Livingstone met them.

In 1867 their price varied from L39 to L42.
" 1868   "   "   "   "   39 " 42.
" 1869   "   "   "   "   41 " 44.
" 1870   "   "   "   "   do. " do.
" 1871   "   "   "   "   do. " do.
" 1872   "   "   "   "   58 " 61.
" 1873   "   "   "   "   68 " 72.
" 1874   "   "   "   "   53 " 58.

Single tusks vary in weight from 1 lb. to 165 lbs.: the average of a pair of tusks may be put at 28 lbs., and therefore 44,000 elephants, large and small, must be killed yearly to supply the ivory which **comes to England alone**, and when we remember that an enormous quantity goes to America, to India and China, for consumption there, and of which we have no account, some faint notion may be formed of the destruction that goes on amongst the herds of elephants.

Although naturalists distinguish only two living species of elephants, viz. the African and the Asiatic, nevertheless there is a great difference in the size, character, and colour of their tusks, which may arise from variations in climate, soil, and food. The largest tusks are yielded by the African elephant, and find their way hither from the port of Zanzibar: they are noted for being opaque, soft or "mellow" to work, and free from cracks or defects.

The tusks from India, Ceylon, &c, are smaller in size, partly of an opaque character, and partly translucent (or, as it is technically called "bright"), and harder and more cracked, but those from Siam and the neighbouring countries are very "bright," soft, and fine grained; they are much sought after for carvings and ornamental work. Tusks from Mozambique and the Cape of Good Hope seldom exceed 70 lbs. in weight each: they are similar in character to the Zanzibar kind.

Tusks which come through Alexandria and Malta differ considerably in quality: some resemble those from Zanzibar, whilst others are white and opaque, harder to work, and more cracked at the points; and others again are very translucent and hard, besides being liable to crack: this latter description fetches a much lower price in the market.

From the West Coast of Africa we get ivory which is always translucent, with a dark outside or coating, but partly hard and partly soft.

The soft ivory which comes from Ambriz, the Gaboon River, and the ports south of the equator, is more highly valued than any other, and is called "silver grey": this sort retains its whiteness when exposed to the air, and is free from that tendency to become yellowish in time which characterises Asiatic and East African ivory.

Hard tusks, as a rule, are proportionately smaller in diameter, sharper, and less worn than soft ones, and they come to market much more cracked, fetching in consequence a lower price.

In addition to the above a few tons of Mammoth ivory are received from time to time from the Arctic regions and Siberia, and although of unknown antiquity, some tusks are equal in every respect to ivory which is obtained in the present day from elephants newly killed; this, no doubt, is owing to the preservative effects of the ice in which the animals have been imbedded for many thousands of years. In the year 1799 the entire carcase of a mammoth was taken from the ice, and the skeleton and portions of the skin, still covered with reddish hair, are preserved in the Museum of St. Petersburg: it is said that portions of the flesh were eaten by the men who dug it out of the ice.]

24th December, 1870. --Between twenty-five and thirty slaves have died in the present epidemic, and many Manyuema; two yesterday at Kandawara. The feet swell, then the hands and face, and in a day or two they drop dead; it came from the East, and is very fatal, for few escape who take it.

A woman was accused of stealing maize, and the chief here sent all his people yesterday, plundered all she had in her house and garden, and brought her husband bound in thongs till he shall pay a goat: she is said to be innocent.

Monangoi does this by fear of the traders here; and, as the people tell him, as soon as they are gone the vengeance he is earning by injustice on all sides will be taken: I told the chief that his head would be cut off as soon as the traders leave, and so it will be; and Kasessa's also.

Three men went from Katomba to Kasongo's to buy Viramba, and a man was speared belonging to Kasongo, these three then fired into a mass of men who collected, one killed two, another three, and so on; so now that place is shut up from traders, and all this country will be closed as soon as the Manyuema learn that guns are limited in their power of killing, and especially in the hands of slaves, who cannot shoot, but only make a noise. These Suaheli are the most cruel and bloodthirsty missionaries in existence, and withal so impure in talk and acts, spreading disease everywhere. The Lord sees it.

28th December, 1870.—Moenembegg, the most intelligent of the two sons of Moenekuss, in power, told us that a man was killed and eaten a few miles from this yesterday: hunger was the reason assigned. On speaking of tainted meat, he said that the Manyuema put meat in water for two days to make it putrid and smell high. The love of high meat is the only reason I know for their cannibalism, but the practice is now hidden on account of the disgust that the traders expressed against open man-eating when they first arrived.

Lightning was very near us last night. The Manyuema say that when it is so loud fishes of large size fall with it, an opinion shared by the Arabs, but the large fish is really the ***Clarias Capensis*** of Smith, and it is often seen migrating in single file along the wet grass for miles: it is probably this that the Manyuema think falls from the lightning.

The strangest disease I have seen in this country seems really to be broken-heartedness, and it attacks free men who have been captured and made slaves. My attention was drawn to it when the elder brother of Syde bin Habib was killed in Rua by a night attack, from a spear being pitched through his tent into his side. Syde then vowed vengeance for the blood of his brother, and assaulted all he could find, killing the elders, and making the young men captives. He had secured a very large number, and they endured the chains until they saw the broad River Lualaba roll between them and their free homes; they then lost heart. Twenty-one were unchained as being now safe; however, all ran away at once, but eight, with many others still in chains, died in three days after crossing. They ascribed their only pain to the heart, and placed the hand correctly on the spot, though many think that the organ stands high up under the breast bone. Some slavers expressed surprise to me that they should die, seeing they had plenty to eat and no work. One fine boy of about twelve years was carried, and when about to expire, was kindly laid down on the side of the path, and a hole dug to deposit the body in. He, too, said he had nothing the matter with him, except pain in his heart: as it attacks only the free (who are captured and never slaves), it seems to be really broken-hearts of which they die.

[Livingstone's servants give some additional particulars in answer to questions put to them about this dreadful history. The sufferings endured by these unfortunate captives, whilst they were hawked about in different directions, must have been shocking indeed; many died because it was impossible for them to carry a burden on the head whilst marching in the heavy yoke or "taming stick," which weighs from 30 lbs. to 40 lbs. as a rule, and the Arabs knew that if once the stick were taken off, the captive would escape on the first opportunity. Children for a time would keep up with wonderful endurance, but it happened sometimes that the sound of dancing and the merry tinkle of the small drums would fall on their ears in passing near to a village; then the memory of home and happy days proved too much for them; they cried and sobbed, the "broken-heart" came on, and they rapidly sank.

The adults as a rule came into the slave-sticks from treachery, and had never been slaves before. Very often the Arabs would promise a present of dried fish to villagers if they would act as guides to some distant point, and as soon as they were far enough away from their friends they were seized and pinned into the yoke from which there is no escape. These poor fellows would expire in the way the Doctor mentions, talking to the last of their wives and children who would never know what had become of them. On one occasion twenty captives succeeded in escaping as follows. Chained together by the neck, and in the custody of an Arab armed with a gun, they were sent off to collect wood; at a given signal, one of them called the guard to look at something which he pretended he had found: when he stooped down they threw themselves upon him and overpowered him, and after he was dead managed to break the chain and make off in all directions.]

Rice sown on 19th October was in ear in seventy days. A leopard killed my goat, and a gun set for him went off at 10 P.M.--the ball broke both hind legs and one fore leg, yet he had power to spring up and bite a man badly afterwards; he was a male, 2 feet 4 inches at withers, and 6 feet 8 inches from tip of nose to end of tail.

1st January, 1871.--O Father! help me to finish this work to Thy honour.

Still detained at Bambarre, but a caravan of 500 muskets is reported from the coast: it may bring me other men and goods.

Rain daily. A woman was murdered without cause close by the camp; the murderer said she was a witch and speared her: the body is exposed till the affair is settled, probably by a fine of goats.

The Manyuema are the most bloody, callous savages I know; one puts a scarlet feather from a parrot's tail on the ground, and challenges those near to stick it in the hair: he who does so must kill a man or woman!

Another custom is that none dare wear the skin of the musk cat, Ngawa, unless he has murdered somebody: guns alone prevent them from killing us all, and for no reason either.

16th January, 1871.--Ramadan ended last night, and it is probable my people and others from the coast will begin to travel after three days of feasting. It has been so rainy I could have done little though I had had people.

22nd January, 1871.--A party is reported to be on the way hither. This is likely enough, but reports are so often false that doubts arise. Mohamad says he will give men when the party of Hassani comes, or when Dugumbe arrives.

24th January, 1871.--Mohamad mentioned this morning that Moene-mokaia, and Moeneghera his brother, brought about thirty slaves from Katanga to Ujiji, affected with swelled thyroid glands or "**Goitre**," and that drinking the water of Tanganyika proved a perfect cure to all in a very few days. Sometimes the swelling went down in two days after they began to use the water, in their ordinary way of cooking, washing, and drinking: possibly some ingredient of the hot fountain that flows into it affects the cure, for the people on the Lofubu, in Nsama's country, had the swelling. The water in bays is decidedly brackish, while the body of Tanganyika is quite fresh.

The odour of putrid elephant's meat in a house kills parrots: the Manyuema keep it till quite rotten, but know its fatal effects on their favourite birds.

27th January, 1871.--Safari or caravan reported to be near, and my men and goods at Ujiji.

28th January, 1871.--A safari, under Hassani and Ebed, arrived with news of great mortality by cholera (**Towny**), at Zanzibar, and my "brother," whom I conjecture to be Dr. Kirk, has fallen. The men I wrote for have come to Ujiji, but did not know my whereabouts; when told by Katomba's men they will come here, and bring my much longed for letters and goods. 70,000 victims in Zanzibar alone from cholera, and it spread inland to the Masoi and Ugogo! Cattle shivered, and fell dead: the fishes in the sea died in great numbers; here the fowls were first seized and died, but not from cholera, only from its companion. Thirty men perished in our small camp, made still smaller by all the able men being off trading at the Metamba, and how many Manyuema died we do not know; the survivors became afraid of eating the dead.

Formerly the Cholera kept along the sea-shore, now it goes far inland, and will spread all over Africa; this we get from Mecca filth, for nothing was done to prevent the place being made a perfect cesspool of animals' guts and ordure of men[11]. A piece of skin bound round the chest of a man, and half of it hanging down, prevents waste of strength, and he forgets and fattens.

Ebed's party bring 200 frasilahs of all sorts of beads; they will cross Lualaba, and open a new field on the other, or Young's Lualaba: all Central Africa will soon be known: the evils inflicted by these Arabs are enormous, but probably not greater than the people inflict on each other. Merere has turned against the Arabs, and killed one; robbing several others of all they had, though he has ivory sufficient to send down 7000 lbs. to the coast, and receive loads of goods for 500 men in return. He looks as if insane, and probably is so, and will soon be killed. His insanity may be the effect of pombe, of which he drinks largely, and his people may have told him that the Arabs were plotting with Goambari. He restored Mohamad's ivory and slaves, and sent for the other traders who had fled, saying his people had spoken badly, and he would repay all losses.

The Watuta (who are the same as the Mazitu) came stealing Banyamwezi cattle, and Mteza's men went out to them, and twenty-two were killed, but the Lewale's people did nothing. The Governor's sole anxiety is to obtain ivory, and no aid is rendered to traders. Seyed Suleiman the Wazeer is the author of the do-nothing policy, and sent away all the sepoys as too expensive, consequently the Wagogo plunder

---

11 The epidemic here mentioned reached Zanzibar Island from the interior of Africa by way of the Masai caravan route and Pangani. Dr. Kirk says it again entered Africa from Zanzibar, and followed the course of the caravans to Ujiji and Manyuema.--ED.

traders unchecked. It is reported that Egyptian Turks came up and attacked Mteza, but lost many people, and fled. The report of a Moslem Mission to his country was a falsehood, though the details given were circumstantial: falsehood is so common, one can believe nothing the Arabs say, unless confirmed by other evidence: they are the followers of the Prince of lies--Mohamad, whose cool appropriation of the knowledge gained at Damascus, and from the Jews, is perfectly disgusting. All his deeds were done when unseen by any witnesses. It is worth noticing that all admit the decadence of the Moslem power, and they ask how it is so fallen? They seem sincere in their devotion and in teaching the Koran, but its meaning is comparatively hid from most of the Suaheli. The Persian Arabs are said to be gross idolators, and awfully impure. Earth from a grave at Kurbelow (?) is put in the turban and worshipped: some of the sects won't say "Amen."

Moenyegumbe never drank more than a mouthful of pombe. When young, he could make his spear pass right through an elephant, and stick in the ground on the other side. He was a large man, and all his members were largely developed, his hands and fingers were all in proportion to his great height; and he lived to old age with strength unimpaired: Goambari inherits his white colour and sharp nose, but not his wisdom or courage. Merere killed five of his own people for exciting him against the Arabs. The half-caste is the murderer of many of Charura's descendants. His father got a daughter of Moenyegumbe for courage in fighting the Babema of Ubena.

Cold-blooded murders are frightfully common here. Some kill people in order to be allowed to wear the red tail feathers of a parrot in their hair, and yet they are not ugly like the West Coast Negroes, for many men have as finely formed heads as could be found in London. We English, if naked, would make but poor figures beside the strapping forms and finely shaped limbs of Manyuema men and women. Their cannibalism is doubtful, but my observations raise grave suspicions. A Scotch jury would say, "Not proven." The women are not guilty.

4th February, 1871. --Ten of my men from the coast have come near to Bambarre, and will arrive to-day. I am extremely thankful to hear it, for it assures me that my packet of letters was not destroyed; they know at home by this time what has detained me, and the end to which I strain.

Only one letter reached, and forty are missing! James was killed to-day by an arrow: the assassin was hid in the forest till my men going to buy food came up[12]. I propose to leave on the 12th. I have sent Dr. Kirk a cheque for Rs. 4000: great havoc was made by cholera, and in the midst of it my friend exerted himself greatly to get men off to me with goods; the first gang of porters all died.

8th February, 1871. --The ten men refusing to go north are influenced probably by Shereef, and my two ringleaders, who try this means to compel me to take them.

9th February, 1871. --The man who contrived the murder of James came here, drawn by the pretence that he was needed to lead a party against the villages, which he led to commit the outrage. His thirst for blood is awful: he was bound, and word sent to bring the actual murderers within three days, or he suffers death. He brought five goats, thinking that would smooth the matter over.

11th February, 1871. --Men struck work for higher wages: I consented to give them six dollars a month if they behaved well; if ill I diminish it, so we hope to start to-morrow. Another hunting quelled by Mohamad and me.

The ten men sent are all slaves of the Banians, who are English subjects, and they come with a lie in their mouth: they will not help me, and swear that the Consul told them not to go forward, but to force me back, and they spread the tale all over the country that a certain letter has been sent to me with orders to return forthwith. They swore so positively that I actually looked again at Dr. Kirk's letter to see if his orders had been rightly understood by me. But for Mohamad Bogharib and fear of pistol-shot they would gain their own and their Banian masters' end to baffle me completely; they demand an advance of one dollar, or six dollars a month, though this is double freeman's pay at Zanzibar. Their two headmen, Shereef and Awathe, refused to come past Ujiji, and are revelling on my goods there.

13th February, 1871. --Mabruki being seized with choleraic purging detains us to-day. I gave Mohamad five pieces Americano, five ditto Kanike[13], and two frasilahs samisami beads. He gives me a note to Hassani for twenty thick copper bracelets. Yesterday crowds came to eat the meat of the man who misled James to his death spot: but we want the men who set the Mbanga men to shoot him: they were

---

12 The men give indisputable proof that his body was eaten by the Manyuema who lay in ambush.--ED.

13 Kanike is a blue calico.

much disappointed when they found that no one was killed, and are undoubtedly cannibals.

16th, February, 1871.--Started to-day. Mabruki making himself out very ill, Mohamad roused him out by telling him I travelled when much worse. The chief gave me a goat, and Mohamad another, but in coming through the forest on the neck of the mountain the men lost three, and have to go back for them, and return to-morrow. Simon and Ibram were bundled out of the camp, and impudently followed me: when they came up, I told them to be off.

17th February, 1871.--Waiting at a village on the Western slope for the men to come up with the goats, if they have gone back to the camp. Mohamad would not allow the deserters to remain among his people, nor would I. It would only be to imbue the minds of my men with their want of respect for all English, and total disregard of honesty and honour: they came after me with inimitable effrontery, believing that though I said I would not take them, they were so valuable, I was only saying what I knew to be false. The goats were brought by a Manyuema man, who found one fallen into a pitfall and dead; he ate it, and brought one of his own in lieu of it. I gave him ten strings of beads, and he presented a fowl in token of goodwill.

18th February, 1871.--Went on to a village on the Lulwa, and on the 19th reached Moenemgoi, who dissuaded me so earnestly against going to Moenekurumbo for the cause of Molembalemba that I agreed not to venture.

20th February, 1871.--To the ford with only one canoe now, as two men of Katomba were swept away in the other, and drowned. They would not sell the remaining canoe, so I go N.W. on foot to Moene Lualaba, where fine large canoes are abundant. The grass and mud are grievous, but my men lift me over the waters.

21st February, 1871.--Arrived at Monandewa's village, situated on a high ridge between two deep and difficult gullies. These people are obliging and kind: the chief's wife made a fire for me in the evening unbidden.

22nd February, 1871.--On N.W. to a high hill called Chibande a Yunde, with a spring of white water at the village on the top. Famine from some unknown cause here, but the people are cultivating now on the plain below with a will.

23rd February, 1871.--On to two large villages with many banana plants around, but the men said they were in fear of the traders, and shifted their villages to avoid them: we then went on to the village Kahombogola, with a feeble old man as chief. The country is beautiful and undulating: light-green grass covers it all, save at the brooks, where the eye is relieved by the dark-green lines of trees. Grass tears the hands and wets the extremities constantly. The soil is formed of the debris of granitic rocks; rough and stony, but everywhere fertile. One can rarely get a bare spot to sit down and rest.

24th February, 1871. --To a village near Lolande River. Then across the Loengadye, sleeping on the bank of the Luha, and so to Mamohela, where we were welcomed by all the Arabs, and I got a letter from Dr. Kirk and another from the Sultan, and from Mohamad bin Nassib who was going to Karagwe: all anxious to be kind. Katomba gave flour, nuts, fowls, and goat. A new way is opened to Kasongo's, much shorter than that I followed. I rest a few days, and then go on.

25th February, 1871. --So we went on, and found that it was now known that the Lualaba flowed west-south-west, and that our course was to be west across this other great bend of the mighty river. I had to suspend my judgment, so as to be prepared to find it after all perhaps the Congo. No one knew anything about it except that when at Kasongo's nine days west, and by south it came sweeping round and flowed north and north and by east.

Katomba presented a young soko or gorillah that had been caught while its mother was killed; she sits eighteen inches high, has fine long black hair all over, which was pretty so long as it was kept in order by her dam. She is the least mischievous of all the monkey tribe I have seen, and seems to know that in me she has a friend, and sits quietly on the mat beside me. In walking, the first thing observed is that she does not tread on the palms of her hands, but on the backs of the second line of bones of the hands: in doing this the nails do not touch the ground, nor do the knuckles; she uses the arms thus supported crutch fashion, and hitches herself along between them; occasionally one hand is put down before the other, and alternates with the feet, or she walks upright and holds up a hand to any one to carry her. If refused, she turns her face down, and makes grimaces of the most bitter human weeping, wringing her hands, and sometimes adding a fourth hand or foot to make the appeal more touching. Grass or leaves she draws around her to make a nest, and resents anyone meddling with her property. She is a most friendly little beast, and came up to me at once, making her chirrup of welcome, smelled my clothing, and held out her hand to be shaken. I slapped her palm without offence, though she winced. She began to untie the cord with which she was afterwards bound, with fingers and thumbs, in quite a systematic way, and on being interfered with by a man looked daggers, and screaming tried to beat him with her hands: she was afraid of his stick, and faced him, putting her back to me as a friend. She holds out her hand for people to lift her up and carry her, quite like a spoiled child; then bursts into a passionate cry, somewhat like that of a kite, wrings her hands quite naturally, as if in despair. She eats everything, covers herself with a mat to sleep, and makes a nest of grass or leaves, and wipes her face with a leaf.

I presented my double-barrelled gun which is at Ujiji to Katomba, as he has been very kind when away from Ujiji: I pay him thus for all his services. He gave me the soko, and will carry it to Ujiji for me; I have tried to refund all that the Arabs expended on me.

1st March, 1871. --I was to start this morning, but the Arabs asked me to take seven of their people going to buy biramba, as they know the new way: the offer was gladly accepted.

2nd to 5th March, 1871. --Left Mamohela, and travelled over fine grassy plains, crossing in six hours fourteen running rills, from three to ten or fifteen feet broad, and from calf to thigh deep. Tree-covered mountains on both sides. The natives know the rills by names, and readily tell their courses, and which falls into which, before all go into the great Lualaba; but without one as a guide, no one can put them in a map. We came to Monanbunda's villages, and spent the night. Our next stage was at Monangongo's. A small present of a few strings of beads satisfies, but is not asked: I give it invariably as acknowledgment for lodgings. The headman of our next stage hid himself in fear, as we were near to the scene of Bin Juma's unprovoked slaughter of five men, for tusks that were not stolen, but thrown down. Our path lay through dense forest, and again, on 5th, our march was in the same dense jungle of lofty trees and vegetation that touch our arms on each side. We came to some villages among beautiful tree-covered hills, called Basilange or Mobasilange. The villages are very pretty, standing on slopes. The main street generally lies east and west, to allow the bright sun to stream his clear hot rays from one end to the other, and lick up quickly the moisture from the frequent showers which is not drained off by the slopes. A little verandah is often made in front of the door, and here at dawn the family gathers round a fire, and, while enjoying the heat needed in the cold that always accompanies the first darting of the light or sun's rays across the atmosphere, inhale the delicious air, and talk over their little domestic affairs. The various shaped leaves of the forest all around their village and near their nestlings are bespangled with myriads of dewdrops. The cocks crow vigorously, and strut and ogle; the kids gambol and leap on the backs of their dams quietly chewing the cud; other goats make believe fighting. Thrifty wives often bake their new clay pots in a fire, made by lighting a heap of grass roots: the next morning they extract salt from the ashes, and so two birds are killed with one stone. The beauty of this morning scene of peaceful enjoyment is indescribable. Infancy gilds the fairy picture with its own lines, and it is probably never forgotten, for the young, taken up from slavers, and treated with all philanthropic missionary care and kindness, still revert to the period of infancy as the finest and fairest they have known. They would go back to freedom and enjoyment as fast as would our own sons of the soil, and be heedless to the charms of hard work and no play which we think so much better for them if not for us.

In some cases we found all the villages deserted; the people had fled at our approach, in dread of repetitions of the outrages of Arab slaves. The doors were all shut: a bunch of the leaves of reeds or of green reeds placed across them, means "no entrance here." A few stray chickens wander about wailing, having hid themselves while the rest were caught and carried off into the deep forest, and the still smoking fires tell the same tale of recent flight from the slave-traders.

Many have found out that I am not one of their number, so in various cases they stand up and call out loudly, "Bolongo, Bolongo!" "Friendship, Friendship!" They sell their fine iron bracelets eagerly for a few beads; for (bracelets seem out of fashion since beads came in), but they are of the finest quality of iron, and were they nearer Europe would be as eagerly sought and bought as horse-shoe nails are for the best gun-barrels. I overhear the Manyuema telling each other that I am the "good one." I have no slaves, and I owe this character to the propagation of a good name by the slaves of Zanzibar, who are anything but good themselves. I have seen slaves belonging to the seven men now with us slap the cheeks of grown men who had offered food for sale; it was done in sheer wantonness, till I threatened to thrash them if I saw it again; but out of my sight they did it still, and when I complained to the masters they confessed that all the mischief was done by slaves; for the Manyuema, on being insulted, lose temper and use their spears on the nasty curs, and then vengeance is taken with guns. Free men behave better than slaves; the bondmen are not responsible. The Manyuema are far more beautiful than either the bond or free of Zanzibar; I overhear the remark often, "If we had Manyuema wives what beautiful children we should beget." The men are usually handsome, and many of the women are very pretty; hands, feet, limbs, and forms perfect in shape and the colour light-brown, but the orifices of the nose are widened by snuff-takers, who ram it up as far as they can with the finger and thumb: the teeth are not filed, except a small space between the two upper front teeth.

5th March, 1871. --We heard to-day that Mohamad's people passed us on the west, with much ivory. I lose thus twenty copper rings I was to take from them, and all the notes they were to make for me of the rivers they crossed.

6th March, 1871. --Passed through very large villages, with many forges in active work; some men followed us, as if to fight, but we got them to turn peaceably: we don't know who are enemies, so many have been maltreated and had relatives killed. The rain of yesterday made the paths so slippery that the feet of all were sorely fatigued, and on coming to Manyara's, I resolved to rest on 7th near Mount Kimazi. I gave a cloth and beads in lieu of a fine fat goat from the chief, a clever, good man.

9th March, 1871. --We marched about five hours across a grassy plain without trees--buga or prairie. The torrid sun, nearly vertical, sent his fierce rays down, and fatigued us all: we crossed two Sokoye streams by bridges, and slept at a village on a ridge of woodland overlooking Kasonga. After two hours this morning, we came to villages of this chief, and at one were welcomed by the Safari of Salem Mokadam, and I was given a house. Kasonga is a very fine young man, with European features, and "very clever and good." He is clever, and is pronounced good, because he eagerly joins the Arabs in marauding! Seeing the advantage of firearms, he has bought four muskets. Mohamad's people were led by his, and spent all their copper for some fifty frasilahs of good ivory. From this party men have been sent over Lualaba, and about fifty frasilahs obtained: all praise Kasonga. We were now only six miles from Lualaba, and yet south of Mamohela; this great river, in fact, makes a second great sweep to the west of some 130 miles, and there are at least

30' of southing; but now it comes rolling majestically to the north, and again makes even easting. It is a mighty stream, with many islands in it, and is never wadeable at any point or at any time of the year.

10th March, 1871. --Mohamad's people are said to have gone to Luapanya, a powerful chief, who told them they were to buy all their ivory from him: he had not enough, and they wanted to go on to a people who have ivory door-posts; but he said, "You shall go neither forward nor backwards, but remain here," and he then called an immense body of archers, and said, "You must fight these." The consequence was they killed Luapanya and many of his people, called Bahika, then crossed a very large river, the Morombya or Morombwe, and again the Pembo River, but don't seem to have gone very far north. I wished to go from this in canoes, but Kasonga has none, so I must tramp for five or six days to Moene Lualaba to buy one, if I have credit with Abed.

11th March, 1871. --I had a long, fierce oration from Amur, in which I was told again and again that I should be killed and eaten--the people wanted a "white one" to eat! I needed 200 guns; and "must not go to die." I told him that I was thankful for advice, if given by one who had knowledge, but his vehement threats were dreams of one who had never gone anywhere, but sent his slaves to kill people. He was only frightening my people, and doing me an injury. I told him that Baker had only twelve people, and came near to this: to this he replied "Were the people cannibals?" &c. &c.

I left this noisy demagogue, after saying I thanked him for his warnings, but saw he knew not what he was saying. The traders from Ujiji are simply marauders, and their people worse than themselves, they thirst for blood more than for ivory, each longs to be able to tell a tale of blood, and the Manyuema are an easy prey. Hassani assaulted the people at Moene Lualaba's, and now they keep to the other bank, and I am forced to bargain with Kasonga for a canoe, and he sends to a friend for one to be seen on the 13th. This Hassani declared to me that he would not begin hostilities, but he began nothing else; the prospect of getting slaves overpowers all else, and blood flows in horrid streams. The Lord look on it! Hassani will have some tale to tell Mohamad Bogharib.

[At the outset of his explorations Livingstone fancied that there were degrees in the sufferings of slaves, and that the horrors perpetrated by the Portuguese of

Tette were unknown in the system of slave hunting which the Arabs pursue: we now see that a further acquaintance with the slave-trade of the Interior has restored the balance of infamy, and that the same tale of murder and destruction is common wherever the traffic extends, no matter by whom it is carried on.]

15th March, 1871.--Falsehood seems ingrained in their constitutions: no wonder that in all this region they have never tried to propagate Islamism; the natives soon learn to hate them, and slaving, as carried on by the Kilwans and Ujijians, is so bloody, as to prove an effectual barrier against proselytism.

My men are not come back: I fear they are engaged in some broil. In confirmation of what I write, some of the party here assaulted a village of Kasonga's, killed three men and captured women and children; they pretended that they did not know them to be his people, but they did not return the captives.

20th March, 1871.--I am heartsore, and sick of human blood.

21st March, 1871.--Kasongo's brother's child died, and he asked me to remain to-day while he buried the dead, and he would give me a guide to-morrow; being rainy I stop willingly. Dugumbe is said to purpose going down the river to Kanagumbe River to build on the land Kanagumbe, which is a loop formed by the river, and is large. He is believed to possess great power of divination, even of killing unfaithful women.

22nd March, 1871.--I am detained another day by the sickness of one of the party. Very cold rain yesterday from the north-west. I hope to go to-morrow towards the Lakoni, or great market of this region.

23rd March, 1871.--Left Kasongo, who gave me a goat and a guide. The country is gently undulating, showing green slopes fringed with wood, with grass from four to six feet. We reached Katenga's, about five miles off. There are many villages, and people passed us carrying loads of provisions, and cassava, from the chitoka or market.

24th March, 1871.--Great rain in the night and morning, and sickness of the men prevented our march.

25th March, 1871.--Went to Mazimwe, 7-1/2 miles off.

26th March, 1871.--Went four miles and crossed the Kabwimaji; then a mile beyond Kahembai, which flows into the Kunda, and it into the Lualaba; the country is open, and low hills appear in the north. We met a party from the traders at Kasenga, chiefly Matereka's people under Salem and Syde bin Sultan; they had eighty-two captives, and say they fought ten days to secure them and two of the Malongwana, and two of the Banyamwezi. They had about twenty tusks, and carried one of their men who broke his leg in fighting; we shall be safe only when past the bloodshed and murder.

27th March, 1871. --We went along a ridge of land overhanging a fine valley of denudation, with well-cultivated hills in the distance (N.), where Hassani's feat of bloodshed was performed. There are many villages on the ridge, some rather tumbledown ones, which always indicate some misrule. Our march was about seven miles. A headman who went with us plagued another chief to give me a goat; I refused to take what was not given willingly, but the slaves secured it; and I threatened our companion, Kama, with dismissal from our party if he became a tool in slave hands. The arum is common.

28th March, 1871. --The Banian slaves are again trying compulsion--I don't know what for. They refused to take their bead rations, and made Chakanga spokesman: I could not listen to it, as he has been concocting a mutiny against me. It is excessively trying, and so many difficulties have been put in my way I doubt whether the Divine favour and will is on my side.

We came six miles to-day, crossing many rivulets running to the Kunda, which also we crossed in a canoe; it is almost thirty yards wide and deep: afterwards, near the village where we slept, we crossed the Luja about twenty yards wide, going into the Kunda and Lualaba. I am greatly distressed because there is no law here; they probably mean to create a disturbance at Abed's place, to which we are near: the Lord look on it.

29th March, 1871. --Crossed the Liya, and next day the Moangoi, by two well-made wattle bridges at an island in its bed: it is twenty yards, and has a very strong current, which makes all the market people fear it. We then crossed the Molembe in a canoe, which is fifteen yards, but swelled by rains and many rills. Came 7-1/2 miles to sleep at one of the outlying villages of Nyangwe: about sixty market people came past us from the Chitoka or marketplace, on the banks of Lualaba; they go thither at night, and come away about mid-day, having disposed of most of their goods by barter. The country is open, and dotted over with trees, chiefly a species of Bauhinia, that resists the annual grass burnings; there are trees along the watercourses, and many villages, each with a host of pigs. This region is low as compared with Tanganyika; about 2000 feet above the sea.

The headman's house, in which I was lodged, contained the housewife's little conveniences, in the shape of forty pots, dishes, baskets, knives, mats, all of which she removed to another house: I gave her four strings of beads, and go on to-morrow. Crossed the Kunda River and seven miles more brought us to Nyangwe, where we found Abed and Hassani had erected their dwellings, and sent their people over Lualaba, and as far west as the Loeki or Lomame. Abed said that my words against bloodshedding had stuck into him, and he had given orders to his people to give presents to the chiefs, but never fight unless actually attacked.

31st March, 1871. --I went down to take a good look at the Lualaba here. It is narrower than it is higher up, but still a mighty river, at least 3000 yards broad, and always deep: it can never be waded at any point, or at any time of the year; the people unhesitatingly declare that if any one tried to ford it, he would assuredly be lost. It has many large islands, and at these it is about 2000 yards or one mile. The banks are steep and deep: there is clay, and a yellow-clay schist in their structure; the other rivers, as the Luya and Kunda, have gravelly banks. The current is about two miles an hour away to the north.

CHAPTER V.

The Chitoka or market gathering. The broken watch. Improvises ink. Builds a new house at Nyangwe on the bank of the Lualaba. Marketing. Cannibalism. Lake Kamalondo. Dreadful effect of slaving. News of country across the Lualaba. Tiresome frustration. The Bakuss. Feeble health. Busy scene at market. Unable to procure canoes. Disaster to Arab canoes. Rapids in Lualaba. Project for visiting Lake Lincoln and the Lomame. Offers large reward for canoes and men. The slave's mistress. Alarm of natives at market. Fiendish slaughter of women by Arabs. Heartrending scene. Death on land and in the river. Tagamoio's assassinations. Continued slaughter across the river. Livingstone becomes desponding.

1st April, 1871. --The banks are well peopled, but one must see the gathering at the market, of about 3000, chiefly women, to judge of their numbers. They hold market one day, and then omit attendance here for three days, going to other markets at other points in the intervals. It is a great institution in Manyuema: numbers seem to inspire confidence, and they enforce justice for each other. As a rule, all prefer to buy and sell in the market, to doing business anywhere else; if one says, "Come, sell me that fowl or cloth," the reply is, "Come to the 'Chitoka,' or marketplace."

2nd April, 1871. --To-day the market contained over a thousand people, carrying earthen pots and cassava, grass cloth, fishes, and fowls; they were alarmed at my coming among them and were ready to flee, many stood afar off in suspicion; some came from the other side of the river with their goods. To-morrow market is held up river.

3rd April, 1871. --I tried to secure a longitude by fixing a weight on the key of the watch, and so helping it on: I will try this in a quiet place to-morrow. The people all fear us, and they have good reason for it in the villainous conduct of many of the blackguard half-castes which alarms them: I cannot get a canoe, so I wait to see what will turn up. The river is said to overflow all its banks annually, as the Nile does further down. I sounded across yesterday. Near the bank it is 9 feet, the rest 15 feet, and one cast in the middle was 20 feet: between the islands 12 feet, and 9 feet again in shore: it is a mighty river truly. I took distances and altitudes alternately with a bullet for a weight on the key of the chronometer, taking successive altitudes of the sun and distances of the moon. Possibly the first and last altitudes may give the rate of going, and the frequent distances between may give approximate longitude.

4th April, 1871. --Moon, the fourth of the Arabs, will appear in three or four days. This will be a guide in ascertaining the day of observing the lunars, with the weight.

The Arabs ask many questions about the Bible, and want to know how many prophets have appeared, and probably say that they believe in them all; while we believe all but reject Mohamad. It is easy to drive them into a corner by questioning, as they don't know whither the inquiries lead, and they are not offended when their knowledge is, as it were, admitted. When asked how many false prophets are known, they appeal to my knowledge, and evidently never heard of Balaam, the son of Beor, or of the 250 false prophets of Jezebel and Ahab, or of the many lying prophets referred to in the Bible.

6th April, 1871. --Ill from drinking two cups of very sweet malofu, or beer, made from bananas: I shall touch it no more.

7th April, 1871. --Made this ink with the seeds of a plant, called by the Arabs Zugifare; it is known in India, and is used here by the Manyuema to dye virambos and ornament faces and heads[14]. I sent my people over to the other side to cut wood

---

14 The reader will best judge of the success of the experiment by looking at a specimen of the writing. An old sheet of the Standard newspaper, made into rough copy-books, sufficed for paper in the absence of all other material, and by writing across the print no doubt the notes were tolerably legible at the time. The colour of the decoction used instead of ink has faded so much that if Dr. Livingstone's handwriting had not at all times been beautifully clear and distinct it would have been impossible to decipher this part of his diary.--Ed.

to build a house for me; the borrowed one has mud walls and floors, which are damp, foul, smelling, and unwholesome. I shall have grass walls, and grass and reeds on the floor of my own house; the free ventilation will keep it sweet. This is the season called Masika, the finishing rains, which we have in large quantities almost every night, and I could scarcely travel even if I had a canoe; still it is trying to be kept back by suspicion, and by the wickedness of the wicked.

Some of the Arabs try to be kind, and send cooked food every day: Abed is the chief donor. I taught him to make a mosquito-curtain of thin printed calico, for he had endured the persecution of these insects helplessly, except by sleeping on a high stage, when they were unusually bad. The Manyuema often bring evil on themselves by being untrustworthy. For instance, I paid one to bring a large canoe to cross the Lualaba, he brought a small one, capable of carrying three only, and after wasting some hours we had to put off crossing till next day.

8th April, 1871. --Every headman of four or five huts is a mologhwe, or chief, and glories in being called so. There is no political cohesion. The Ujijian slavery is an accursed system; but it must be admitted that the Manyuema, too, have faults, the result of ignorance of other people: their isolation has made them as unconscious of danger in dealing with the cruel stranger, as little dogs in the presence of lions. Their refusal to sell or lend canoes for fear of blame by each other will be ended by the party of Dugumbe, which has ten headmen, taking them by force; they are unreasonable and bloody-minded towards each other: every Manyuema would like every other headman slain; they are subjected to bitter lessons and sore experience. Abed went over to Mologhwe Kahembe and mixed blood with him; he was told that two large canoes were hollowed out, and nearly ready to be brought for sale; if this can be managed peaceably it is a great point gained, and I may get one at our Arabs' price, which may be three or four times the native price. There is no love lost among the three Arabs here.

9th April, 1871. --Cut wood for my house. The Loeki is said by slaves who have come thence to be much larger than the Lualaba, but on the return of Abed's people from the west we shall obtain better information.

10th April, 1871. --Chitoka, or market, to-day. I counted upwards of 700 passing my door. With market women it seems to be a pleasure of life to haggle and joke, and laugh and cheat: many come eagerly, and retire with careworn faces;

many are beautiful, and many old; all carry very heavy loads of dried cassava and earthen pots, which they dispose of very cheaply for palm-oil, fish, salt, pepper, and relishes for their food. The men appear in gaudy lambas, and carry little save their iron wares, fowls, grass cloth, and pigs.

Bought the fish with the long snouts: very good eating.

12th April, 1871. --New moon last night; fourth Arab month: I am at a loss for the day of the month. My new house is finished; a great comfort, for the other was foul and full of vermin: bugs (Tapazi, or ticks), that follow wherever Arabs go, made me miserable, but the Arabs are insensible to them; Abed alone had a mosquito-curtain, and he never could praise it enough. One of his remarks is, "If slaves think you fear them, they will climb over you." I clothed mine for nothing, and ever after they have tried to ride roughshod over me, and mutiny on every occasion!

14th April, 1871. --Kahembe came over, and promises to bring a canoe; but he is not to be trusted; he presented Abed with two slaves, and is full of fair promises about the canoe, which he sees I am anxious to get. They all think that my buying a canoe means carrying war to the left bank; and now my Banian slaves encourage the idea: "He does not wish slaves nor ivory," say they, "but a canoe, in order to kill Manyuema." Need it be wondered at that people, who had never heard of strangers or white men before I popped down among them, believed the slander? The slaves were aided in propagating the false accusation by the half-caste Ujijian slaves at the camp. Hassani fed them every day; and, seeing that he was a bigoted Moslem, they equalled him in prayers in his sitting-place seven or eight times a day! They were adepts at lying, and the first Manyuema words they learned were used to propagate falsehood.

I have been writing part of a despatch, in case of meeting people from the French settlement on the Gaboon at Loeki, but the canoe affair is slow and tedious: the people think only of war: they are a bloody-minded race.

15th April, 1871. --The Manyuema tribe, called Bagenya, occupy the left bank, opposite Nyangwe. A spring of brine rises in the bed of a river, named Lofubu, and this the Bayenga inspissate by boiling, and sell the salt at market. The Lomame is about ten days west of Lualaba, and very large; the confluence of Lomame, or Loeki, is about six days down below Nyangwe by canoe; the river Nyanze is still less distant.

16th April, 1871.--On the Nyanze stands the principal town and market of the chief, Zurampela. Rashid visited him, and got two slaves on promising to bring a war-party from Abed against Chipange, who by similar means obtained the help of Salem Mokadam to secure eighty-two captives: Rashid will leave this as soon as possible, sell the slaves, and leave Zurampela to find out the fraud! This deceit, which is an average specimen of the beginning of half-caste dealings, vitiates his evidence of a specimen of cannibalism which he witnessed; but it was after a fight that the victims were cut up, and this agrees with the fact that the Manyuema eat only those who are killed in war. Some have averred that captives, too, are eaten, and a slave is bought with a goat to be eaten; but this I very strongly doubt.

17th April, 1871.--Rainy.

18th April, 1871.--I found that the Lepidosiren is brought to market in pots with water in them, also white ants roasted, and the large snail, achetina, and a common snail: the Lepidosiren is called "**sembe**."

Abed went a long way to examine a canoe, but it was still further, and he turned back.

19th April, 1871.--Dreary waiting, but Abed proposes to join and trade along with me: this will render our party stronger, and he will not shoot people in my company; we shall hear Katomba's people's story too.

20th April, 1871.--Katomba a chief was to visit us yesterday, but failed, probably through fear.

The chief Mokandira says that Loeki is small where it joins Lualaba, but another, which they call Lomame, is very much larger, and joins Lualaba too: rapids are reported on it.

21st April, 1871.--A common salutation reminds me of the Bechuana's "U le hatsi" (thou art on earth); "Ua tala" (thou lookest); "Ua boka," or byoka (thou awakest); "U ri ho" (thou art here); "U li koni" (thou art here)--about pure "Sichuana," and "Nya," No, is identical. The men here deny that cannibalism is common: they eat only those killed in war, and, it seems, in revenge, for, said Mokandira, "the meat is not nice; it makes one dream of the dead man." Some west of Lualaba eat even those bought for the purpose of a feast; but I am not quite positive on this point: all agree in saying that human flesh is saltish, and needs but little condiment. And yet they are a fine-looking race; I would back a company of Manyuema men to be far superior in shape of head and generally in physical form too against the whole Anthropological Society. Many of the women are very light-coloured and very pretty; they dress in a kilt of many folds of gaudy lambas.

22nd April, 1871. --In Manyuema, here Kusi, Kunzi, is north; Mhuru, south; Nkanda, west, or other side Lualaba; Mazimba, east. The people are sometimes confused in name by the directions; thus Bankanda is only "the other side folk." The Bagenya Chimburu came to visit me, but I did not see him, nor did I know Moene Nyangwe till too late to do him honour; in fact, every effort was made to keep me in the dark while the slavers of Ujiji made all smooth for themselves to get canoes. All chiefs claim the privilege of shaking hands, that is, they touch the hand held out with their palm, then clap two hands together, then touch again, and clap again, and the ceremony concludes: this frequency of shaking hands misled me when the great man came.

24th April, 1871. --Old feuds lead the Manyuema to entrap the traders to fight: they invite them to go to trade, and tell them that at such a village plenty of ivory lies; then when the trader goes with his people, word is sent that he is coming to fight, and he is met by enemies, who compel him to defend himself by their onslaught. We were nearly entrapped in this way by a chief pretending to guide us through the country near Basilange; he would have landed us in a fight, but we detected his drift, changed our course so as to mislead any messengers he might have sent, and dismissed him with some sharp words.

Lake Kamolondo is about twenty-five miles broad. The Lufira at Katanga is a full bow-shot wide; it goes into Kamolondo. Chakomo is east of Lufira Junction. Kikonze Kalanza is on the west of it, and Mkana, or the underground dwellings, still further west: some are only two days from Katanga. The Chorwe people are friendly. Kamolondo is about ten days distant from Katanga.

25th April, 1871. --News came that four men sent by Abed to buy ivory had been entrapped, and two killed. The rest sent for aid to punish the murderers, and Abed wished me to send my people to bring the remaining two men back. I declined; because, no matter what charges I gave, my Banian slaves would be sure to shed human blood. We can go nowhere but the people of the country ask us to kill their fellow-men, nor can they be induced to go to villages three miles off, because there, in all probability, live the murderers of fathers, uncles, or grandfathers--a dreadful state truly. The traders are as bloodthirsty every whit as the Manyuema, where no danger exists, but in most cases where the people can fight they are as civil as possible. At Moere Mpanda's, the son of Casembe, Mohamad Bogharib left a debt of twenty-eight slaves and eight bars of copper, each seventy pounds, and did not dare to fire a shot because they saw they had met their match: here his headmen are said to have bound the headmen of villages till a ransom was paid in tusks! Had they only gone three days further to the Babisa, to whom Moene-mokaia's men went, they would have got fine ivory at two rings a tusk, while they had paid from ten to eighteen. Here it is as sad a tale to tell as was that of the Manganja scattered and peeled by the Waiyau agents of the Portuguese of Tette. The good Lord look on it.

26th April, 1871.--Chitovu called nine slaves bought by Abed's people from the Kuss country, west of the Lualaba, and asked them about their tribes and country for me. One, with his upper front teeth extracted, was of the tribe Maloba, on the other side of the Loeki, another comes from the River Lombadzo, or Lombazo, which is west of Loeki (this may be another name for the Lomame), the country is called Nanga, and the tribe Nongo, chief Mpunzo. The Malobo tribe is under the chiefs Yunga and Lomadyo. Another toothless boy said that he came from the Lomame: the upper teeth extracted seem to say that the tribe have cattle; the knocking out the teeth is in imitation of the animals they almost worship. No traders had ever visited them; this promises ivory to the present visitors: all that is now done with the ivory there is to make rude blowing horns and bracelets.

27th April, 1871.--Waiting wearily and anxiously; we cannot move people who are far off and make them come near with news. Even the owners of canoes say, "Yes, yes; we shall bring them," but do not stir; they doubt us, and my slaves increase the distrust by their lies to the Manyuema.

28th April, 1871.--Abed sent over Manyuema to buy slaves for him and got a pretty woman for 300 cowries and a hundred strings of beads; she can be sold again to an Arab for much more in ivory. Abed himself gave $130 for a woman-cook, and she fled to me when put in chains for some crime: I interceded, and she was loosed: I advised her not to offend again, because I could not beg for her twice.

Hassani with ten slaves dug at the malachite mines of Katanga for three months, and gained a hundred frasilahs of copper, or 3500 lbs. We hear of a half-caste reaching the other side of Lomame, probably from Congo or Ambriz, but the messengers had not seen him.

1st May, 1871. --Katomba's people arrived from the Babisa, where they sold all their copper at two rings for a tusk, and then found that abundance of ivory still remained: door-posts and house-pillars had been made of ivory which now was rotten. The people of Babisa kill elephants now and bring tusks by the dozen, till the traders get so many that in this case they carried them by three relays. They dress their hair like the Bashukulompo, plaited into upright basket helmets: no quarrel occurred, and great kindness was shown to the strangers. A river having very black water, the Nyengere, flows into Lualaba from the west, and it becomes itself very large: another river or water, Shamikwa, falls into it from the south-west, and it becomes still larger: this is probably the Lomame. A short-horned antelope is common.

3rd May, 1871. --Abed informs me that a canoe will come in five days. Word was sent after me by the traders south of us not to aid me, as I was sure to die where I was going: the wish is father to the thought! Abed was naturally very anxious to get first into the Babisa ivory market, yet he tried to secure a canoe for me before he went, but he was too eager, and a Manyuema man took advantage of his desire, and came over the river and said that he had one hollowed out, and he wanted goats and beads to hire people to drag it down to the water. Abed on my account advanced five goats, a thousand cowries, and many beads, and said that he would tell me what he wished in return: this was debt, but I was so anxious to get away I was content to take the canoe on any terms. However, it turned out that the matter on the part of the headman whom Abed trusted was all deception: he had no canoe at all, but knew of one belonging to another man, and wished to get Abed and me to send men to see it--in fact, to go with their guns, and he would manage to embroil them with the real owner, so that some old feud should be settled to his satisfaction. On finding that I declined to be led into his trap, he took a female slave to the owner, and on his refusal to sell the canoe for her, it came out that he had adopted a system of fraud to Abed. He had victimized Abed, who was naturally inclined to believe his false statements, and get off to the ivory market. His people came from the Kuss country in the west with sixteen tusks, and a great many slaves bought and not murdered for. The river is rising fast, and bringing down large quantities of aquatic grass, duckweed, &c. The water is a little darker in colour than at Cairo. People remove and build their huts on the higher forest lands adjacent. Many white birds (the paddy bird) appear, and one Ibis religiosa; they pass north.

The Bakuss live near Lomame; they were very civil and kind to the strangers, but refused passage into the country. At my suggestion, the effect of a musket-shot was shown on a goat: they thought it supernatural, looked up to the clouds, and offered to bring ivory to buy the charm that could draw lightning down. When it was afterwards attempted to force a path, they darted aside on seeing the Banyamwezi's followers putting the arrows into the bowstrings, but stood in mute amazement looking at the guns, which mowed them down in large numbers. They thought that muskets were the insignia of chieftainship. Their chiefs all go with a long straight staff of rattan, having a quantity of black medicine smeared on each end, and no weapons in their hands: they imagined that the guns were carried as insignia of the same kind; some, jeering in the south, called them big tobacco-pipes; they have no fear on seeing a gun levelled at them.

They use large and very long spears very expertly in the long grass and forest of their country, and are terrible fellows among themselves, and when they become acquainted with firearms will be terrible to the strangers who now murder them. The Manyuema say truly, "If it were not for your guns, not one of you would ever return to your country." The Bakuss cultivate more than the southern Manyuema, especially Pennisetum and dura, or **Holcus sorghum;** common coffee is abundant, and they use it, highly scented with vanilla, which must be fertilized by insects; they hand round cups of it after meals. Pineapples too are abundant. They bathe regularly twice a day: their houses are of two storeys. The women have rather compressed heads, but very pleasant countenances; and ancient Egyptian, round, wide-awake eyes. Their numbers are prodigious; the country literally swarms with people, and a chief's town extends upwards of a mile. But little of the primeval forest remains. Many large pools of standing water have to be crossed, but markets are held every eight or ten miles from each other, and to these the people come from far, for the market is as great an institution as shopping is with the civilized. Illicit intercourse is punished by the whole of the offender's family being enslaved.

The Bakuss smelt copper from the ore and sell it very cheaply to the traders for beads. The project of going in canoes now appeared to the half-castes so plausible, that they all tried to get the Bagenya on the west bank to lend them, and all went over to mix blood and make friends with the owners, then all slandered me as not to be trusted, as they their blood-relations were; and my slaves mutinied and would go no further. They mutinied three times here, and Hassani harboured them till I told him that, if an English officer harboured an Arab slave he would be compelled by the Consul to refund the price, and I certainly would not let him escape; this frightened him; but I was at the mercy of slaves who had no honour, and no interest in going into danger.

16th May, 1871. --Abed gave me a frasilah of Matunda beads, and I returned fourteen fathoms of fine American sheeting, but it was an obligation to get beads from one whose wealth depended on exchanging beads for ivory.

16th May, 1871. --At least 3000 people at market to-day, and my going among them has taken away the fear engendered by the slanders of slaves and traders, for all are pleased to tell me the names of the fishes and other things. Lepidosirens are caught by the neck and lifted out of the pot to show their fatness. Camwood ground and made into flat cakes for sale and earthen balls, such as are eaten in the disease safura or earth-eating, are offered and there is quite a roar of voices in the multitude, haggling. It was pleasant to be among them compared to being with the slaves, who were all eager to go back to Zanzibar: some told me that they were slaves, and required a free man to thrash them, and proposed to go back to Ujiji for one. I saw no hope of getting on with them, and anxiously longed for the arrival of Dugumbe; and at last Abed overheard them plotting my destruction. "If forced to go on, they would watch till the first difficulty arose with the Manyuema, then fire off their guns, run away, and as I could not run as fast as they, leave me to perish." Abed overheard them speaking loudly, and advised me strongly not to trust myself to them any more, as they would be sure to cause my death. He was all along a sincere friend, and I could not but take his words as well-meant and true.

18th May, 1871. --Abed gave me 200 cowries and some green beads. I was at the point of disarming my slaves and driving them away, when they relented, and professed to be willing to go anywhere; so, being eager to finish my geographical work, I said I would run the risk of their desertion, and gave beads to buy provisions for a start north. I cannot state how much I was worried by these wretched slaves, who did much to annoy me, with the sympathy of all the slaving crew. When baffled by untoward circumstances the bowels plague me too, and discharges of blood relieve the headache, and are as safety-valves to the system. I was nearly persuaded to allow Mr. Syme to operate on me when last in England, but an old friend told me that his own father had been operated on by the famous John Hunter, and died in consequence at the early age of forty. His advice saved me, for this complaint has been my safety-valve.

The Zingifure, or red pigment, is said to be a cure for itch common among both natives and Arab slaves and Arab children.

20th May, 1871.--Abed called Kalonga the headman, who beguiled him as I soon found, and delivered the canoe he had bought formally to me, and went off down the Lualaba on foot to buy the Babisa ivory. I was to follow in the canoe and wait for him in the River Luera, but soon I ascertained that the canoe was still in the forest, and did not belong to Kalonga. On demanding back the price he said, "Let Abed come and I will give it to him;" then when I sent to force him to give up the goods, all his village fled into the forest: I now tried to buy one myself from the Bagenya, but there was no chance; so long as the half-caste traders needed any they got all--nine large canoes, and I could not secure one.

24th May, 1871.--The market is a busy scene--everyone is in dead earnest--little time is lost in friendly greetings; vendors of fish run about with potsherds full of snails or small fishes or young **Clarias capensis** smoke-dried and spitted on twigs, or other relishes to exchange for cassava roots dried after being steeped about three days in water--potatoes, vegetables, or grain, bananas, flour, palm-oil, fowls, salt, pepper; each is intensely eager to barter food for relishes, and makes strong assertions as to the goodness or badness of everything: the sweat stands in beads on their faces--cocks crow briskly, even when slung over the shoulder with their heads hanging down, and pigs squeal. Iron knobs, drawn out at each end to show the goodness of the metal, are exchanged for cloth of the Muabe palm. They have a large funnel of basket-work below the vessel holding the wares, and slip the goods down if they are not to be seen. They deal fairly, and when differences arise they are easily settled by the men interfering or pointing to me: they appeal to each other, and have a strong sense of natural justice. With so much food changing hands amongst the three thousand attendants much benefit is derived; some come from twenty to twenty-five miles. The men flaunt about in gaudy-coloured lambas of many folded kilts--the women work hardest--the potters slap and ring their earthenware all round, to show that there is not a single flaw in them. I bought two finely shaped earthen bottles of porous earthenware, to hold a gallon each, for one string of beads, the women carry huge loads of them in their funnels above the baskets, strapped to the shoulders and forehead, and their hands are full besides; the roundness of the vessels is wonderful, seeing no machine is used: no slaves could be induced to carry half as much as they do willingly. It is a scene of the finest natural acting imaginable. The eagerness with which all sorts of assertions are made--the eager earnestness with which apparently all creation, above, around, and beneath, is called on to attest the truth of what they allege--and then the intense surprise and withering scorn cast on those who despise their goods: but they show no concern when the buyers turn up their noses at them. Little girls run about selling cups of water for a few small fishes to the half-exhausted wordy combatants. To me it was an amusing scene. I could not understand the words that flowed off their glib tongues, but the gestures were too expressive to need interpretation.

27th May, 1871.--Hassani told me that since he had come, no Manyuema had ever presented him with a single mouthful of food, not even a potato or banana, and he had made many presents. Going from him into the market I noticed that one man presented a few small fishes, another a sweet potato and a piece of cassava, and a third two small fishes, but the Manyuema are not a liberal people. Old men and women who remained in the half-deserted villages we passed through in coming north, often ran forth to present me with bananas, but it seemed through fear; when I sat down and ate the bananas they brought beer of bananas, and I paid for all. A stranger in the market had ten human under jaw-bones hung by a string over his shoulder: on inquiry he professed to have killed and eaten the owners, and showed with his knife how he cut up his victim. When I expressed disgust he and others laughed. I see new faces every market-day. Two nice girls were trying to sell their venture, which was roasted white ants, called "Gumbe."

30th May, 1871.--The river fell four inches during the last four days; the colour is very dark brown, and large quantities of aquatic plants and trees float down. Mologhwe, or chief Ndambo, came and mixed blood with the intensely bigoted Moslem, Hassani: this is to secure the nine canoes. He next went over to have more palaver about them, and they do not hesitate to play me false by detraction.

The Manyuema, too, are untruthful, but very honest; we never lose an article by them: fowls and goats are untouched, and if a fowl is lost, we know that it has been stolen by an Arab slave. When with Mohamad Bogharib, we had all to keep our fowls at the Manyuema villages to prevent them being stolen by our own slaves, and it is so here. Hassani denies complicity with them, but it is quite apparent that he and others encourage them in mutiny.

5th June, 1871.--The river rose again six inches and fell three. Rain nearly ceased, and large masses of fleecy clouds float down here from the north-west, with accompanying cold.

7th June, 1871.--I fear that I must march on foot, but the mud is forbidding.

11th June, 1871.--New moon last night, and I believe Dugumbe will leave Kasonga's to-day. River down three inches.

14th June, 1871.--Hassani got nine canoes, and put sixty-three persons in three; I cannot get one. Dugumbe reported near, but detained by his divination, at which he is an expert; hence his native name is "Molembalemba"--"writer, writing."

16th June, 1871.--The high winds and drying of soap and sugar tell that the rains are now over in this part.

18th June, 1871.--Dugumbe arrived, but passed to Moene Nyangwe's, and found that provisions were so scarce, and dear there, as compared with our market, that he was fain to come back to us. He has a large party and 500 guns. He is determined to go into new fields of trade, and has all his family with him, and intends to remain six or seven years, sending regularly to Ujiji for supplies of goods.

20th June, 1871.--Two of Dugumbe's party brought presents of four large fundos of beads each. All know that my goods are unrighteously detained by Shereef and they show me kindness, which I return by some fine calico which I have. Among the first words Dugumbe said to me were, "Why your own slaves are your greatest enemies: I will buy you a canoe, but the Banian slaves' slanders have put all the Manyuema against you." I knew that this was true, and that they were conscious of the sympathy of the Ujijian traders, who hate to have me here.

24th June, 1871.--Hassani's canoe party in the river were foiled by narrows, after they had gone down four days. Rocks jut out on both sides, not opposite, but alternate to each other; and the vast mass of water of the great river jammed in, rushes round one promontory on to another, and a frightful whirlpool is formed in which the first canoe went and was overturned, and five lives lost. Had I been there, mine would have been the first canoe, for the traders would have made it a point of honour to give me the precedence (although actually to make a feeler of me), while they looked on in safety. The men in charge of Hassani's canoes were so frightened by this accident that they at once resolved to return, though they had arrived in the country of the ivory: they never looked to see whether the canoes could be dragged past the narrows, as anyone else would have done. No better luck could be expected after all their fraud and duplicity in getting the canoes; no harm lay in obtaining them, but why try to prevent me getting one?

27th June, 1871. --In answer to my prayers for preservation, I was prevented going down to the narrows, formed by a dyke of mountains cutting across country, and jutting a little ajar, which makes the water in an enormous mass wheel round behind it helplessly, and if the canoes reach the rock against which the water dashes, they are almost certainly overturned. As this same dyke probably cuts across country to Lomame, my plan of going to the confluence and then up won't do, for I should have to go up rapids there. Again, I was prevented from going down Luamo, and on the north of its confluence another cataract mars navigation in the Lualaba, and my safety is thereby secured. We don't always know the dangers that we are guided past.

28th June, 1871. --The river has fallen two feet: dark brown water, and still much wreck floating down.

Eight villages are in flames, set fire to by a slave of Syde bin Habib, called Manilla, who thus shows his blood friends of the Bagenya how well he can fight against the Mohombo, whose country the Bagenya want! The stragglers of this camp are over on the other side helping Manilla, and catching fugitives and goats. The Bagenya are fishermen by taste and profession, and sell the produce of their nets and weirs to those who cultivate the soil, at the different markets. Manilla's foray is for an alleged debt of three slaves, and ten villages are burned.

30th June, 1871. --Hassani pretended that he was not aware of Manilla's foray, and when I denounced it to Manilla himself, he showed that he was a slave, by cringing and saying nothing except something about the debt of three slaves.

1st July, 1871. --I made known my plan to Dugumbe, which was to go west with his men to Lomame, then by his aid buy a canoe and go up Lake Lincoln to Katanga and the fountains, examine the inhabited caves, and return here, if he would let his people bring me goods from Ujiji; he again referred to all the people being poisoned in mind against me, but was ready to do everything in his power for my success. My own people persuaded the Bagenya not to sell a canoe: Hassani knows it all, but swears that he did not join in the slander, and even points up to Heaven in attestation of innocence of all, even of Manilla's foray. Mohamadans are certainly famous as liars, and the falsehood of Mohamad has been transmitted to his followers in a measure unknown in other religions.

2nd July, 1871. --The upper stratum of clouds is from the north-west, the lower from the south-east; when they mix or change places the temperature is much lowered, and fever ensues. The air evidently comes from the Atlantic, over the low swampy lands of the West Coast. Morning fogs show that the river is warmer than the air.

4th July, 1871. --Hassani off down river in high dudgeon at the cowards who turned after reaching the ivory country. He leaves them here and goes himself, entirely on land. I gave him hints to report himself and me to Baker, should he meet any of his headmen.

5th July, 1871. --The river has fallen three feet in all, that is one foot since 27th June.

I offer Dugumbe $2000, or 400 *l.*, for ten men to replace the Banian slaves, and enable me to go up the Lomame to Katanga and the underground dwellings, then return and go up by Tanganyika to Ujiji, and I added that I would give all the goods I had at Ujiji besides: he took a few days to consult with his associates.

6th July, 1871. --Mokandira, and other headmen, came with a present of a pig and a goat on my being about to depart west. I refused to receive them till my return, and protested against the slander of my wishing to kill people, which they all knew, but did not report to me: this refusal and protest will ring all over the country.

7th July, 1871. --I was annoyed by a woman frequently beating a slave near my house, but on my reproving her she came and apologized. I told her to speak softly to her slave, as she was now the only mother the girl had; the slave came from beyond Lomame, and was evidently a lady in her own land; she calls her son

Mologwe, or chief, because his father was a headman.

Dugumbe advised my explaining my plan of procedure to the slaves, and he evidently thinks that I wish to carry it towards them with a high hand. I did explain all the exploration I intended to do: for instance, the fountains of Herodotus--beyond Katanga--Katanga itself, and the underground dwellings, and then return. They made no remarks, for they are evidently pleased to have me knuckling down to them; when pressed on the point of proceeding, they say they will only go with Dugumbe's men to the Lomame, and then return. River fallen three inches since the 5th.

10th July, 1871. --Manyuema children do not creep, as European children do, on their knees, but begin by putting forward one foot and using one knee. Generally a Manyuema child uses both feet and both hands, but never both knees: one Arab child did the same; he never crept, but got up on both feet, holding on till he could walk.

New moon last night of seventh Arab month.

11th July, 1871. --I bought the different species of fish brought to market, in order to sketch eight of them, and compare them with those of the Nile lower down: most are the same as in Nyassa. A very active species of Glanis, of dark olive-brown, was not sketched, but a spotted one, armed with offensive spikes in the dorsal and pectoral fins, was taken. Sesamum seed is abundant just now and cakes are made of ground-nuts, as on the West Coast. Dugumbe's horde tried to deal in the market in a domineering way. "I shall buy that," said one. "These are mine," said another; "no one must touch them but me," but the market-women taught them that they could not monopolize, but deal fairly. They are certainly clever traders, and keep each other in countenance, they stand by each other, and will not allow overreaching, and they give food astonishingly cheap: once in the market they have no fear.

12th and 13th July 1871. --The Banian slaves declared before Dugumbe that they would go to the River Lomame, but no further: he spoke long to them, but they will not consent to go further. When told that they would thereby lose all their pay, they replied, "Yes, but not our lives," and they walked off from him muttering, which is insulting to one of his rank. I then added, "I have goods at Ujiji; I don't know how many, but they are considerable, take them all, and give me men to finish my work; if not enough, I will add to them, only do not let me be forced to return now I am so near the end of my undertaking." He said he would make a plan in conjunction with his associates, and report to me.

14th July, 1871. --I am distressed and perplexed what to do so as not to be foiled, but all seems against me.

15th July, 1871. --The reports of guns on the other side of the Lualaba all the morning tell of the people of Dugumbe murdering those of Kimburu and others who mixed blood with Manilla. "Manilla is a slave, and how dares he to mix blood with chiefs who ought only to make friends with free men like us"--this is their complaint. Kimburu gave Manilla three slaves, and he sacked ten villages in token of friendship; he proposed to give Dugumbe nine slaves in the same operation, but Dugumbe's people destroy his villages, and shoot and make his people captives to punish Manilla; to make an impression, in fact, in the country that they alone are to be dealt with--"make friends with us, and not with Manilla or anyone else"--such is what they insist upon.

About 1500 people came to market, though many villages of those that usually come from the other side were now in flames, and every now and then a number of shots were fired on the fugitives.

It was a hot, sultry day, and when I went into the market I saw Adie and Manilla, and three of the men who had lately come with Dugumbe. I was surprised to see these three with their guns, and felt inclined to reprove them, as one of my men did, for bringing weapons into the market, but I attributed it to their ignorance, and, it being very hot, I was walking away to go out of the market, when I saw one of the fellows haggling about a fowl, and seizing hold of it. Before I had got thirty yards out, the discharge of two guns in the middle of the crowd told me that slaughter had begun: crowds dashed off from the place, and threw down their wares in confusion, and ran. At the same time that the three opened fire on the mass of people near the upper end of the marketplace volleys were discharged from a party down near the creek on the panic-stricken women, who dashed at the canoes. These, some fifty or more, were jammed in the creek, and the men forgot their paddles in the terror that seized all. The canoes were not to be got out, for the creek was too small for so many; men and women, wounded by the balls, poured into them, and leaped and scrambled into the water, shrieking. A long line of heads in the river showed that great numbers struck out for an island a full mile off: in going towards it they had to put the left shoulder to a current of about two miles an hour; if they had struck away diagonally to the opposite bank, the current would have aided them, and, though nearly three miles off, some would have gained land: as it was, the heads above water showed the long line of those that would inevitably perish.

Shot after shot continued to be fired on the helpless and perishing. Some of the long line of heads disappeared quietly; whilst other poor creatures threw their arms high, as if appealing to the great Father above, and sank. One canoe took in as many as it could hold, and all paddled with hands and arms: three canoes, got out in haste, picked up sinking friends, till all went down together, and disappeared. One man in a long canoe, which could have held forty or fifty, had clearly lost his head; he had been out in the stream before the massacre began, and now paddled up the river nowhere, and never looked to the drowning. By-and-bye all the heads disappeared; some had turned down stream towards the bank, and escaped. Dugumbe put people into one of the deserted vessels to save those in the water, and saved twenty-one, but one woman refused to be taken on board from thinking that she was to be made a slave of; she preferred the chance of life by swimming, to the lot of a slave: the Bagenya women are expert in the water, as they are accustomed to dive for oysters, and those who went down stream may have escaped, but the Arabs themselves estimated the loss of life at between 330 and 400 souls. The shooting-party near the canoes were so reckless, they killed two of their own people; and a Banyamwezi follower, who got into a deserted canoe to plunder, fell into the water, went down, then came up again, and down to rise no more.

My first impulse was to pistol the murderers, but Dugumbe protested against my getting into a blood-feud, and I was thankful afterwards that I took his advice. Two wretched Moslems asserted "that the firing was done by the people of the English;" I asked one of them why he lied so, and he could utter no excuse: no other falsehood came to his aid as he stood abashed, before me, and so telling him not to tell palpable falsehoods, I left him gaping.

After the terrible affair in the water, the party of Tagamoio, who was the chief perpetrator, continued to fire on the people there and fire their villages. As I write I hear the loud wails on the left bank over those who are there slain, ignorant of their many friends now in the depths of Lualaba. Oh, let Thy kingdom come! No one will ever know the exact loss on this bright sultry summer morning, it gave me the impression of being in Hell. All the slaves in the camp rushed at the fugitives on land, and plundered them: women were for hours collecting and carrying loads of what had been thrown down in terror.

Some escaped to me, and were protected: Dugumbe saved twenty-one, and of his own accord liberated them, they were brought to me, and remained over night near my house. One woman of the saved had a musket-ball through the thigh, another in the arm. I sent men with our flag to save some, for without a flag they might have been victims, for Tagamoio's people were shooting right and left like fiends. I counted twelve villages burning this morning. I asked the question of Dugumbe and others, "Now for what is all this murder?" All blamed Manilla as its cause, and in one sense he was the cause; but it is hardly credible that they repeat it is in order to be avenged on Manilla for making friends with headmen, he being a slave. I cannot believe it fully. The wish to make an impression in the country as to the importance and greatness of the new comers was the most potent motive; but it was terrible that the murdering of so many should be contemplated at all. It made me sick at heart. Who could accompany the people of Dugumbe and Tagamoio to Lomame and be free from blood-guiltiness?

I proposed to Dugumbe to catch the murderers, and hang them up in the marketplace, as our protest against the bloody deeds before the Manyuema. If, as he and others added, the massacre was committed by Manilla's people, he would have consented; but it was done by Tagamoio's people, and others of this party, headed by Dugumbe. This slaughter was peculiarly atrocious, inasmuch as we have always heard that women coming to or from market have never been known to be molested: even when two districts are engaged in actual hostilities, "the women," say they, "pass among us to market unmolested," nor has one ever been known to be plundered by the men. These Nigger Moslems are inferior to the Manyuema in justice and right. The people under Hassani began the superwickedness of capture and pillage of all indiscriminately. Dugumbe promised to send over men to order Tagamoio's men to cease firing and burning villages; they remained over among the ruins, feasting on goats and fowls all night, and next day (16th) continued their infamous work till twenty-seven villages were destroyed.

16th July, 1871. --I restored upwards of thirty of the rescued to their friends: Dugumbe seemed to act in good faith, and kept none of them; it was his own free will that guided him. Women are delivered to their husbands, and about thirty-three canoes left in the creek are to be kept for the owners too.

12 A.M.--Shooting still going on on the other side, and many captives caught. At 1 P.M. Tagamoio's people began to cross over in canoes, beating their drums, firing their guns, and shouting, as if to say, "See the conquering heroes come;" they are answered by the women of Dugumba's camp lullilooing, and friends then fire off their guns in joy. I count seventeen villages in flames, and the smoke goes straight up and forms clouds at the top of the pillar, showing great heat evolved, for the houses are full of carefully-prepared firewood. Dugumbe denies having sent Tagamoio on this foray, and Tagamoio repeats that he went to punish the friends made by Manilla, who, being a slave, had no right to make war and burn villages, that could only be done by free men. Manilla confesses to me privately that he did wrong in that, and loses all his beads and many friends in consequence.

2 P.M.--An old man, called Kabobo, came for his old wife; I asked her if this were her husband, she went to him, and put her arm lovingly around him, and said "Yes." I gave her five strings of beads to buy food, all her stores being destroyed with her house; she bowed down, and put her forehead to the ground as thanks, and old Kabobo did the same: the tears stood in her eyes as she went off. Tagamoio caught 17 women, and other Arabs of his party, 27; dead by gunshot, 25. The heads of two headmen were brought over to be redeemed by their friends with slaves.

3 P.M.--Many of the headmen who have been burned out by the foray came over to me, and begged me to come back with them, and appoint new localities for them to settle in again, but I told them that I was so ashamed of the company in which I found myself, that I could scarcely look the Manyuema in the face. They had believed that I wished to kill them--what did they think now? I could not remain among bloody companions, and would flee away, I said, but they begged me hard not to leave until they were again settled.

The open murder perpetrated on hundreds of unsuspecting women fills me with unspeakable horror: I cannot think of going anywhere with the Tagamoio crew; I must either go down or up Lualaba, whichever the Banian slaves choose.

4 P.M.--Dugumbe saw that by killing the market people he had committed a great error, and speedily got the chiefs who had come over to me to meet him at his house, and forthwith mix blood: they were in bad case. I could not remain to

see to their protection, and Dugumbe, being the best of the whole horde, I advised them to make friends, and then appeal to him as able to restrain to some extent his infamous underlings. One chief asked to have his wife and daughter restored to him first, but generally they were cowed, and the fear of death was on them. Dugumbe said to me, "I shall do my utmost to get all the captives, but he must make friends now, in order that the market may not be given up." Blood was mixed, and an essential condition was, "You must give us chitoka," or market. He and most others saw that in theoretically punishing Manilla, they had slaughtered the very best friends that strangers had. The Banian slaves openly declare that they will go only to Lomame, and no further. Whatever the Ujijian slavers may pretend, they all hate to have me as a witness of their cold-blooded atrocities. The Banian slaves would like to go with Tagamoio, and share in his rapine and get slaves. I tried to go down Lualaba, then up it, and west, but with bloodhounds it is out of the question. I see nothing for it but to go back to Ujiji for other men, though it will throw me out of the chance of discovering the fourth great Lake in the Lualaba line of drainage, and other things of great value.

At last I said that I would start for Ujiji, in three days, on foot. I wished to speak to Tagamoio about the captive relations of the chiefs, but he always ran away when he saw me coming.

17th July, 1871. --All the rest of Dugumbe's party offered me a share of every kind of goods they had, and pressed me not to be ashamed to tell them what I needed. I declined everything save a little gunpowder, but they all made presents of beads, and I was glad to return equivalents in cloth. It is a sore affliction, at least forty-five days in a straight line--equal to 300 miles, or by the turnings and windings 600 English miles, and all after feeding and clothing the Banian slaves for twenty-one months! But it is for the best though; if I do not trust to the riffraff of Ujiji, I must wait for other men at least ten months there. With help from above I shall yet go through Rua, see the underground excavations first, then on to Katanga, and the four ancient fountains eight days beyond, and after that Lake Lincoln.

18th July, 1871. --The murderous assault on the market people felt to me like Gehenna, without the fire and brimstone; but the heat was oppressive, and the firearms pouring their iron bullets on the fugitives, was not an inapt representative of burning in the bottomless pit.

The terrible scenes of man's inhumanity to man brought on severe headache, which might have been serious had it not been relieved by a copious discharge of blood; I was laid up all yesterday afternoon, with the depression the bloodshed made,--it filled me with unspeakable horror. "Don't go away," say the Manyuema chiefs to me; but I cannot stay here in agony.

19th July, 1871. --Dugumbe sent me a fine goat, a maneh of gunpowder, a maneh of fine blue beads, and 230 cowries, to buy provisions in the way. I proposed to leave a doti Merikano and one of Kanike to buy specimens of workmanship. He sent me two very fine large Manyuema swords, and two equally fine spears, and said that I must not leave anything; he would buy others with his own goods, and divide them equally with me: he is very friendly.

River fallen 4-1/2 feet since the 5th ult.

A few market people appear to-day, formerly they came in crowds: a very few from the west bank bring salt to buy back the baskets from the camp slaves, which they threw away in panic, others carried a little food for sale, about 200 in all, chiefly those who have not lost relatives: one very beautiful woman had a gunshot wound in her upper arm tied round with leaves. Seven canoes came instead of fifty; but they have great tenacity and hopefulness, an old established custom has great charms for them, and the market will again be attended if no fresh outrage is committed. No canoes now come into the creek of death, but land above, at Ntambwe's village: this creek, at the bottom of the long gentle slope on which the market was held, probably led to its selection.

A young Manyuema man worked for one of Dugumbe's people preparing a space to build on; when tired, he refused to commence to dig a pit, and was struck on the loins with an axe, and soon died: he was drawn out of the way, and his relations came, wailed over him, and buried him: they are too much awed to complain to Dugumbe!!

CHAPTER VI.

Leaves for Ujiji. Dangerous journey through forest. The Manyuema understand Livingstone's kindness. Zanzibar slaves. Kasongo's. Stalactite caves. Consequences of eating parrots. Ill. Attacked in the forest. Providential deliverance. Another extraordinary escape. Taken for Mohamad Bogharib. Running the gauntlet for five hours. Loss of property. Reaches place of safety. Ill. Mamohela. To the Luamo. Severe disappointment. Recovers. Severe marching. Reaches Ujiji. Despondency. Opportune arrival of Mr. Stanley. Joy and thankfulness of the old traveller. Determines to examine north end of Lake Tanganyika. They start. Reach the Lusize. No outlet. "Theoretical discovery" of the real outlet. Mr. Stanley ill. Returns to Ujiji. Leaves stores there. Departure for Unyanyembe with Mr. Stanley. Abundance of game.--Attacked by bees. Serious illness of Mr. Stanley. Thankfulness at reaching Unyatiyembe.

20th July, 1871. --I start back for Ujiji. All Dugumbe's people came to say good bye, and convoy me a little way. I made a short march, for being long inactive it is unwise to tire oneself on the first day, as it is then difficult to get over the effects.

21st July, 1871. --One of the slaves was sick, and the rest falsely reported him to be seriously ill, to give them time to negotiate for women with whom they had cohabited: Dugumbe saw through the fraud, and said "Leave him to me: if he lives, I will feed him; if he dies, we will bury him: do not delay for any one, but travel in a compact body, as stragglers now are sure to be cut off." He lost a woman of his party, who lagged behind, and seven others were killed besides, and the forest hid the murderers. I was only too anxious to get away quickly, and on the 22nd started off at daylight, and went about six miles to the village of Mankwara, where I spent the night when coming this way. The chief Mokandira convoyed us hither:

I promised him a cloth if I came across from Lomame. He wonders much at the underground houses, and never heard of them till I told him about them. Many of the gullies which were running fast when we came were now dry. Thunder began, and a few drops of rain fell.

23rd-24th July, 1871.--We crossed the River Kunda, of fifty yards, in two canoes, and then ascended from the valley of denudation, in which it flows to the ridge Lobango. Crowds followed, all anxious to carry loads for a few beads. Several market people came to salute, who knew that we had no hand in the massacre, as we are a different people from the Arabs. In going and coming they must have a march of 25 miles with loads so heavy no slave would carry them. They speak of us as "good:" the anthropologists think that to be spoken of as wicked is better. Ezekiel says that the Most High put His comeliness upon Jerusalem: if He does not impart of His goodness to me I shall never be good: if He does not put of His comeliness on me I shall never be comely in soul, but be like these Arabs in whom Satan has full sway--the god of this world having blinded their eyes.

25th July, 1871.--We came over a beautiful country yesterday, a vast hollow of denudation, with much cultivation, intersected by a ridge some 300 feet high, on which the villages are built: this is Lobango. The path runs along the top of the ridge, and we see the fine country below all spread out with different shades of green, as on a map. The colours show the shapes of the different plantations in the great hollow drained by the Kunda. After crossing the fast flowing Kahembai, which flows into the Kunda, and it into Lualaba, we rose on to another intersecting ridge, having a great many villages burned by Matereka or Salem Mokadam's people, since we passed them in our course N.W. They had slept on the ridge after we saw them, and next morning, in sheer wantonness, fired their lodgings,--their slaves had evidently carried the fire along from their lodgings, and set fire to houses of villages in their route as a sort of horrid Moslem Nigger joke; it was done only because they could do it without danger of punishment: it was such fun to make the Mashense, as they call all natives, houseless. Men are worse than beasts of prey, if indeed it is lawful to call Zanzibar slaves men. It is monstrous injustice to compare free Africans living under their own chiefs and laws, and cultivating their own free lands, with what slaves afterwards become at Zanzibar and elsewhere.

26th July, 1871.--Came up out of the last valley of denudation--that drained by Kahembai, and then along a level land with open forest. Four men passed us in hot haste to announce the death of a woman at their village to her relations living at another. I heard of several deaths lately of dysentery. Pleurisy is common from cold winds from N.W. Twenty-two men with large square black shields, capable of completely hiding the whole person, came next in a trot to receive the body of their relative and all her gear to carry her to her own home for burial: about twenty women followed them, and the men waited under the trees till they should have wound the body up and wept over her. They smeared their bodies with clay, and their faces with soot. Reached our friend Kama.

27th July, 1871. --Left Kama's group of villages and went through many others before we reached Kasongo's, and were welcomed by all the Arabs of the camp at this place. Bought two milk goats reasonably, and rest over Sunday. (*28th and 29th*). They asked permission to send a party with me for goods to Ujiji; this will increase our numbers, and perhaps safety too, among the justly irritated people between this and Bambarre. All are enjoined to help me, and of course I must do the same to them. It is colder here than at Nyangwe. Kasongo is off guiding an ivory or slaving party, and doing what business he can on his own account; he has four guns, and will be the first to maraud on his own account.

30th July, 1871. --They send thirty tusks to Ujiji, and seventeen Manyuema volunteers to carry thither and back: these are the very first who in modern times have ventured fifty miles from the place of their birth. I came only three miles to a ridge overlooking the River Shokoye, and slept at village on a hill beyond it.

31st July, 1871. --Passed through the defile between Mount Kimazi and Mount Kijila. Below the cave with stalactite pillar in its door a fine echo answers those who feel inclined to shout to it. Come to Mangala's numerous villages, and two slaves being ill, rest on Wednesday.

1st August, 1871. --A large market assembles close to us.

2nd August, 1871. --Left Mangala's, and came through a great many villages all deserted on our approach on account of the vengeance taken by Dugumbe's party for the murder of some of their people. Kasongo's men appeared eager to plunder their own countrymen: I had to scold and threaten them, and set men to watch their deeds. Plantains are here very abundant, good, and cheap. Came to Kittette, and lodge in a village of Loembo. About thirty foundries were passed; they are very high in the roof, and thatched with leaves, from which the sparks roll off as sand would. Rain runs off equally well.

3rd August, 1871. --Three slaves escaped, and not to abandon ivory we wait a day, Kasongo came up and filled their places.

I have often observed effigies of men made of wood in Manyuema; some of clay are simply cones with a small hole in the top; on asking about them here, I for the first time obtained reliable information. They are called Bathata--fathers or ancients--and the name of each is carefully preserved. Those here at Kittette were evidently the names of chiefs, Molenda being the most ancient, whilst Mbayo Yamba, Kamoanga, Kitambwe, Nongo, Aulumba, Yenge Yenge, Simba Mayanga, Loembwe, are more recently dead. They were careful to have the exact pronunciation of the names. The old men told me that on certain occasions they offer goat's flesh to them: men eat it, and allow no young person or women to partake. The flesh of the parrot is only eaten by very old men. They say that if eaten by young men their children will have the waddling gait of the bird. They say that originally those who preceded Molenda came from Kongolakokwa, which conveys no idea to my mind. It was interesting to get even this little bit of history here. (Nkongolo = Deity; Nkongolokwa as the Deity.)

4th August, 1871. --Came through miles of villages all burned because the people refused a certain Abdullah lodgings! The men had begun to re-thatch the huts, and kept out of our way, but a goat was speared by some one in hiding, and we knew danger was near. Abdullah admitted that he had no other reason for burning them than the unwillingness of the people to lodge him and his slaves without payment, with the certainty of getting their food stolen and utensils destroyed.

5th and 6th August, 1871. --Through many miles of palm-trees and plantains to a Boma or stockaded village, where we slept, though the people were evidently suspicious and unfriendly.

7th August, 1871. --To a village, ill and almost every step in pain. The people all ran away, and appeared in the distance armed, and refused to come near--then came and threw stones at us, and afterwards tried to kill those who went for water. We sleep uncomfortably, the natives watching us all round. Sent men to see if the way was clear.

8th August, 1871. --They would come to no parley. They knew their advantage, and the wrongs they had suffered from Bin Juma and Mohamad's men when they threw down the ivory in the forest. In passing along the narrow path with a wall of dense vegetation touching each hand, we came to a point where an ambush had been placed, and trees cut down to obstruct us while they speared us; but for some reason it was abandoned. Nothing could be detected; but by stooping down to the earth and peering up towards the sun, a dark shade could sometimes be seen: this was an infuriated savage, and a slight rustle in the dense vegetation meant a spear. A large spear from my right lunged past and almost grazed my back, and stuck firmly into the soil. The two men from whom it came appeared in an opening in the forest only ten yards off and bolted, one looking back over his shoulder as he ran. As they are expert with the spear I don't know how it missed, except that he was too sure of his aim and the good hand of God was upon me.

I was behind the main body, and all were allowed to pass till I, the leader, who was believed to be Mohamad Bogharib, or Kolokolo himself, came up to the point where they lay. A red jacket they had formerly seen me wearing was proof to them, that I was the same that sent Bin Juma to kill five of their men, capture eleven women and children, and twenty-five goats. Another spear was thrown at me by an unseen assailant, and it missed me by about a foot in front. Guns were fired into the dense mass of forest, but with no effect, for nothing could be seen; but we heard the men jeering and denouncing us close by: two of our party were slain.

Coming to a part of the forest cleared for cultivation I noticed a gigantic tree, made still taller by growing on an ant-hill 20 feet high; it had fire applied near its roots, I heard a crack which told that the fire had done its work, but felt no alarm till I saw it come straight towards me: I ran a few paces back, and down it came to the ground one yard behind me, and breaking into several lengths, it covered me with a cloud of dust. Had the branches not previously been rotted off, I could scarcely have escaped.

Three times in one day was I delivered from impending death.

My attendants, who were scattered in all directions, came running back to me, calling out, "Peace! peace! you will finish all your work in spite of these people, and in spite of everything." Like them, I took it as an omen of good success to crown me yet, thanks to the "Almighty Preserver of men."

We had five hours of running the gauntlet, waylaid by spearmen, who all felt that if they killed me they would be revenging the death of relations. From each hole in the tangled mass we looked for a spear; and each moment expected to hear the rustle which told of deadly weapons hurled at us. I became weary with the constant strain of danger, and--as, I suppose, happens with soldiers on the field of battle--not courageous, but perfectly indifferent whether I were killed or not.

When at last we got out of the forest and crossed the Liya on to the cleared lands near the villages of Monan-bundwa, we lay down to rest, and soon saw Muanampunda coming, walking up in a stately manner unarmed to meet us. He had heard the vain firing of my men into the bush, and came to ask what was the matter. I explained the mistake that Munangonga had made in supposing that I was Kolokolo, the deeds of whose men he knew, and then we went on to his village together.

In the evening he sent to say that if I would give him all my people who had guns, he would call his people together, burn off all the vegetation they could fire, and punish our enemies, bringing me ten goats instead of the three milch goats I had lost. I again explained that the attack was made by a mistake in thinking I was Mohamad Bogharib, and that I had no wish to kill men: to join in his old feud would only make matters worse. This he could perfectly understand.

I lost all my remaining calico, a telescope, umbrella, and five spears, by one of the slaves throwing down the load and taking up his own bundle of country cloth.

9th August, 1871.--Went on towards Mamohela, now deserted by the Arabs. Monanponda convoyed me a long way, and at one spot, with grass all trodden down, he said, "Here we killed a man of Moezia and ate his body." The meat cut up had been seen by Dugumbe.

10th August, 1871.--In connection with this affair the party that came through from Mamalulu found that a great fight had taken place at Muanampunda's, and they saw the meat cut up to be cooked with bananas. They did not like the strangers to look at their meat, but said, "Go on, and let our feast alone," they did not want to be sneered at. The same Muanampunda or Monambonda told me frankly that they ate the man of Moezia: they seem to eat their foes to inspire courage, or in revenge. One point is very remarkable; it is not want that has led to the custom, for the country is full of food: nobody is starved of farinaceous food; they have maize, dura, pennisetum, cassava and sweet potatoes, and for fatty ingredients of diet, the palm-oil, ground-nuts, sessamum, and a tree whose fruit yields a fine sweet oil: the saccharine materials needed are found in the sugar-cane, bananas, and plantains.

Goats, sheep, fowls, dogs, pigs, abound in the villages, whilst the forest affords elephants, zebras, buffaloes, antelopes, and in the streams there are many varieties of fish. The nitrogenous ingredients are abundant, and they have dainties in palm-toddy, and tobacco or Bange: the soil is so fruitful that mere scraping off the weeds is as good as ploughing, so that the reason for cannibalism does not lie in starvation or in want of animal matter, as was said to be the case with the New Zealanders. The only feasible reason I can discover is a depraved appetite, giving an extraordinary craving for meat which we call "high." They are said to bury a dead body for a couple of days in the soil in a forest, and in that time, owing to the climate, it soon becomes putrid enough for the strongest stomachs.

The Lualaba has many oysters in it with very thick shells. They are called *Makessi*, and at certain seasons are dived for by the Bagenya women: pearls are said to be found in them, but boring to string them has never been thought of. *Kanone*, Ibis religiosa. *Uruko*, Kuss name of coffee.

The Manyuema are so afraid of guns, that a man borrows one to settle any dispute or claim: he goes with it over his shoulder, and quickly arranges the matter by the pressure it brings, though they all know that he could not use it.

Gulu, Deity above, or heaven. *Mamvu*, earth or below. *Gulu* is a person, and men, on death, go to him. *Nkoba,* lightning. *Nkongolo*, Deity (?). *Kula* or *Nkula*, salt spring west of Nyangwe. *Kalunda*, ditto. *Kiria*, rapid down river. *Kirila*, islet in sight of Nyangwe. *Magoya*, ditto.

Note.--The chief Zurampela is about N.W. of Nyangwe, and three days off. The Luive River, of very red water, is crossed, and the larger Mabila River receives it into its very dark water before Mabila enters Lualaba.

A ball of hair rolled in the stomach of a lion, as calculi are, is a great charm among the Arabs: it scares away other animals, they say.

Lion's fat smeared on the tails of oxen taken through a country abounding in tsetse, or bungo, is a sure preventive; when I heard of this, I thought that lion's fat would be as difficult of collection as gnat's brains or mosquito tongues, but I was assured that many lions are killed on the Basango highland, and they, in common with all beasts there, are extremely fat: so it is not at all difficult to buy a calabash of the preventive, and Banyamwezi, desirous of taking cattle to the coast for sale, know the substance, and use it successfully (?).

11th August, 1871.--Came on by a long march of six hours across plains of grass and watercourses, lined with beautiful trees, to Kassessa's, the chief of Mamohela, who has helped the Arabs to scourge several of his countrymen for old feuds: he gave them goats, and then guided them by night to the villages, where they got more goats and many captives, each to be redeemed with ten goats more. During the last foray, however, the people learned that every shot does not kill, and they came up to the party with bows and arrows, and compelled the slaves to throw down their guns and powder-horns. They would have shown no mercy had Manyuema been thus in slave power; but this is a beginning of the end, which will exclude Arab traders from the country. I rested half a day, as I am still ill. I do most devoutly thank the Lord for sparing my life three times in one day. The Lord is good, a stronghold in the day of trouble, and He knows them that trust in Him.

[The brevity of the following notes is fully accounted for: Livingstone was evidently suffering too severely to write more.]

12th August, 1871.--Mamohela camp all burned off. We sleep at Mamohela village.

13th August, 1871.--At a village on the bank of River Lolindi, I am suffering greatly. A man brought a young, nearly full-fledged, kite from a nest on a tree: this is the first case of their breeding, that I am sure of, in this country: they are migratory into these intertropical lands from the south, probably.

14th August, 1871.--Across many brisk burns to a village on the side of a mountain range. First rains 12th and 14th, gentle; but near Luamo, it ran on the paths, and caused dew.

15th August, 1871.--To Muanambonyo's. Golungo, a bush buck, with stripes across body, and two rows of spots along the sides (?)

16th August, 1871.--To Luamo River. Very ill with bowels.

17th August, 1871.--Cross river, and sent a message to my friend. Katomba sent a bountiful supply of food back.

18th August, 1871.--Reached Katomba, at Moenemgoi's, and was welcomed by all the heavily-laden Arab traders. They carry their trade spoil in three relays. Kenyengere attacked before I came, and 150 captives were taken and about 100 slain; this is an old feud of Moenemgoi, which the Arabs took up for their own gain.

No news whatever from Ujiji, and M. Bogharib is still at Bambarre, with all my letters.

19th-20th August, 1871.--Rest from weakness. (***21st August, 1871.***) Up to the palms on the west of Mount Kanyima Pass. (***22nd August, 1871.***) Bambarre. (***28th August, 1871.***) Better and thankful. Katomba's party has nearly a thousand frasilahs of ivory, and Mohamad's has 300 frasilahs.

29th August, 1871.--Ill all night, and remain. (***30th August, 1871.***) Ditto, ditto; but go on to Monandenda's on River Lombonda.

31st August, 1871.--Up and half over the mountain range, (***1st September, 1871***) and sleep in dense forest, with several fine running streams.

2nd September, 1871.--Over the range, and down on to a marble-capped hill, with a village on top.

3rd September, 1871.--Equinoctial gales. On to Lohombo.

5th September, 1871.--To Kasangangazi's. (***6th September, 1871.***) Rest. (***7th September, 1871.***) Mamba's. Rest on 8th. (***9th September, 1871.***) Ditto ditto. People falsely accused of stealing; but I disproved it to the confusion of the Arabs, who wish to be able to say, "the people of the English steal too." A very rough road from Kasangangazi's hither, and several running rivulets crossed.

10th September, 1871.--Manyuema boy followed us, but I insisted on his father's consent, which was freely given: marching proved too hard for him, however, and in a few days he left.

Down into the valley of the Kapemba through beautiful undulating country, and came to village of Amru: this is a common name, and is used as "man," or "comrade," or "mate."

11th September, 1871.--Up a very steep high mountain range, Moloni or Mononi, and down to a village at the bottom on the other side, of a man called Molembu.

12th September, 1871.--Two men sick. Wait, though I am now comparatively sound and well. Dura flour, which we can now procure, helps to strengthen me: it is nearest to wheaten flour; maize meal is called "cold," and not so wholesome as the ***Holeus sorghum*** or dura. A lengthy march through a level country, with high mountain ranges on each hand; along that on the left our first path lay, and it was very fatiguing. We came to the Rivulet Kalangai. I had hinted to Mohamad that if he harboured my deserters, it might go hard with him; and he came after me for two marches, and begged me not to think that he did encourage them. They came impudently into the village, and I had to drive them out: I suspected that he had sent them. I explained, and he gave me a goat, which I sent back for.

13th September, 1871. --This march back completely used up the Manyuema boy: he could not speak, or tell what he wanted cooked, when he arrived. I did not see him go back, and felt sorry for the poor boy, who left us by night. People here would sell nothing, so I was glad of the goat.

14th September, 1871. --To Pyanamosinde's. (15th September, 1871.) ***To Karungamagao's; very fine undulating green country.*** (16th and 17th September, 1871.) Rest, as we could get food to buy.

(18th September, 1871.) To a stockaded village, where the people ordered us to leave. We complied, and went out half a mile and built our sheds in the forest: I like sheds in the forest much better than huts in the villages, for we have no mice or vermin, and incur no obligation.

19th September, 1871. --Found that Barua are destroying all the Manyuema villages not stockaded.

20th September, 1871. --We came to Kunda's on the River Katemba, through great plantations of cassava, and then to a woman chief's, and now regularly built our own huts apart from the villages, near the hot fountain called Kabila which is about blood-heat, and flows across the path. Crossing this we came to Mokwaniwa's, on the River Gombeze, and met a caravan, under Nassur Masudi, of 200 guns. He presented a fine sheep, and reported that Seyed Majid was dead--he had been ailing and fell from some part of his new house at Darsalam, and in three days afterwards expired. He was a true and warm friend to me and did all he could to aid me with his subjects, giving me two Sultan's letters for the purpose. Seyed Burghash succeeds him; this change causes anxiety. Will Seyed Burghash's goodness endure now that he has the Sultanate? Small-pox raged lately at Ujiji.

22nd September, 1871. --Caravan goes northwards, and we rest, and eat the sheep kindly presented.

23rd September, 1871. --We now passed through the country of mixed Barua and Baguha, crossed the River Longumba twice and then came near the great mountain mass on west of Tanganyika. From Mokwaniwa's to Tanganyika is about ten good marches through open forest. The Guha people are not very friendly; they know strangers too well to show kindness: like Manyuema, they are also keen traders. I was sorely knocked up by this march from Nyangwe back to Ujiji. In the latter part of it, I felt as if dying on my feet. Almost every step was in pain, the appetite failed, and a little bit of meat caused violent diarrhoea, whilst the mind, sorely depressed, reacted on the body. All the traders were returning successful: I alone had failed and experienced worry, thwarting, baffling, when almost in sight of the end towards which I strained.

3rd October, 1871. --I read the whole Bible through four times whilst I was in Manyuema.

8th October, 1871. --The road covered with angular fragments of quartz was very sore to my feet, which are crammed into ill-made French shoes. How the bare feet of the men and women stood out, I don't know; it was hard enough on mine though protected by the shoes. We marched in the afternoons where water at this season was scarce. The dust of the march caused ophthalmia, like that which afflicted Speke: this was my first touch of it in Africa. We now came to the Lobumba River, which flows into Tanganyika, and then to the village Loanda and sent to Kasanga, the Guha chief, for canoes. The Longumba rises, like the Lobumba, in the mountains called Kabogo West. We heard great noises, as if thunder, as far as twelve days off, which were ascribed to Kabogo, as if it had subterranean caves into which the waves rushed with great noise, and it may be that the Longumba is the outlet of Tanganyika: it becomes the Luasse further down, and then the Luamo before it joins the Lualaba: the country slopes that way, but I was too ill to examine its source.

9th October, 1871. --On to islet Kasenge. After much delay got a good canoe for three dotis, and on *15th October, 1871* went to the islet Kabiziwa.

18th October, 1871. --Start for Kabogo East, and *19th* reach it 8 A.M.

20th October, 1871. --Rest men.

22nd October, 1871. --To Rombola.

23rd October, 1871. --At dawn, off and go to Ujiji. Welcomed by all the Arabs, particularly by Moenyeghere. I was now reduced to a skeleton, but the market being held daily, and all kinds of native food brought to it, I hoped that food and rest would soon restore me, but in the evening my people came and told me that Shereef had sold off all my goods, and Moenyeghere confirmed it by saying, "We protested, but he did not leave a single yard of calico out of 3000, nor a string of beads out of 700 lbs." This was distressing. I had made up my mind, if I could not get people at Ujiji, to wait till men should come from the coast, but to wait in beggary was what I never contemplated, and I now felt miserable. Shereef was evidently a moral idiot, for he came without shame to shake hands with me, and when I refused, assumed an air of displeasure, as having been badly treated; and afterwards came with his "Balghere," good-luck salutation, twice a day, and on leaving said, "I am going to pray," till I told him that were I an Arab, his hand and both ears would be cut off for thieving, as he knew, and I wanted no salutations from him. In my distress it was annoying to see Shereef's slaves passing from the market with all the good things that my goods had bought.

24th October, 1871. --My property had been sold to Shereef's friends at merely nominal prices. Syed bin Majid, a good man, proposed that they should be returned, and the ivory be taken from Shereef; but they would not restore stolen property, though they knew it to be stolen. Christians would have acted differently, even those of the lowest classes. I felt in my destitution as if I were the man who went down from Jerusalem to Jericho, and fell among thieves; but I could not hope for Priest, Levite, or good Samaritan to come by on either side, but one morning Syed bin Majid said to me, "Now this is the first time we have been alone together; I have no goods, but I have ivory; let me, I pray you, sell some ivory, and give the goods to you." This was encouraging; but I said, "Not yet, but by-and-bye." I had still a few barter goods left, which I had taken the precaution to deposit with Mohamad bin Saleh before going to Manyuema, in case of returning in extreme need. But when my spirits were at their lowest ebb, the good Samaritan was close at hand, for one morning Susi came running at the top of his speed and gasped out, "An Englishman! I see him!" and off he darted to meet him. The American flag at the head of a caravan told of the nationality of the stranger. Bales of goods, baths of tin, huge kettles, cooking pots, tents, &c, made me think "This must be a luxurious traveller, and not one at his wits' end like me." (28th October, 1871.) **It was Henry Moreland Stanley, the travelling correspondent of the** New York Herald, **sent by James Gordon Bennett, junior, at an expense of more than 400**0l.**, to obtain**

*accurate information about Dr. Livingstone if living, and if dead to bring home my bones. The news he had to tell to one who had been two full years without any tidings from Europe made my whole frame thrill. The terrible fate that had befallen France, the telegraphic cables successfully laid in the Atlantic, the election of General Grant, the death of good Lord Clarendon--my constant friend, the proof that Her Majesty's Government had not forgotten me in voting 1000*l. for supplies, and many other points of interest, revived emotions that had lain dormant in Manyuema. Appetite returned, and instead of the spare, tasteless, two meals a day, I ate four times daily, and in a week began to feel strong. I am not of a demonstrative turn; as cold, indeed, as we islanders are usually reputed to be, but this disinterested kindness of Mr. Bennett, so nobly carried into effect by Mr. Stanley, was simply overwhelming. I really do feel extremely grateful, and at the same time I am a little ashamed at not being more worthy of the generosity. Mr. Stanley has done his part with untiring energy; good judgment in the teeth of very serious obstacles. His helpmates turned out depraved blackguards, who, by their excesses at Zanzibar and elsewhere, had ruined their constitutions, and prepared their systems to be fit provender for the grave. They had used up their strength by wickedness, and were of next to no service, but rather downdrafts and unbearable drags to progress.

16th November, 1871. --As Tanganyika explorations are said by Mr. Stanley to be an object of interest to Sir Roderick, we go at his expense and by his men to the north of the Lake.

[Dr. Livingstone on a previous occasion wrote from the interior of Africa to the effect that Lake Tanganyika poured its waters into the Albert Nyanza Lake of Baker. At the time perhaps he hardly realized the interest that such an announcement was likely to occasion. He was now shown the importance of ascertaining by actual observation whether the junction really existed, and for this purpose he started with Mr. Stanley to explore the region of the supposed connecting link in the North, so as to verify the statements of the Arabs.]

16th November, 1871. --Four hours to Chigoma.

20th and 21st November, 1871. --Passed a very crowded population, the men calling to us to land to be fleeced and insulted by way of Mahonga or Mutuari: they threw stones in rage, and one, apparently slung, lighted close to the canoe. We came on until after dark, and landed under a cliff to rest and cook, but a crowd came and made inquiries, then a few more came as if to investigate more perfectly: they told us to sleep, and to-morrow friendship should be made. We put our luggage on board and set a watch on the cliff. A number of men came along, cowering behind rocks, which then aroused suspicion, and we slipped off quietly; they called after us, as men baulked of their prey. We went on five hours and slept, and then this morning came on to Magala, where the people are civil, but Mukamba had war with some one. The Lake narrows to about ten miles, as the western mountains come towards the eastern range, that being about N.N.W. magnetic. Many stumps of trees killed by water show an encroachment by the Lake on the east side. A transverse range seems to shut in the north end, but there is open country to the east and west of its ends.

24th November, 1871. --To Point Kizuka in Mukamba's country. A Molongwana came to us from Mukamba and asserted most positively that all the water of Tanganyika flowed into the River Lusize, and then on to Ukerewe of Mteza; nothing could be more clear than his statements.

25th November, 1871. --We came on about two hours to some villages on a high bank where Mukamba is living. The chief, a young good-looking man like Mugala, came and welcomed us. Our friend of yesterday now declared as positively as before that the water of Lusize flowed into Tanganyika, and not the way he said yesterday! I have not the smallest doubt but Tanganyika discharges somewhere, though we may be unable to find it. Lusize goes to or comes from Luanda and Karagwe. This is hopeful, but I suspend my judgment. War rages between Mukamba and Wasmashanga or Uasmasane, a chief between this and Lusize: ten men were killed of Mukamba's people a few days ago. Vast numbers of fishermen ply their calling night and day as far as we can see. Tanganyika closes in except at one point N. and by W. of us. The highest point of the western range, about 7000 feet above the sea, is Sumburuza. We are to go to-morrow to Luhinga, elder brother of Mukamba, near Lusize, and the chief follows us next day.

26th November, 1871. --Sunday. Mr. Stanley has severe fever. I gave Mukamba 9 dotis and 9 fundos. The end of Tanganyika seen clearly is rounded off about 4' broad from east to west.

27th November, 1871. --Mr. Stanley is better. We started at sunset westwards, then northwards for seven hours, and at 4 A.M. reached Lohinga, at the mouth of the Lusize.

28th November, 1871. --Shot an ***Ibis religiosa.*** In the afternoon Luhinga, the superior of Mukambe, came and showed himself very intelligent. He named eighteen rivers, four of which enter Tanganyika, and the rest Lusize: all come into, none leave Tanganyika[15]. Lusize is said to rise in Kwangeregere in the Kivo lagoon, between Mutumbe and Luanda. Nyabungu is chief of Mutumbe. Luhinga is the most intelligent and the frankest chief we have seen here.

29th November, 1871. --We go to see the Lusize Eiver in a canoe. The mouth is filled with large reedy sedgy islets: there are three branches, about twelve to fifteen yards broad, and one fathom deep, with a strong current of 2' per hour: water discoloured. The outlet of the Lake is probably by the Longumba River into Lualaba as the Luamo, but this as yet must be set down as a "theoretical discovery."

30th November, 1871. --A large present of eggs, flour, and a sheep came from Mukamba. Mr. Stanley went round to a bay in the west, to which the mountains come sheer down.

1st December, 1871, Friday. --Latitude last night 3 deg. 18' 3" S. I gave fifteen cloths to Lohinga, which pleased him highly. Kuansibura is the chief who lives near Kivo, the lagoon from which the Lusize rises: they say it flows under a rock.

2nd December, 1871. --Ill from bilious attack.

3rd December, 1871. --Better and thankful. Men went off to bring Mukamba, whose wife brought us a handsome present of milk, beer, and cassava. She is a good-looking young woman, of light colour and full lips, with two children of eight or ten years of age. We gave them cloths, and sheasked beads, so we made them a present of two fundos. By lunars I was one day wrong to-day.

4th December, 1871. --Very heavy rain from north all night. Baker's Lake cannot be as near as he puts it in his map, for it is unknown to Lohinge. He thinks that he is a hundred years old, but he is really about forty-five! Namataranga is the name of birds which float high in air in large flocks.

5th December, 1871. --We go over to a point on our east. The bay is about 12' broad: the mountains here are very beautiful. We visited the chief Mukamba, at his village five miles north of Lohinga's; he wanted us to remain a few days, but I

---

15   Thus the question of the Lusize was settled at once: the previous notion of its outflow to the north proved a myth.--ED.

declined. We saw two flocks of *Ibis religiosa,* numbering in all fifty birds, feeding like geese.

6th December, 1871.--Remain at Luhinga's.

7th December, 1871.--Start and go S.W. to Lohanga: passed the point where Speke turned, then breakfasted at the marketplace.

8th December, 1871.--Go on to Mukamba; near the boundary of Babembe and Bavira. We pulled six hours to a rocky islet, with two rocks covered with trees on its western side. The Babembe are said to be dangerous, on account of having been slaughtered by the Malongwana. The Lat. of these islands is 3 deg. 41' S.

9th December, 1871.--Leave New York Herald Islet and go S. to Lubumba Cape. The people now are the Basansas along the coast. Some men here were drunk and troublesome: we gave them a present and left them about 4-1/2 in afternoon and went to an islet at the north end in about three hours, good pulling, and afterwards in eight hours to the eastern shore; this makes the Lake, say, 28 or 30 miles broad. We coasted along to Mokungos and rested.

10th December, 1871.--Kisessa is chief of all the islet Mozima. His son was maltreated at Ujiji and died in consequence; this stopped the dura trade, and we were not assaulted because not Malongwana.

11th December, 1871.--Leave Mokungo at 6 A.M. and coast along 6-1/2 hours to Sazzi.

12th December, 1871.--Mr. Stanley ill with fever. Off, and after three hours, stop at Masambo village.

13th December, 1871.--Mr. Stanley better. Go on to Ujiji. Mr. Stanley received a letter from Consul Webb (American) of 11th June last, and telegrams from Aden up to 29th April.

14th December, 1871.--Many people off to fight Mirambo at Unyanyembe: their wives promenade and weave green leaves for victory.

15th December, 1871.--At Ujiji. Getting ready to march east for my goods.

16th December, 1871.--Engage paddlers to Tongwe and a guide.

17th December, 1871.--S. *18th.*--Writing. *19th-20th.*--Still writing despatches. Packed up the large tin box with Manyuema swords and spear heads, for transmission home by Mr. Stanley. Two chronometers and two watches--anklets of

Nzige and of Manyuema. Leave with Mohamad bin Saleh a box with books, shirts, paper, &c.; also large and small beads, tea, coffee and sugar.

21st December, 1871.--Heavy rains for planting now.

22nd December, 1871.--Stanley ill of fever.

23rd December, 1871.--Do. very ill. Rainy and uncomfortable.

24th December, 1871.--S. *25th.--Christmas*. I leave here one bag of beads in a skin, 2 bags of Sungo mazi 746 and 756 blue. Gardner's bag of beads, soap 2 bars in 3 boxes (wood). 1st, tea and matunda; 2nd, wooden box, paper and shirts; 3rd, iron box, shoes, quinine, 1 bag of coffee, sextant stand, one long wooden box empty. These are left with Mohamad bin Saleh at Ujiji, Christmas Day, 1871. Two bags of beads are already here and table cloths.

26th December, 1871.--Had but a sorry Christmas yesterday.

27th December, 1871.--Mem. To send Moenyeghere some coffee and tell his wishes to Masudi.

27th December, 1871.--Left Ujiji 9 A.M., and crossed goats, donkeys, and men over Luiche. Sleep at the Malagarasi.

29th December, 1871.--Crossed over the broad bay of the Malagarasi to Kagonga and sleep.

30th December, 1871.--Pass Viga Point, red sandstone, and cross the bay of the River Lugufu and Nkala village, and transport the people and goats: sleep.

31st December, 1871.--Send for beans, as there are no provisions in front of this. Brown water of the Lugufu bent away north: the high wind is S.W. and W. Having provisions we went round Munkalu Point. The water is slightly discoloured for a mile south of it, but brown water is seen on the north side of bay bent north by a current.

1st January, 1872.--May the Almighty help me to finish my work this year for Christ's sake! We slept in Mosehezi Bay. I was storm-stayed in Kifwe Bay, which is very beautiful--still as a millpond. We found 12 or 13 hippopotami near a high bank, but did not kill any, for our balls are not hardened. It is high rocky tree-covered shore, with rocks bent and twisted wonderfully; large slices are worn off the land with hillsides clad with robes of living green, yet very, very steep.

2nd January, 1872.--A very broad Belt of large tussocks of reeds lines the shore near Mount Kibanga or Boumba. We had to coast along to the south. Saw a village nearly afloat, the people having there taken refuge from their enemies. There are many hippopotami and crocodiles in Tanganyika. A river 30 yards wide, the Kibanga, flows in strongly. We encamped on an open space on a knoll and put up flags to guide our land party to us.

3rd January, 1872. --We send off to buy food. Mr. Stanley shot a fat zebra, its meat was very good.

4th January, 1872. --The Ujijians left last night with their canoes. I gave them 14 fundos of beads to buy food on the way. We are now waiting for our land party. I gave headmen here at Burimba 2 dotis and a Kitamba. Men arrived yesterday or 4-1/2 days from the Lugufu.

5th January, 1872. --Mr. Stanley is ill of fever. I am engaged in copying notes into my journal. All men and goats arrived safely.

6th January, 1872. --Mr. Stanley better, and we prepare to go.

7th January, 1872. --Mr. Stanley shot a buffalo at the end of our first march up. East and across the hills. The River Luajere is in front. We spend the night at the carcase of the buffalo.

8th January, 1872. --We crossed the river, which is 30 yards wide and rapid. It is now knee and waist deep. The country is rich and beautiful, hilly and tree-covered, reddish soil, and game abundant.

9th January, 1872. --Rainy, but we went on E. and N.N.E. through a shut-in valley to an opening full of all kinds of game. Buffalo cows have calves now: one was wounded. Rain came down abundantly.

10th January, 1872. --Across a very lovely green country of open forest all fresh, and like an English gentleman's park. Game plentiful. Tree-covered mountains right and left, and much brown haematite on the levels. Course E. A range of mountains appears about three miles off on our right.

11th January, 1872. --Off through open forest for three hours east, then cook, and go on east another three hours, over very rough rocky, hilly country. River Mtambahu.

12th January, 1872. --Off early, and pouring rain came down; as we advance the country is undulating. We cross a rivulet 15 yards wide going north, and at another of 3 yards came to a halt; all wet and uncomfortable.

The people pick up many mushrooms and manendinga roots, like turnips. There are buffaloes near us in great numbers.

13th January, 1872. --Fine morning. Went through an undulating hilly country clothed with upland trees for three hours, then breakfast in an open glade, with bottom of rocks of brown haematite, and a hole with rain-water in it. We are over 1000 feet higher than Tanganyika. It became cloudy, and we finished our march in a pouring rain, at a rivulet thickly clad with aquatic trees on banks. Course E.S.E.

14th January, 1872. --Another fine morning, but miserably wet afternoon. We went almost 4' E.S.E., and crossed a strong rivulet 8 or 10 yards wide: then on and up to a ridge and along the top of it, going about south. We had breakfast on the edge of the plateau, looking down into a broad lovely valley. We now descended, and saw many reddish monkeys, which made a loud outcry: there was much game, but scattered, and we got none. Miserably wet crossing another stream, then up a valley to see a deserted Boma or fenced village.

15th January, 1872. --Along a valley with high mountains on each hand, then up over that range on our left or south. At the top some lions roared. We then went on on high land, and saw many hartebeests and zebra, but did not get one, though a buffalo was knocked over. We crossed a rivulet, and away over beautiful and undulating hills and vales, covered with many trees and jambros fruit. Sleep at a running rill.

16th January, 1872. --A very cold night after long-continued and heavy rain. Our camp was among brakens. Went E. and by S. along the high land, then we saw a village down in a deep valley into which we descended. Then up another ridge in a valley and along to a village well cultivated--up again 700 feet at least, and down to Merera's village, hid in a mountainous nook, about 140 huts with doors on one side. The valleys present a lovely scene of industry, all the people being eagerly engaged in weeding and hoeing to take advantage of the abundant rains which have drenched us every afternoon.

17th January, 1872. --We remain at Merera's to buy food for our men and ourselves.

18th January, 1872. --March, but the Mirongosi wandered and led us round about instead of S.S.E. We came near some tree-covered hills, and a river Monya

Mazi--Mtamba River in front. I have very sore feet from bad shoes.

19th January, 1872. --Went about S.E. for four hours, and crossed the Mbamba River and passed through open forest. There is a large rock in the river, and hills thickly tree-covered, 2' East and West, down a steep descent and camp. Came down River Mpokwa over rough country with sore feet, to ruins of a village Basivira and sleep. *21st.* --Rest. *22nd.* --Rest. Mr. Stanley shot two zebras yesterday, and a she giraffe to-day, the meat of the giraffe was 1000 lbs. weight, the two zebras about 800 lbs.

23rd January, 1872. --Rest. Mr. Stanley has fever. *24th.* --Ditto. *25th.* --Stanley ill. *26th.* --Stanley better and off.

26th January, 1872. --Through low hills N.E. and among bamboos to open forest--on in undulating bushy tract to a river with two rounded hills east, one having three mushroom-shaped trees on it.

27th January, 1872. --On across long land waves and the only bamboos east of Mpokwa Rill to breakfast. In going on a swarm of bees attacked a donkey Mr. Stanley bought for me, and instead of galloping off, as did the other, the fool of a beast rolled down, and over and over. I did the same, then ran, dashed into a bush like an ostrich pursued, then ran whisking a bush round my head. They gave me a sore head and face, before I got rid of the angry insects: I never saw men attacked before: the donkey was completely knocked up by the stings on head, face, and lips, and died in two days, in consequence. We slept in the stockade of Misonghi.

28th January, 1872. --We crossed the river and then away E. to near a hill. Crossed two rivers, broad and marshy, and deep with elephants plunging. Rain almost daily, but less in amount now. Bombay says his greatest desire is to visit Speke's grave ere he dies: he has a square head with the top depressed in the centre.

29th January, 1872. --We ascended a ridge, the edge of a flat basin with ledges of dark brown sandstone, the brim of ponds in which were deposited great masses of brown haematite, disintegrated into gravel, flat open forest with short grass. We crossed a rill of light-coloured water three times and reached a village. After this in 1-1/2 hour we came to Merera's.

30th January, 1872. --At Merera's, the second of the name. Much rain and very heavy; food abundant. Baniayamwezi and Yukonongo people here.

31st January, 1872.--Through scraggy bush, then open forest with short grass, over a broad rill and on good path to village Mwaro; chief Kamirambo.

1st February, 1872.--We met a caravan of Syde bin Habib's people yesterday who reported that Mirambo has offered to repay all the goods he has robbed the Arabs of, all the ivory, powder, blood, &c., but his offer was rejected. The country all around is devastated, and Arab force is at Simba's. Mr. Stanley's man Shaw is dead. There is very great mortality by small-pox amongst the Arabs and at the coast. We went over flat upland forest, open and bushy, then down a deep descent and along N.E. to a large tree at a deserted stockade.

2nd February, 1872.--Away over ridges of cultivation and elephant's footsteps. Cultivators all swept away by Basavira. Very many elephants feed here. We lost our trail and sent men to seek it, then came to the camp in the forest. Lunched at rill running into Ngombe Nullah.

Ukamba is the name of the Tsetse fly here.

3rd February, 1872.--Mr. Stanley has severe fever, with great pains in the back and loins: an emetic helped him a little, but resin of jalap would have cured him quickly. Rainy all day.

4th February, 1872.--Mr. Stanley so ill that we carried him in a cot across flat forest and land covered with short grass for three hours, about north-east, and at last found a path, which was a great help. As soon as the men got under cover continued rains began. There is a camp of Malongwana here.

5th February, 1872.--Off at 6 A.M. Mr. Stanley a little better, but still carried across same level forest; we pass water in pools, and one in haematite. Saw a black rhinoceros, and come near people.

6th February, 1872.--Drizzly morning, but we went on, and in two hours got drenched with cold N.W. rain: the paths full of water we splashed along to our camp in a wood. Met a party of native traders going to Mwara.

7th February, 1872.--Along level plains, and clumps of forest, and hollows filled at present with water, about N.E., to a large pool of Ngombe Nullah. Send off two men to Unyanyembe for letters and medicine.

8th February, 1872.--Removed from the large pool of the nullah, about an hour north, to where game abounds. Saw giraffes and zebras on our way. The nullah is covered with lotus-plants, and swarms with crocodiles.

9th February, 1872.--Remained for game, but we were unsuccessful. An eland was shot by Mr. Stanley, but it was lost. Departed at 2 P.M., and reached Manyara, a kind old chief. The country is flat, and covered with detached masses of forest, with open glades and flats.

10th February, 1872.--Leave Manyara and pass along the same park-like country, with but little water. The rain sinks into the sandy soil at once, and the collection is seldom seen. After a hard tramp we came to a pool by a sycamore-tree, 28 feet 9 inches in circumference, with broad fruit-laden branches. Ziwane.

11th February, 1872.--Rain nearly all night. Scarcely a day has passed without rain and thunder since we left Tanganyika Across a flat forest again, meeting a caravan for Ujiji. The grass is three feet high, and in seed. Reach Chikuru, a stockaded village, with dura plantations around it and pools of rain-water.

12th February, 1872.--Rest.

13th February, 1872.--Leave Chikuru, and wade across an open flat with much standing-water. They plant rice on the wet land round the villages. Our path lies through an open forest, where many trees are killed for the sake of the bark, which is used as cloth, and for roofing and beds. Mr. Stanley has severe fever.

14th February, 1872.--Across the same flat open forest, with scraggy trees and grass three feet long in tufts. Came to a Boma. N.E. Gunda.

15th February, 1872.--Over the same kind of country, where the water was stagnant, to camp in the forest.

16th February, 1872.--Camp near Kigando, in a rolling country with granite knolls.

17th February, 1872.--Over a country, chiefly level, with stagnant water; rounded hills were seen. Cross a rain torrent and encamp in a new Boma, Magonda.

18th February, 1872.--Go through low tree-covered hills of granite, with blocks of rock sticking out: much land cultivated, and many villages. The country now opens out and we come to the Tembe[16], in the midst of many straggling villages. Unyanyembe. Thanks to the Almighty.

---

16 Tembe, a flat-roofed Arab house.

CHAPTER VII.

Determines to continue his work. Proposed route. Refits. Robberies discovered. Mr. Stanley leaves. Parting messages. Mteza's people arrive. Ancient geography. Tabora. Description of the country. The Banyamwezi. A Baganda bargain. The population of Unyanyembe. The Mirambo war. Thoughts on Sir S. Baker's policy. The cat and the snake. Firm faith. Feathered neighbours. Mistaken notion concerning mothers. Prospects for missionaries. Halima. News of other travellers. Chuma is married.

By the arrival of the fast Ramadan on the 14th November, and a Nautical Almanac, I discovered that I was on that date twenty-one days too fast in my reckoning. Mr. Stanley used some very strong arguments in favour of my going home, recruiting my strength, getting artificial teeth, and then returning to finish my task; but my judgment said, "All your friends will wish you to make a complete work of the exploration of the sources of the Nile before you retire." My daughter Agnes says, "Much as I wish you to come home, I would rather that you finished your work to your own satisfaction than return merely to gratify me." Rightly and nobly said, my darling Nannie. Vanity whispers pretty loudly, "She is a chip of the old block." My blessing on her and all the rest.

It is all but certain that four full-grown gushing fountains rise on the watershed eight days south of Katanga, each of which at no great distance off becomes a large river; and two rivers thus formed flow north to Egypt, the other two to Inner Ethiopia; that is, Lufira or Bartle Frere's River, flows into Kamolondo, and that into Webb's Lualaba, the main line of drainage. Another, on the north side of the sources, Sir Paraffin Young's Lualaba, flows through Lake Lincoln, otherwise named Chibungo and Lomame, and that too into Webb's Lualaba. Then Liambai Fountain, Palmerston's, forms the Upper Zambesi; and the Lunga (Lunga), Oswell's

Fountain, is the Kafue; both flowing into Inner Ethiopia. It may be that these are not the fountains of the Nile mentioned to Herodotus by the secretary of Minerva, in Sais, in Egypt; but they are worth discovery, as in the last hundred of the seven hundred miles of the watershed, from which nearly all the Nile springs do unquestionably arise.

I propose to go from Unyanyembe to Fipa; then round the south end of Tanganyika, Tambete, or Mbete; then across the Chambeze, and round south of Lake Bangweolo, and due west to the ancient fountains; leaving the underground excavations till after visiting Katanga. This route will serve to certify that no other sources of the Nile can come from the south without being seen by me. No one will cut me out after this exploration is accomplished; and may the good Lord of all help me to show myself one of His stout-hearted servants, an honour to my children, and, perhaps, to my country and race.

Our march extended from 26th December, 1871, till 18th February, 1872, or fifty-four days. This was over 300 miles, and thankful I am to reach Unyanyembe, and the Tembe Kwikuru.

I find, also, that the two headmen selected by the notorious, but covert slave-trader, Ludha Damji, have been plundering my stores from the 20th October, 1870, to 18th February, 1872, or nearly sixteen months. One has died of small-pox, and the other not only plundered my stores, but has broken open the lock of Mr. Stanley's storeroom, and plundered his goods. He declared that all my goods were safe, but when the list was referred to, and the goods counted, and he was questioned as to the serious loss, he at last remembered a bale of seven pieces of merikano, and three kanike--or 304 yards, that he evidently had hidden. On questioning him about the boxes brought, he was equally ignorant, but at last said, "Oh! I remember a box of brandy where it went, and every one knows as well as I."

18th February, 1872.--This, and Mr. Stanley's goods being found in his possession, make me resolve to have done with him. My losses by the robberies of the Banian employed slaves are more than made up by Mr. Stanley, who has given me twelve bales of calico; nine loads = fourteen and a half bags of beads; thirty-eight coils of brass wire; a tent; boat; bath; cooking pots; twelve copper sheets; air beds; trowsers; jackets, &c. Indeed, I am again quite set up, and as soon as he can send men, not slaves, from the coast I go to my work, with a fair prospect of finishing it.

19th February, 1872.--Rest. Receive 38 coils of brass wire from Mr. Stanley, 14-1/2 bags of beads, 12 copper sheets, a strong canvas tent, boat-trowsers, nine loads of calico, a bath, cooking pots, a medicine chest, a good lot of tools, tacks, screw nails, copper nails, books, medicines, paper, tar, many cartridges, and some shot.

20th February, 1872.--To my great joy I got four flannel shirt from Agnes, and I was delighted to find that two pairs of fine English boots had most considerately been sent by my friend Mr. Waller. Mr. Stanley and I measured the calico and found that 733-3/4 yards were wanting, also two frasilahs of samsam, and one case of brandy. Othman pretended sickness, and blamed the dead men, but produced a bale of calico hidden in Thani's goods; this reduced the missing quantity to 436-1/2 yards.

21st February, 1872.--Heavy rains. I am glad we are in shelter. Masudi is an Arab, near to Ali bin Salem at Bagamoio. Bushir is an Arab, for whose slave he took a bale of calico. Masudi took this Chirongozi, who is not a slave, as a pagazi or porter. Robbed by Bushir at the 5th camp from Bagamoio. Othman confessed that he knew of the sale of the box of brandy, and brought also a shawl which he had forgotten: I searched him, and found Mr. Stanley's stores which he had stolen.

22nd February, 1872.--Service this morning, and thanked God for safety thus far. Got a packet of letters from an Arab.

23rd February, 1872.--Send to Governor for a box which he has kept for four years: it is all eaten by white ants: two fine guns and a pistol are quite destroyed, all the wood-work being eaten. The brandy bottles were broken to make it appear as if by an accident, but the corks being driven in, and corks of maize cobs used in their place, show that a thief has drunk the brandy and then broken the bottles. The tea was spoiled, but the china was safe, and the cheese good.

24th February, 1872.--Writing a despatch to Lord Granville against Banian slaving, and in favour of an English native settlement transfer.

25th February, 1872.--A number of Batusi women came to-day asking for presents. They are tall and graceful in form, with well-shaped small heads, noses, and mouths. They are the chief owners of cattle here. The war with Mirambo is still going on. The Governor is ashamed to visit me.

26th February, 1872. --Writing journal and despatch.

27th February, 1872. --Moene-mokaia is ill of heart disease and liver abscess. I sent him some blistering fluid. To-day we hold a Christmas feast.

28th February, 1872. --Writing journal. Syde bin Salem called; he is a China-looking man, and tried to be civil to us.

5th March, 1872. --My friend Moene-mokaia came yesterday; he is very ill of abscess in liver, which has burst internally. I gave him some calomel and jalap to open his bowels. He is very weak; his legs are swollen, but body emaciated.

6th March, 1872. --Repairing tent, and receiving sundry stores, Moenemokaia died.

7th March, 1872. --Received a machine for filling cartridges.

8th and 9th March, 1872. --Writing.

10th March, 1872. --Writing. Gave Mr. Stanley a cheque for 5000 rupees on Stewart and Co., Bombay. This 500 *l.* is to be drawn if Dr. Kirk has expended the rest of the 1000 *l.* If not, then the cheque is to be destroyed by Mr. Stanley.

12th March, 1872. --Writing.

13th March, 1872. --Finished my letter to Mr. Bennett of the **New York Herald**, and Despatch No. 3 to Lord Granville.

14th March, 1872. --Mr. Stanley leaves. I commit to his care my journal sealed with five seals: the impressions on them are those of an American gold coin, anna, and half anna, and cake of paint with royal arms. Positively not to be opened.

[We must leave each heart to know its own bitterness, as the old explorer retraces his steps to the Tembe at Kwihara, there to hope and pray that good fortune may attend his companion of the last few months on his journey to the coast; whilst Stanley, duly impressed with the importance of that which he can reveal to the outer world, and laden with a responsibility which by this time can be fully comprehended, thrusts on through every difficulty.

There is nothing for it now but to give Mr. Stanley time to get to Zanzibar, and to shorten by any means at hand the anxious period which must elapse before evidence can arrive that he has carried out the commission entrusted to him.

As we shall see, Livingstone was not without some material to afford him occupation. Distances were calculated from native report; preparations were pushed on for the coming journey to Lake Bangweolo; apparatus was set in order. Travellers from all quarters dropped in from time to time: each contributed something about his own land; whilst waifs and strays of news from the expedition sent by the Arabs against Mirambo kept the settlement alive. To return to his Diary.

How much seems to lie in their separating, when we remember that with the last shake of the hand, and the last adieu, came the final parting between Livingstone and all that could represent the interest felt by the world in his travels, or the sympathy of the white man!]

15th March, 1872. --Writing to send after Mr. Stanley by two of his men, who wait here for the purpose. Copied line of route, observations from Kabuire to Casembe's, the second visit, and on to Lake Bangweolo; then the experiment of weight on watch-key at Nyangwe and Lusize.

16th March, 1872. --Sent the men after Mr. Stanley, and two of mine to bring his last words, if any.

[Sunday was kept in the quiet of the Tembe, on the 17th March. Two days after, and his birthday again comes round--that day which seems always to have carried with it such a special solemnity. He has yet time to look back on his marvellous deliverances, and the venture he is about to launch forth upon.]

19th March, 1872. --Birthday. My Jesus, my king, my life, my all; I again dedicate my whole self to Thee. Accept me, and grant, Gracious Father, that ere this year is gone I may finish my task. In Jesus' name I ask it. Amen, so let it be.

DAVID LIVINGSTONE.

[Many of his astronomical observations were copied out at this time, and minute records taken of the rainfall. Books saved up against a rainy day were read in the middle of the "Masika" and its heavy showers.]

21st March, 1872. --Read Baker's book. It is artistic and clever. He does good service in exploring the Nile slave-trade; I hope he may be successful in suppressing it.

The Batusi are the cattle herds of all this Unyanyembe region. They are very polite in address. The women have small compact, well-shaped heads and pretty faces; colour, brown; very pleasant to speak to; well-shaped figures, with small hands and feet; the last with high insteps, and springy altogether. Plants and grass are collected every day, and a fire with much smoke made to fumigate the cattle and keep off flies: the cattle like it, and the valleys are filled with smoke in the evening in consequence. The Baganda are slaves in comparison; black, with a tinge of copper-colour sometimes; bridgeless noses, large nostrils and lips, but well-made limbs and feet.

[We see that the thread by which he still draws back a lingering word or two from Stanley has not parted yet.]

25th March, 1872.--Susi brought a letter back from Mr. Stanley. He had a little fever, but I hope he will go on safely.

26th March, 1872.--Rain of Masika chiefly by night. The Masika of 1871 began on 23rd of March, and ended 30th of April.

27th March, 1872.--Reading. Very heavy rains.

28th March, 1872.--Moenyembegu asked for the loan of a "doti." He is starving, and so is the war-party at M'Futu; chaining their slaves together to keep them from running away to get food anywhere.

29th, 30th, 31st March, 1872.--Very rainy weather. Am reading 'Mungo Park's Travels;' they look so truthful.

1st April, 1872.--Read Young's 'Search after Livingstone;' thankful for many kind words about me. He writes like a gentleman.

2nd April, 1872.--Making a sounding-line out of lint left by Mr. Stanley. Whydah birds are now building their nests. The cock-bird brings fine grass seed-stalks off the top of my Tembe. He takes the end inside the nest and pulls it all in, save the ear. The hen keeps inside, constantly arranging the grass with all her might, sometimes making the whole nest move by her efforts. Feathers are laid in after the grass.

4th April, 1872.--We hear that Dugumbe's men have come to Ujiji with fifty tusks. He went down Lualaba with three canoes a long way and bought much ivory. They were not molested by Monangungo as we were.

My men whom I had sent to look for a book left by accident in a hut some days' journey off came back stopped by a flood in their track. Copying observations for Sir T. Maclear.

8th April, 1872.--An Arab called Seyed bin Mohamad Magibbe called. He proposes to go west to the country west of Katanga (Urange).

[It is very interesting to find that the results of the visit paid by Speke and

Grant to Mteza, King of Uganda, have already become well marked. As we see, Livingstone was at Unyanyembe when a large trading party dropped in on their way back to the king, who, it will be remembered, lives on the north-western shores of the Victoria Nyassa.]

9th April, 1872.--About 150 Waganga of Mteza carried a present to Seyed Burghash, Sultan of Zanzibar, consisting of ivory and a young elephant[17]. He spent all the ivory in buying return presents of gunpowder, guns, soap, brandy, gin, &c., and they have stowed it all in this Tembe. This morning they have taken everything out to see if anything is spoilt. They have hundreds of packages.

One of the Baganda told me yesterday that the name of the Deity is Dubale in his tongue.

15th April, 1872.--Hung up the sounding-line on poles 1 fathom apart and tarred it. 375 fathoms of 5 strands.

Ptolemy's geography of Central Africa seems to say that the science was then (second century A.D.) in a state of decadence from what was known to the ancient Egyptian priests as revealed to Herodotus 600 years before his day (or say B.C. 440). They seem to have been well aware by the accounts of travellers or traders that a great number of springs contributed to the origin of the Nile, but none could be pointed at distinctly as the "Fountains," except those I long to discover, or rather rediscover. Ptolemy seems to have gathered up the threads of ancient explorations, and made many springs (six) flow into two Lakes situated East and West of each other--the space above them being unknown. If the Victoria Lake were large, then it and the Albert would probably be the Lakes which Ptolemy meant, and it would be pleasant to call them Ptolemy's sources, rediscovered by the toil and enterprise of our countrymen Speke, Grant, and Baker--but unfortunately Ptolemy has inserted the small Lake "Coloe," nearly where the Victoria Lake stands, and one cannot say where his two Lakes are. Of Lakes Victoria, Bangweolo, Moero, Kamolondo--Lake Lincoln and Lake Albert, which two did he mean? The science in his time was in a state of decadence. Were two Lakes not the relics of a greater number previously known? What says the most ancient map known of Sethos II.'s time?

---

17 This elephant was subsequently sent by Dr. Kirk to Sir Philip
Wodehouse, Governor of Bombay. When in Zanzibar it was perfectly tame.
We understand it is now in the possession of Sir Solar Jung, to whom
it was presented by Sir Philip Wodehouse.--Ed.

16th April, 1872.--Went over to visit Sultan bin Ali near Tabora--country open, plains sloping very gently down from low rounded granite hills covered with trees. Rounded masses of the light grey granite crop out all over them, but many are hidden by the trees: Tabora slopes down from some of the same hills that overlook Kwihara, where I live. At the bottom of the slope swampy land lies, and during the Masika it is flooded and runs westwards. The sloping plain on the North of the central drain is called Kaze--that on the South is Tabora, and this is often applied to the whole space between the hills north and south. Sultan bin Ali is very hospitable. He is of the Bedawee Arabs, and a famous marksman with his long Arab gun or matchlock. He often killed hares with it, always hitting them in the head. He is about sixty-five years of age, black eyed, six feet high and inclined to stoutness, and his long beard is nearly all grey. He provided two bountiful meals for self and attendants.

Called on Mohamad bin Nassur--recovering from sickness. He presented a goat and a large quantity of guavas. He gave the news that came from Dugumbe's underling Nserere, and men now at Ujiji; they went S.W. to country called Nombe, it is near Rua, and where copper is smelted. After I left them on account of the massacre at Nyangwe, they bought much ivory, but acting in the usual Arab way, plundering and killing, they aroused the Bakuss' ire, and as they are very numerous, about 200 were killed, and none of Dugumbe's party. They brought fifty tusks to Ujiji. We dare not pronounce positively on any event in life, but this looks like prompt retribution on the perpetrators of the horrible and senseless massacre of Nyangwe. It was not vengeance by the relations of the murdered ones we saw shot and sunk in the Lualaba, for there is no communication between the people of Nyangwe and the Bakuss or people of Nombe of Lomame--that massacre turned my heart completely against Dugumbe's people. To go with them to Lomame as my slaves were willing to do, was so repugnant I preferred to return that weary 400 or 600 miles to Ujiji. I mourned over my being baffled and thwarted all the way, but tried to believe that it was all for the best--this news shows that had I gone with these people to Lomame, I could not have escaped the Bakuss spears, for I could not have run like the routed fugitives. I was prevented from going in order to save me from death. Many escapes from danger I am aware of: some make me shudder, as I think how near to death's door I came. But how many more instances of Providential protecting there may be of which I know nothing! But I thank most sincerely the good Lord of all for His goodness to me.

18th April, 1872.--I pray the good Lord of all to favour me so as to allow me to discover the ancient fountains of Herodotus, and if there is anything in the underground excavations to confirm the precious old documents (τβιβλα), the Scriptures of truth, may He permit me to bring it to light, and give me wisdom to make a proper use of it.

Some seem to feel that their own importance in the community is enhanced by an imaginary connection with a discovery or discoverer of the Nile sources, and are only too happy to figure, if only in a minor part, as theoretical discoverers--a theoretical discovery being a contradiction in terms.

The cross has been used--not as a Christian emblem certainly, but from time immemorial as the form in which the copper ingot of Katanga is moulded--this is met with quite commonly, and is called Handiple Mahandi. Our capital letter I (called Vigera) is the large form of the bars of copper, each about 60 or 70 lbs. weight, seen all over Central Africa and from Katanga.

19th April, 1872.--A roll of letters and newspapers, apparently, came to-day for Mr. Stanley. The messenger says he passed Mr. Stanley on the way, who said, "Take this to the Doctor;" this is erroneous. The Prince of Wales is reported to be dying of typhoid fever: the Princess Louise has hastened to his bedside.

20th April, 1872.--Opened it on 20th, and found nine 'New York Heralds' of December 1-9, 1871, and one letter for Mr. Stanley, which. I shall forward, and one stick of tobacco.

21st April, 1872.--Tarred the tent presented by Mr. Stanley.

23rd April, 1872.--Visited Kwikuru, and saw the chief of all the Banyamwezi (around whose Boma it is), about sixty years old, and partially paralytic. He told me that he had gone as far as Katanga by the same Fipa route I now propose to take, when a little boy following his father, who was a great trader.

The name Banyamwezi arose from an ivory ornament of the shape of the new moon hung to the neck, with a horn reaching round over either shoulder. They believe that they came from the sea-coast, Mombas (?) of old, and when people inquired for them they said, "We mean the men of the moon ornament." It is very popular even now, and a large amount of ivory is cut down in its manufacture; some are made of the curved tusks of hippopotami. The Banyamwezi have turned out good porters, and they do most of the carrying work of the trade to and from the East Coast; they are strong and trustworthy. One I saw carried six frasilahs, or 200 lbs., of ivory from Unyanyembe to the sea-coast.

The prefix "*Nya*" in Nyamwezi seems to mean place or locality, as Mya does on the Zambesi. If the name referred to the "moon ornament," as the people believe, the name would be Ba or Wamwezi, but Banyamwezi means probably the Ba--they or people--Nya, place--Mwezi, moon, people of the moon locality or moon-land.

Unyanyembe, place of hoes.
Unyambewa.
Unyangoma, place of drums.
Nyangurue, place of pigs.
Nyangkondo.
Nyarukwe.

It must be a sore affliction to be bereft of one's reason, and the more so if the insanity takes the form of uttering thoughts which in a sound state we drive from us as impure.

25th and 26th April, 1872. --A touch of fever from exposure.

27th April, 1872. --Better, and thankful. Zahor died of small-pox here, after collecting much ivory at Fipa and Urungu. It is all taken up by Lewale[18].

The rains seem nearly over, and are succeeded by very cold easterly winds; these cause fever by checking the perspiration, and are well known as eminently febrile. The Arabs put the cause of the fever to the rains drying up. In my experience it is most unhealthy during the rains if one gets wet; the chill is brought on, the bowels cease to act, and fever sets in. Now it is the cold wind that operates, and possibly this is intensified by the malaria of the drying-up surface. A chill from bathing on the 25th in cold water gave me a slight attack.

1st May, 1872. --Unyanyembe: bought a cow for 11 dotis of merikano (and 2 kanike for calf), she gives milk, and this makes me independent.

Headman of the Baganda from whom I bought it said, "I go off to pray." He has been taught by Arabs, and is the first proselyte they have gained. Baker thinks that

---

18 Lewale appears to be the title by which the Governor of the town is called.

the first want of Africans is to teach them to ***want***. Interesting, seeing he was bored almost to death by Kamrasi wanting everything he had.

Bought three more cows and calves for milk, they give good quantity enough for me and mine, and are small shorthorns: one has a hump--two black with white spots and one white--one black with white face: the Baganda were well pleased with the prices given, and so am I. Finished a letter for the **New York Herald,** trying to enlist American zeal to stop the East Coast slave-trade: I pray for a blessing on it from the All-Gracious. [Through a coincidence a singular interest attaches to this entry. The concluding words of the letter he refers to are as follows:--]

"All I can add in my loneliness is, may Heaven's rich blessing come down on everyone, American, English, or Turk, who will help to heal the open sore of the world."

[It was felt that nothing could more palpably represent the man, and this quotation has consequently been inscribed upon the tablet erected to his memory near his grave in Westminster Abbey. It was noticed some time after selecting it that Livingstone wrote these words exactly one year before his death, which, as we shall see, took place on the 1st May, 1873.]

3rd May, 1872.--The entire population of Unyanyembe called Arab is eighty males, many of these are country born, and are known by the paucity of beard and bridgeless noses, as compared with men from Muscat; the Muscatees are more honourable than the mainlanders, and more brave--altogether better looking and better everyway.

If we say that the eighty so-called Arabs here have twenty dependants each, 1500 or 1600 is the outside population of Unyanyembe in connection with the Arabs. It is called an ivory station, that means simply that elephant's tusks are the chief articles of trade. But little ivory comes to market, every Arab who is able sends bands of his people to different parts to trade: the land being free they cultivate patches of maize, dura, rice, beans, &c., and after one or two seasons, return with what ivory they may have secured. Ujiji is the only mart in the country, and it is chiefly for oil, grain, goats, salt, fish, beef, native produce of all sorts, and is held daily. A few tusks are sometimes brought, but it can scarcely be called an ivory mart for that. It is an institution begun and carried on by the natives in spite of great drawbacks from unjust Arabs. It resembles the markets of Manyuema, but is attended every day by about 300 people. No dura has been brought lately to Ujiji, because a Belooch man found the son of the chief of Mbwara Island peeping in at his women, and beat the young man, so that on returning home he died. The Mbwara people always brought much grain before that, but since that affair never come.

The Arabs send a few freemen as heads of a party of slaves to trade. These select a friendly chief, and spend at least half these goods brought in presents on him, and in buying the best food the country affords for themselves. It happens frequently that the party comes back nearly empty handed, but it is the Banians that lose, and the Arabs are not much displeased. This point is not again occupied if it has been a dead loss.

4th May, 1872.--Many palavers about Mirambu's death having taken place and being concealed. Arabs say that he is a brave man, and the war is not near its end. Some northern natives called Bagoye get a keg of powder and a piece of cloth, go and attack a village, then wait a month or so eating the food of the captured place, and come back for stores again: thus the war goes on. Prepared tracing paper to draw a map for Sir Thomas Maclear. Lewale invites me to a feast.

7th May, 1872.--New moon last night. Went to breakfast with Lewale. He says that the Mirambo war is virtually against himself as a Seyed Majid man. They wish to have him removed, and this would be a benefit.

The Banyamwezi told the Arabs that they did not want them to go to fight, because when one Arab was killed all the rest ran away and the army got frightened.

"Give us your slaves only and we will fight," say they.

A Magohe man gave charms, and they pressed Mirambo sorely. His brother sent four tusks as a peace-offering, and it is thought that the end is near. His mother was plundered, and lost all her cattle.

9th May, 1872.--No fight, though it was threatened yesterday: they all like to talk a great deal before striking a blow. They believe that in the multitude of counsellors there is safety. Women singing as they pound their grain into meal,--"Oh, the march of Bwanamokolu to Katanga! Oh, the march to Katanga and back to Ujiji!--Oh, oh, oh!" Bwanamokolu means the great or old gentleman. Batusi women are very keen traders, and very polite and pleasing in their address and pretty way of speaking.

I don't know how the great loving Father will bring all out right at last, but He knows and will do it.

The African's idea seems to be that they are within the power of a power superior to themselves--apart from and invisible: good; but frequently evil and dangerous. This may have been the earliest religious feeling of dependence on a Divine power without any conscious feeling of its nature. Idols may have come in to give a definite idea of superior power, and the primitive faith or impression obtained by Revelation seems to have mingled with their idolatry without any sense of incongruity. (See Micah in Judges.)[19]

The origin of the primitive faith in Africans and others, seems always to have been a divine influence on their dark minds, which has proved persistent in all ages. One portion of primitive belief--the continued existence of departed spirits--seems to have no connection whatever with dreams, or, as we should say, with "ghost seeing," for great agony is felt in prospect of bodily mutilation or burning of the body after death, as that is believed to render return to one's native land impossible. They feel as if it would shut them off from all intercourse with relatives after death. They would lose the power of doing good to those onceloved, and evil to those who deserved their revenge. Take the case of the slaves in the yoke, singing songs of hate and revenge against those who sold them into slavery. They thought it right so to harbour hatred, though most of the party had been sold for crimes--adultery, stealing, &c.--which they knew to be sins.

If Baker's expedition should succeed in annexing the valley of the Nile to Egypt, the question arises,--Would not the miserable condition of the natives, when subjected to all the atrocities of the White Nile slave-traders, be worse under Egyptian dominion? The villages would be farmed out to tax-collectors, the women, children and boys carried off into slavery, and the free thought and feeling of the population placed under the dead weight of Islam. Bad as the situation now is, if Baker leaves it matters will grow worse. It is probable that actual experience will correct the fancies he now puts forth as to the proper mode of dealing with Africans.

10th May, 1872.--Hamees Wodin Tagh, my friend, is reported slain by the Makoa of a large village he went to fight. Other influential Arabs are killed, but full information has not yet arrived. He was in youth a slave, but by energy and good conduct in trading with the Masai and far south of Nyassa, and elsewhere, he rose

---

19 Judges xviii.

to freedom and wealth. He had good taste in all his domestic arrangements, and seemed to be a good man. He showed great kindness to me on my arrival at Chitimbwa's.

11th May, 1872. --A serpent of dark olive colour was found dead at my door this morning, probably killed by a cat. Puss approaches very cautiously, and strikes her claws into the head with a blow delivered as quick as lightning; then holds the head down with both paws, heedless of the wriggling mass of coils behind it; she then bites the neck and leaves it, looking with interest to the disfigured head, as if she knew that therein had lain the hidden power of mischief. She seems to possess a little of the nature of the *Ichneumon*, which was sacred in Egypt from its destroying serpents. The serpent is in pursuit of mice when killed by puss.

12th May, 1872. --Singeri, the headman of the Baganda here, offered me a cow and calf yesterday, but I declined, as we were strangers both, and this is too much for me to take. I said that I would take ten cows at Mtesa's if he offered them. I gave him a little medicine (arnica) for his wife, whose face was burned by smoking over gunpowder. Again he pressed the cow and calf in vain.

The reported death of Hamees Wodin Tagh is contradicted. It was so circumstantial that I gave it credit, though the false reports in this land are one of its most marked characteristics. They are "enough to spear a sow."

13th May, 1872. --He will keep His word--the gracious One, full of grace and truth--no doubt of it. He said, "Him that cometh unto me, I will in nowise cast out," and "Whatsoever ye shall ask in my name I will give it." He WILL keep His word: then I can come and humbly present my petition, and it will be all right. Doubt is here inadmissible, surely.--D.L.

Ajala's people, sent to buy ivory in Uganda, were coming back with some ten tusks and were attacked at Ugalla by robbers, and one free man slain: the rest threw everything down and fled. They came here with their doleful tale to-day.

14th May, 1872. --People came from Ujiji to-day, and report that many of Mohamad Bogharib's slaves have died of small-pox--Fundi and Suliman amongst them. Others sent out to get firewood have been captured by the Waha. Mohamad's chief slave, Othman, went to see the cause of their losses received a spear in the back, the point coming out at his breast. It is scarcely possible to tell how many of the slaves have perished since they were bought or captured, but the loss has been grievous.

Lewale off to Mfutu to loiter and not to fight. The Bagoye don't wish Arabs to come near the scene of action, because, say they, "When one Arab is killed all the rest ran away, and they frighten us thereby. Stay at M'futu; we will do all the fighting." This is very acceptable advice.

16th May, 1872. --A man came from Ujiji to say one of the party at Kasongo's reports that a marauding party went thence to the island of Bazula north of them. They ferried them to an island, and in coming back they were assaulted by the islanders in turn. They speared two in canoes shoving off, and the rest, panic-struck, took to the water, and thirty-five were slain. It was a just punishment, and shows what the Manyuema can do, if aroused to right their wrongs. No news of Baker's party; but Abed and Hassani are said to be well, and far down the Lualaba. Nassur Masudi is at Kasongo's, probably afraid by the Zula slaughter to go further. They will shut their own market against themselves. Lewale sends off letters to the Sultan to-day. I have no news to send, but am waiting wearily.

17th May, 1872. --Ailing. Making cheeses for the journey: good, but sour rather, as the milk soon turns in this climate, and we don't use rennet, but allow the milk to coagulate of itself, and it does thicken in half a day.

18th-19th May, 1872. --One of Dugumbe's men came to-day from Ujiji. He confirms the slaughter of Matereka's people, but denies that of Dugumbe's men. They went to Lomame about eleven days west, and found it to be about the size of Luamo; it comes from a Lake, and goes to Lualaba, near the Kisingite, a cataract. Dugumbe then sent his people down Lualaba, where much ivory is to be obtained. They secured a great deal of copper--1000 thick bracelets--on the south-west of Nyangwe, and some ivory, but not so much as they desired. No news of Abed. Lomame water is black, and black scum comes up in it.

20th May, 1872. --Better. Very cold winds. The cattle of the Batusi were captured by the Arabs to prevent them going off with the Baganda: my four amongst them. I sent over for them and they were returned this morning. Thirty-five of Mohamad's slaves died of small-pox.

21st May, 1872. --The genuine Africans of this region have flattened nose-bridges; the higher grades of the tribes have prominent nose-bridges, and are on this account greatly admired by the Arabs. The Batusi here, the Balunda of Casembe, and Itawa of Nsama, and many Manyuema have straight noses, but every now and then you come to districts in which the bridgeless noses give the air of the low English bruiser class, or faces inclining to King Charles the Second's spaniels. The Arab progeny here have scanty beards, and many grow to a very great height--tall, gaunt savages; while the Muscatees have prominent nose-bridges, good beards, and are polite and hospitable.

I wish I had some of the assurance possessed by others, but I am oppressed with the apprehension that after all it may turn out that I have been following the Congo; and who would risk being put into a cannibal pot, and converted into black man for it?

22nd May, 1872.--Baganga are very black, with a tinge of copper colour in some. Bridgeless noses all.

23rd May, 1872.--There seems but little prospect of Christianity spreading by ordinary means among Mohamadans. Their pride is a great obstacle, and is very industriously nurtured by its votaries. No new invention or increase of power on the part of Christians seems to disturb the self-complacent belief that ultimately all power and dominion in this world will fall into the hands of Moslems. Mohamad will appear at last in glory, with all his followers saved by him. When Mr. Stanley's Arab boy from Jerusalem told the Arab bin Saleh that he was a Christian, he was asked, "Why so, don't you know that all the world will soon be Mohamadan? Jerusalem is ours; all the world is ours, and in a short time we shall overcome all." Theirs are great expectations!

A family of ten Whydah birds (Vidua purpurea) come to the pomegranate-trees in our yard. The eight young ones, full-fledged, are fed by the dam, as young pigeons are. The food is brought up from the crop without the bowing and bending of the pigeon. They chirrup briskly for food: the dam gives most, while the red-breasted cock gives one or two, and then knocks the rest away.

24th May, 1872.--Speke at Kasenge islet inadvertently made a general statement thus: "The mothers of these savage people have infinitely less affection than many savage beasts of my acquaintance. I have seen a mother bear, galled by frequent shots, obstinately meet her death by repeatedly returning under fire whilst endeavouring to rescue her young from the grasp of intruding men. But here, for a simple loin-cloth or two, human mothers eagerly exchanged their little offspring, delivering them into perpetual bondage to my Beluch soldiers."-- ***Speke***, pp. 234,5. For the sake of the little story of "a bear mother," Speke made a general assertion on a very small and exceptional foundation. Frequent inquiries among the most intelligent and far-travelled Arabs failed to find confirmation of this child-selling, except in the very rare case of a child cutting the upper front teeth before the under, and because this child is believed to be "moiko" (***unlucky***), and certain to bring death into the family. It is called an Arab child, and sold to the first Arab, or even left at his door. This is the only case the Arabs know of child-selling. Speke had only two Beluch soldiers with him, and the idea that they loaded themselves with infants, at once stamps the tale as fabulous. He may have seen one sold, an extremely rare and exceptional case; but the inferences drawn are just like that of the Frenchman who thought the English so partial to suicide in November, that they might be seen suspended from trees in the common highways.

In crossing Tanganyika three several times I was detained at the islet Kasenge about ten weeks in all. On each occasion Arab traders were present, all eager to buy slaves, but none were offered, and they assured me that they had never seen the habit alleged to exist by Speke, though they had heard of the "unlucky" cases referred to. Everyone has known of poor little foundlings in England, but our mothers are not credited with less affection than she-bears.

I would say to missionaries, Come on, brethren, to the real heathen. You have no idea how brave you are till you try. Leaving the coast tribes, and devoting yourselves heartily to the savages, as they are called, you will find, with some drawbacks and wickednesses, a very great deal to admire and love. Many statements made about them require confirmation. You will never see women selling their infants: the Arabs never did, nor have I. An assertion of the kind was made by mistake.

Captive children are often sold, but not by their mothers. Famine sometimes reduces fathers to part with them, but the selling of children, as a general practice, is quite unknown, and, as Speke put it, quite a mistake.

25th and 26th May, 1872. --Cold weather. Lewale sends for all Arabs to make a grand assault, as it is now believed that Mirambo is dead, and only his son, with few people, remains.

Two Whydah birds, after their nest was destroyed several times, now try again in another pomegranate-tree in the yard. They put back their eggs, as they have the power to do, and build again.

The trout has the power of keeping back the ova when circumstances are unfavourable to their deposit. She can quite absorb the whole, but occasionally the absorbents have too much to do; the ovarium, and eventually the whole abdomen, seems in a state of inflammation, as when they are trying to remove a mortified human limb; and the poor fish, feeling its strength leaving it, true to instinct, goes to the entrance to the burn where it ought to have spawned, and, unable to ascend, dies. The defect is probably the want of the aid of a milter.

27th May, 1872. --Another pair of the kind (in which the cock is redbreasted) had ten chickens, also rebuilds afresh. The red cock-bird feeds all the brood. Each little one puts his head on one side as he inserts his bill, chirruping briskly, and bothering him. The young ones lift up a feather as a child would a doll, and invite others to do the same, in play. So, too, with another pair. The cock skips from side to side with a feather in his bill, and the hen is pleased: nature is full of enjoyment. Near Kasanganga's I saw boys shooting locusts that settled on the ground with little bows and arrows.

Cock Whydah bird died in the night. The brood came and chirruped to it for food, and tried to make it feed them, as if not knowing death!

A wagtail dam refused its young a caterpillar till it had been killed--she ran away from it, but then gave it when ready to be swallowed. The first smile of an infant with its toothless gums is one of the pleasantest sights in nature. It is innocence claiming kinship, and asking to be loved in its helplessness.

28th May, 1872. --Many parts of this interior land present most inviting prospects for well-sustained efforts of private benevolence. Karague, for instance, with its intelligent friendly chief Rumainyika (Speke's Rumanika), and Bouganda, with its teeming population, rain, and friendly chief, who could easily be swayed by an energetic prudent missionary. The evangelist must not depend on foreign support other than an occasional supply of beads and calico; coffee is indigenous, and so is sugar-cane. When detained by ulcerated feet in Manyuema I made sugar by pounding the cane in the common wooden mortar of the country, squeezing out the juice very hard and boiling it till thick; the defect it had was a latent acidity, for which I had no lime, and it soon all fermented. I saw sugar afterwards at Ujiji made in the same way, and that kept for months. Wheat and rice are cultivated by the Arabs in all this upland region; the only thing a missionary needs in order to secure an abundant supply is to follow the Arab advice as to the proper season for sowing. Pomegranates, guavas, lemons and oranges are abundant in Unyanyembe; mangoes flourish, and grape vines are beginning to be cultivated; papaws grow everywhere. Onions, radishes, pumpkins and watermelons prosper, and so would most European vegetables, if the proper seasons were selected for planting, and the most important point attended to in bringing the seeds. These must never be soldered in tins or put in close boxes; a process of sweating takes place when they are confined, as in a box or hold of the ship, and the power of vegetating is destroyed, but garden seeds put up in common brown paper, and hung in the cabin on the voyage, and not exposed to the direct rays of the sun afterwards, I have found to be as good as in England.

It would be a sort of Robinson Crusoe life, but with abundant materials for surrounding oneself with comforts, and improving the improvable among the natives. Clothing would require but small expense: four suits of strong tweed served me comfortably for five years. Woollen clothing is the best; if all wool, it wears long and prevents chills. The temperature here in the beginning of winter ranges from 62 deg. to 75 deg. Fahr. In summer it seldom goes above 84 deg., as the country generally is from 3600 to 4000 feet high. Gently undulating plains with outcropping tree-covered granite hills on the ridges and springs in valleys will serve as a description of the country.

29th May, 1872.--Halima ran away in a quarrel with Ntaoeka: I went over to Sultan bin Ali and sent a note after her, but she came back of her own accord, and only wanted me to come outside and tell her to enter. I did so, and added, "You must not quarrel again." She has been extremely good ever since I got her from Katombo or Moene-mokaia: I never had to reprove her once. She is always very attentive and clever, and never stole, nor would she allow her husband to steal. She is the best spoke in the wheel; this her only escapade is easily forgiven, and I gave her a warm cloth for the cold, by way of assuring her that I had no grudge against her. I shall free her, and buy her a house and garden at Zanzibar, when we get there[20]. Smokes or haze begins, and birds, stimulated by the cold, build briskly.

30th May, 1872, Sunday.--Sent over to Sultan bin Ali, to write another note

---

20   Halima followed the Doctor's remains to Zanzibar. It does seem hard that his death leaves her long services entirely unrequited.--ED.

to Lewale, to say first note not needed.

31st May, 1872. --The so-called Arab war with Mirambo drags its slow length along most wearily. After it is over then we shall get Banyamwezi pagazi in abundance. It is not now known whether Mirambo is alive or not: some say that he died long ago, and his son keeps up his state instead.

In reference to this Nile source I have been kept in perpetual doubt and perplexity. I know too much to be positive. Great Lualaba, or Lualubba, as Manyuema say, may turn out to be the Congo and Nile, a shorter river after all--the fountains flowing north and south seem in favour of its being the Nile. Great westing is in favour of the Congo. It would be comfortable to be positive like Baker. "Every drop from the passing shower to the roaring mountain torrent must fall into Albert Lake, a giant at its birth." How soothing to be positive.

1st June, 1872. --Visited by Jemadar Hamees from Katanga, who gives the following information.

UNYANYEMBE, ***Tuesday***.--Hamees bin Jumaadarsabel, a Beluch, came here from Katanga to-day. He reports that the three Portuguese traders, Jao, Domasiko, and Domasho, came to Katanga from Matiamvo. They bought quantities of ivory and returned: they were carried in Mashilahs[21] by slaves. This Hamees gave them pieces of gold from the rivulet there between the two copper or malachite hills from which copper is dug. He says that Tipo Tipo is now at Katanga, and has purchased much ivory from Kayomba or Kayombo in Rua. He offers to guide me thither, going first to Merere's, where Amran Masudi has now the upper hand, and Merere offers to pay all the losses he has caused to Arabs and others. Two letters were sent by the Portuguese to the East Coast, one is in Amran's hands. Hamees Wodin Tagh is alive and well. These Portuguese went nowhere from Katanga, so that they have not touched the sources of the Nile, for which I am thankful.

Tipo Tipo has made friends with Merosi, the Monyamweze headman at Katanga, by marrying his daughter, and has formed the plan of assaulting Casembe in conjunction with him because Casembe put six of Tipo Tipo's men to death. He will now be digging gold at Katanga till this man returns with gunpowder.

[Many busy calculations are met with here which are too involved to be given in detail. At one point we see a rough conjecture as to the length of the road

---

21 The Portuguese name for palanquin.

through Fipa.]

On looking at the projected route by Merere's I see that it will be a saving of a large angle into Fipa = 350 into Basango country S.S.W. or S. and by W., this comes into Lat. 10' S., and from this W.S.W. 400' to Long. of Katanga, skirting Bangweolo S. shore in 12 deg. S. = the whole distance = 750', say 900'.

[Further on we see that he reckoned on his work occupying him till 1874.]

If Stanley arrived the 1st of May at Zanzibar:--allow = 20 days to get men and settle with them = May 20th, men leave Zanzibar 22nd of May = now 1st of June.

On the road may be	10 days
Still to come 30 days, June	30 "
--	
Ought to arrive 10th or 15th of July	40 "

14th of June = Stanley being away now 3 months; say he left Zanzibar 24th of May = at Aden 1st of June = Suez 8th of June, near Malta 14th of June.

Stanley's men may arrive in July next. Then engage pagazi half a month = August, 5 months of this year will remain for journey, the whole of 1873 will be swallowed up in work, but in February or March, 1874, please the Almighty Disposer of events, I shall complete my task and retire.

2nd June, 1872. --A second crop here, as in Angola. The lemons and pomegranates are flowering and putting out young fruits anew, though the crops of each have just been gathered. Wheat planted a month ago is now a foot high, and in three months will be harvested. The rice and dura are being reaped, and the hoes are busy getting virgin land ready. Beans, and Madagascar underground beans, voandzeia and ground-nuts are ripe now. Mangoes are formed; the weather feels cold, min. 62 deg., max. 74 deg., and stimulates the birds to pair and build, though they are of broods scarcely weaned from being fed by their parents. Bees swarm and pass over us. Sky clear, with fleecy clouds here and there.

7th June, 1872. --Sultan bin Ali called. He says that the path by Fipa is the best, it has plenty of game, and people are friendly[22]. By going to Amran I should

---

22 It will be seen that this was fully confirmed afterwards by Livingstone's men: the fact may be of importance to future travellers.--ED.

get into the vicinity of Merere, and possibly be detained, as the country is in a state of war. The Beluch would naturally wish to make a good thing of me, as he did of Speke. I gave him a cloth and arranged the Sungomaze beads, but the box and beads weigh 140 lbs., or two men's loads. I visited Lewale. Heard of Baker going to Unyoro Water, Lake Albert. Lewale praises the road by Moeneyungo and Merere, and says he will give a guide, but he never went that way.

10th June, 1872.--Othman, our guide from Ujiji hither, called to-day, and says positively that the way by Fipa is decidedly the shortest and easiest: there is plenty of game, and the people are all friendly. He reports that Mirambo's headman, Merungwe, was assaulted and killed, and all his food, cattle, and grain used. Mirambo remains alone. He has, it seems, inspired terror in the Arab and Banyamwezi mind by his charms, and he will probably be allowed to retreat north by flight, and the war for a season close; if so, we shall get plenty of Banyamwezi pagazi, and be off, for which I earnestly long and pray.

13th June, 1872.--Sangara, one of Mr. Stanley's men, returned from Bagamoio, and reports that my caravan is at Ugogo. He arrived to-day, and reports that Stanley and the American Consul acted like good fellows, and soon got a party of over fifty off, as he heard while at Bagamoio, and he left. The main body, he thinks, are in Ugogo. He came on with the news, but the letters were not delivered to him. I do most fervently thank the good Lord of all for His kindness to me through these gentlemen. The men will come here about the end of this month. Bombay happily pleaded sickness as an excuse for not re-engaging, as several others have done. He saw that I got a clear view of his failings, and he could not hope to hoodwink me.

After Sangara came, I went over to Kukuru to see what the Lewale had received, but he was absent at Tabora. A great deal of shouting, firing of guns, and circumgyration by the men who had come from the war just outside the stockade of Nkisiwa (which is surrounded by a hedge of dark euphorbia and stands in a level hollow) was going on as we descended the gentle slope towards it. Two heads had been put up as trophies in the village, and it was asserted that Marukwe, a chief man of Mirambo, had been captured at Uvinza, and his head would soon come too. It actually did come, and was put up on a pole.

I am most unfeignedly thankful that Stanley and Webb have acted nobly.

14th June, 1872.--On 22nd June Stanley was 100 days gone: he must be in

London now.

Seyed bin Mohamad Margibbe called to say that he was going off towards Katanga to-morrow by way of Amran. I feel inclined to go by way of Fipa rather, though I should much like to visit Merere. By the bye, he says too that the so-called Portuguese had filed teeth, and are therefore Mambarre.

15th June, 1872. --Lewale doubts Sangara on account of having brought no letters. Nothing can be believed in this land unless it is in black and white, and but little even then; the most circumstantial details are often mere figments of the brain. The one half one hears may safely be called false, and the other half doubtful or ***not proven.***

Sultan bin Ali doubts Sangara's statements also, but says, "Let us wait and see the men arrive, to confirm or reject them." I incline to belief, because he says that he did not see the men, but heard of them at Bagamoio.

16th June, 1872. --Nsare chief, Msalala, came selling from Sakuma on the north--a jocular man, always a favourite with the ladies. He offered a hoe as a token of friendship, but I bought it, as we are, I hope, soon going off, and it clears the tent floor and ditch round it in wet weather.

Mirambo made a sortie against a headman in alliance with the Arabs, and was quite successful, which shows that he is not so much reduced as reports said.

Boiling points to-day about 9 A.M. There is a full degree of difference between boiling in an open pot and in Casella's apparatus.

205 deg..1 open pot }
                              } 69 deg. air.
206 deg..1 Casella   }

About 200 Baguha came here, bringing much ivory and palm oil for sale because there is no market nor goods at Ujiji for the produce. A few people came also from Buganda, bringing four tusks and an invitation to Seyed Burghash to send for two housefuls of ivory which Mteza has collected.

18th June, 1872. --Sent over a little quinine to Sultan bin Ali--he is ailing of fever--and a glass of "Moiko" the shameful!

The Ptolemaic map defines people according to their food. The Elephantophagi, the Struthiophagi, the Ichthyophagi, and Anthropophagi. If we followed the same sort of classification our definition would be the drink, thus:--the tribe of stout-guzzlers, the roaring potheen-fuddlers, the whisky-fishoid-drinkers, the vin-ordinaire bibbers, the lager-beer-swillers, and an outlying tribe of the brandy cocktail persuasion.

[His keen enjoyment in noticing the habits of animals and birds serves a good purpose whilst waiting wearily and listening to disputed rumours concerning the Zanzibar porters. The little orphan birds seem to get on somehow or other; perhaps the Englishman's eye was no bad protection, and his pity towards the fledglings was a good lesson, we will hope, to the children around the Tembe at Kwihara--]

19th June, 1872. --Whydahs, though full fledged, still gladly take a feed from their dam, putting down the breast to the ground and cocking up the bill and chirruping in the most engaging manner and winning way they know. She still gives them a little, but administers a friendly shove off too. They all pick up feathers or grass, and hop from side to side of their mates, as if saying, "Come, let us play at making little houses." The wagtail has shaken her young quite off, and has a new nest. She warbles prettily, very much like a canary, and is extremely active in catching flies, but eats crumbs of bread-and-milk too. Sun-birds visit the pomegranate flowers and eat insects therein too, as well as nectar. The young whydah birds crouch closely together at night for heat. They look like a woolly ball on a branch. By day they engage in pairing and coaxing each other. They come to the same twig every night. Like children they try and lift heavy weights of feathers above their strength.

[How fully he hoped to reach the hill from which he supposed the Nile to flow is shown in the following words written at this time:--]

I trust in Providence still to help me. I know the four rivers Zambesi, Kafue, Luapula, and Lomame, their fountains must exist in one region.

An influential Muganda is dead of dysentery: no medicine had any effect in stopping the progress of the disease. This is much colder than his country. Another is blind from ophthalmia.

Great hopes are held that the war which has lasted a full year will now be brought to a close, and Mirambo either be killed or flee. As he is undoubtedly an able man, his flight may involve much trouble and guerilla warfare.

Clear cold weather, and sickly for those who have only thin clothing, and not all covered.

The women work very hard in providing for their husbands' kitchens. The rice is the most easily prepared grain: three women stand round a huge wooden mortar with pestles in their hands, a gallon or so of the unhusked rice--called Mopunga here and paddy in India--is poured in, and the three heavy pestles worked in exact time; each jerks up her body as she lifts the pestle and strikes it into the mortar with all her might, lightening the labour with some wild ditty the while, though one hears by the strained voice that she is nearly out of breath. When the husks are pretty well loosened, the grain is put into a large plate-shaped basket and tossed so as to bring the chaff to one side, the vessel is then heaved downwards and a little horizontal motion given to it which throws the refuse out; the partially cleared grain is now returned to the mortar, again pounded and cleared of husks, and a semicircular toss of the vessel sends all the remaining unhusked grain to one side, which is lifted out with the hand, leaving the chief part quite clean: they certainly work hard and well. The maize requires more labour by far: it is first pounded to remove the outer scales from the grain, then steeped for three days in water, then pounded, the scales again separated by the shallow-basket tossings, then pounded fine, and the fine white flour separated by the basket from certain hard rounded particles, which are cooked as a sort of granular porridge--"Mtyelle."

When Ntaoeka chose to follow us rather than go to the coast, I did not like to have a fine-looking woman among us unattached, and proposed that she should marry one of my three worthies, Chuma, Gardner, or Mabruki, but she smiled at the idea. Chuma was evidently too lazy ever to get a wife; the other two were contemptible in appearance, and she has a good presence and is buxom. Chuma promised reform: "he had been lazy, he admitted, because he had no wife." Circumstances led to the other women wishing Ntaoeka married, and on my speaking to her again she consented. I have noticed her ever since working hard from morning to night: the first up in the cold mornings, making fire and hot water, pounding, carrying water, wood, sweeping, cooking.

21st June, 1872.--No jugglery or sleight-of-hand, as was recommended to Napoleon III., would have any effect in the civilization of the Africans; they have too much good sense for that. Nothing brings them to place thorough confidence in

Europeans but a long course of well-doing. They believe readily in the supernatural as effecting any new process or feat of skill, for it is part of their original faith to ascribe everything above human agency to unseen spirits. Goodness or unselfishness impresses their minds more than any kind of skill or power. They say, "You have different hearts from ours; all black men's hearts are bad, but yours are good." The prayer to Jesus for a new heart and right spirit at once commends itself as appropriate. Music has great influence on those who have musical ears, and often leads to conversion.

[Here and there he gives more items of intelligence from the war which afford a perfect representation of the rumours and contradictions which harass the listener in Africa, especially if he is interested, as Livingstone was, in the re-establishment of peace between the combatants.]

Lewale is off to the war with Mirambo; he is to finish it now! A continuous fusilade along his line of march west will expend much powder, but possibly get the spirits up. If successful, we shall get Banyamwezi pagazi in numbers.

Mirambo is reported to have sent 100 tusks and 100 slaves towards the coast to buy gunpowder. If true, the war is still far from being finished; but falsehood is fashionable.

26th June, 1872. --Went over to Kwikuru and engaged Mohamad bin Seyde to speak to Nkasiwa for pagazi; he wishes to go himself. The people sent by Mirambo to buy gunpowder in Ugogo came to Kitambi, he reported the matter to Nkasiwa that they had come, and gave them pombe. When Lewale heard it, he said, "Why did Kitambi not kill them; he is a partaker in Mirambo's guilt?" A large gathering yesterday at M'futu to make an assault on the last stockade in hostility.

[A few notes in another pocket-book are placed under this date. Thus:--]

24th June, 1872. --A continuous covering of forests is a sign of a virgin country. The earlier seats of civilization are bare and treeless according to Humboldt. The civilization of the human race sets bounds to the increase of forests. It is but recently that sylvan decorations rejoice the eyes of the Northern Europeans. The old forests attest the youthfulness of our civilization. The aboriginal woods of Scotland are but recently cut down. (Hugh Miller's **Sketches**, p. 7.)

Mosses often evidence the primitive state of things at the time of the Roman invasion. Roman axe like African, a narrow chisel-shaped tool, left sticking in the stumps.

The medical education has led me to a continual tendency to suspend the judgment. What a state of blessedness it would have been had I possessed the dead certainty of the homoeopathic persuasion, and as soon as I found the Lakes Bangweolo, Moero, and Kamolondo pouring out their waters down the great central valley, bellowed out, "Hurrah! Eureka!" and gone home in firm and honest belief that I had settled it, and no mistake. Instead of that I am even now not at all "cock-sure" that I have not been following down what may after all be the Congo.

25th June, 1872. --Send over to Tabora to try and buy a cow from Basakuma, or northern people, who have brought about 100 for sale. I got two oxen for a coil of brass wire and seven dotis of cloth.

CHAPTER VIII.

Letters arrive at last. Sore intelligence. Death of an old friend. Observations on the climate. Arab caution. Dearth of missionary enterprise. The slave trade and its horrors. Progressive barbarism. Carping benevolence. Geology of Southern Africa. The fountain sources. African elephants. A venerable piece of artillery. Livingstone on Materialism. Bin Nassib. The Baganda leave at last. Enlists a new follower.

[And now the long-looked for letters came in by various hands, but with little regularity. It is not here necessary to refer to the withdrawal of the Livingstone Relief Expedition which took place as soon as Mr. Stanley confronted Lieutenant Dawson on his way inland. Suffice it to say that the various members of this Expedition, of which his second son, Mr. Oswell Livingstone, was one, had already quitted Africa for England when these communications reached Unyanyembe.]

27th June, 1872.--Received a letter from Oswell yesterday, dated Bagamoio, 14th May, which awakened thankfulness, anxiety, and deep sorrow.

28th June, 1872.--Went over to Kwikuru yesterday to speak about pagazi. Nkasiwa was off at M'futu to help in the great assault on Mirambo, which is hoped to be the last. But Mohamad bin Seyed promised to arrange with the chief on his return. I was told that Nkasiwa has the head of Morukwe in a kirindo or band-box, made of the inner bark of a tree, and when Morukwe's people have recovered they will come and redeem it with ivory and slaves, and bury it in his grave, as they did the head of Ishbosheth in Abner's grave in Hebron.

Dugumbe's man, who went off to Ujiji to bring ivory, returned to-day, having been attacked by robbers of Mirambo. The pagazi threw down all their loads and ran; none were killed, but they lost all.

29th June, 1872.--Received a packet from Sheikh bin Nasib containing a letter for him and one 'Pall Mall Gazette,' one Overland Mail and four Punches. Provision has been made for my daughter by Her Majesty's Government of 300 *l.*, but I don't understand the matter clearly.

2nd July, 1872. --Make up a packet for Dr. Kirk and Mr. Webb, of Zanzibar: explain to Kirk, and beg him to investigate and punish, and put blame on right persons. Write Sir Bartle Frere and Agnes: send large packet of astronomical observations and sketch map to Sir Thomas Maclear by a native, Suleiman.

3rd July, 1872. --Received a note from Oswell, written in April last, containing the sad intelligence of Sir Roderick's departure from among us. Alas! alas! this is the only time in my life I ever felt inclined to use the word, and it bespeaks a sore heart: the best friend I ever had--true, warm, and abiding--he loved me more than I deserved: he looks down on me still. I must feel resigned to the loss by the Divine Will, but still I regret and mourn.

Wearisome waiting, this; and yet the men cannot be here before the middle or end of this month. I have been sorely let and hindered in this journey, but it may have been all for the best. I will trust in Him to whom I commit my way.

5th July, 1872. --Weary! weary!

7th July, 1872. --Waiting wearily here, and hoping that the good and loving Father of all may favour me, and help me to finish my work quickly and well.

Temperature at 6 A.M. 61 deg.; feels cold. Winds blow regularly from the east; if it changes to N.W. brings a thick mantle of cold grey clouds. A typhoon did great damage at Zanzibar, wrecking ships and destroying cocoa-nuts, carafu, and all fruits: happened five days after Seyed Burghash's return from Mecca.

At the Loangwa of Zumbo we came to a party of hereditary hippopotamus hunters, called Makembwe or Akombwe. They follow no other occupation, but when their game is getting scanty at one spot they remove to some other part of the Loangwa, Zambesi, or Shire, and build temporary huts on an island, where their women cultivate patches: the flesh of the animals they kill is eagerly exchanged by the more settled people for grain. They are not stingy, and are everywhere welcome guests. I never heard of any fraud in dealing, or that they had been guilty of an outrage on the poorest: their chief characteristic is their courage. Their hunting is the bravest thing I ever saw. Each canoe is manned by two men; they are long light craft, scarcely half an inch in thickness, about eighteen inches beam, and from eighteen to twenty feet long. They are formed for speed, and shaped somewhat like our racing boats. Each man uses a broad short paddle, and as they guide the canoe slowly down stream to a sleeping hippopotamus not a single ripple is raised on the smooth water; they look as if holding in their breath, and communicate by signs only. As they come near the prey the harpooner in the bow lays down his paddle and rises slowly up, and there he stands erect, motionless, and eager, with the long-handled weapon poised at arm's length above his head, till coming close to the beast he plunges it with all his might in towards the heart. During this exciting feat he has to keep his balance exactly. His neighbour in the stern at once backs his paddle, the harpooner sits down, seizes his paddle, and backs too to escape: the animal surprised and wounded seldom returns the attack at this stage of the hunt. The next stage, however, is full of danger.

The barbed blade of the harpoon is secured by a long and very strong rope wound round the handle: it is intended to come out of its socket, and while the iron head is firmly fixed in the animal's body the rope unwinds and the handle floats on the surface. The hunter next goes to the handle and hauls on the rope till he knows that he is right over the beast: when he feels the line suddenly slacken he is prepared to deliver another harpoon the instant that hippo.'s enormous jaws appear with a terrible grunt above the water. The backing by the paddles is again repeated, but hippo. often assaults the canoe, crunches it with his great jaws as easily as a pig would a bunch of asparagus, or shivers it with a kick by his hind foot. Deprived of their canoe the gallant comrades instantly dive and swim to the shore under water: they say that the infuriated beast looks for them on the surface, and being below they escape his sight. When caught by many harpoons the crews of several canoes seize the handles and drag him hither and thither till, weakened by loss of blood, he succumbs.

This hunting requires the greatest skill, courage, and nerve that can be conceived--double armed and threefold brass, or whatever the AEneid says. The Makombwe are certainly a magnificent race of men, hardy and active in their habits, and well fed, as the result of their brave exploits; every muscle is well developed, and though not so tall as some tribes, their figures are compact and finely proportioned: being a family occupation it has no doubt helped in the production of fine physical development. Though all the people among whom they sojourn would like the profits they secure by the flesh and curved tusks, and no game is preserved, I have met with no competitors to them except the Wayeiye of Lake Ngami and adjacent rivers.

I have seen our dragoon officers perform fencing and managing their horses so dexterously that every muscle seemed trained to its fullest power and efficiency, and perhaps had they been brought up as Makombwe they might have equalled their daring and consummate skill: but we have no sport, except perhaps Indian tiger shooting, requiring the courage and coolness this enterprise demands. The danger may be appreciated if one remembers that no sooner is blood shed in the water than all the crocodiles below are immediately drawn up stream by the scent, and are ready to act the part of thieves in a London crowd, or worse.

8th July, 1872. --At noon, wet bulb 66 deg., dry 74 deg.. These observations are taken from thermometers hung four feet from the ground on the cool side (south) of the house, and beneath an earthen roof with complete protection from wind and radiation. Noon known by the shadows being nearly perpendicular. To show what is endured by a traveller, the following register is given of the heat on a spot, four feet from the ground, protected from the wind by a reed fence, but exposed to the sun's rays, slanting a little.

Noon.	*Wet Bulb 78 deg.*	*Dry Bulb 102 deg.*
2 P.M.	*77 deg.*	*99 deg.*
3 P.M.	*78 deg.*	*102 deg.*
4 P.M.	*72 deg.*	*88 deg. (Agreeable marching now.)*
6 P.M.	*66 deg.*	*77 deg.*

9th July, 1872. --Clear and cold the general weather: cold is penetrating. War forces have gone out of M'futu and built a camp. Fear of Mirambo rules them all: each one is nervously anxious not to die, and in no way ashamed to own it. The Arabs keep out of danger: "Better to sleep in a whole skin" is their motto.

Noon.--Spoke to Singeri about the missionary reported to be coming: he seems to like the idea of being taught and opening up the country by way of the Nile. I told him that all the Arabs confirmed Mtesa's cruelties, and that his people were more to blame than he: it was guilt before God. In this he agreed fully, but said,

"What Arab was killed?" meaning, if they did not suffer how can they complain?

6 A.M.   Wet Bulb 55 deg.   Dry Bulb 57 deg. min. 55 deg.
9 A.M.   74 deg.   82 deg.
*Noon.   74 deg.   98 deg. (**Now becomes too hot to march.**)*
3.30 P.M.   75 deg.   90 deg.

10th July, 1872.

6 A.M.   59 deg.   65 deg. min. 55 deg.
Noon.   67 deg.   77 deg. shady.
3 P.M.   69 deg.   81 deg. cloudy.
5 P.M.   65 deg.   75 deg. cloudy.

10th July, 1872. --No great difficulty would be encountered in establishing a Christian Mission a hundred miles or so from the East Coast. The permission of the Sultan of Zanzibar would be necessary, because all the tribes of any intelligence claim relationship, or have relations with him; the Banyamwezi even call themselves his subjects, and so do others. His permission would be readily granted, if respectfully applied for through the English Consul. The Suaheli, with their present apathy on religious matters, would be no obstacle. Care to speak politely, and to show kindness to them, would not be lost labour in the general effect of the Mission on the country, but all discussion on the belief of the Moslems should be avoided; they know little about it. Emigrants from Muscat, Persia, and India, who at present possess neither influence nor wealth, would eagerly seize any formal or offensive denial of the authority of their Prophet to fan their own bigotry, and arouse that of the Suaheli. A few now assume an air of superiority in matters of worship, and would fain take the place of Mullams or doctors of the law, by giving authoritative dicta as to the times of prayer; positions to be observed; lucky and unlucky days; using cabalistic signs; telling fortunes; finding from the Koran when an attack may be made on any enemy, &c.; but this is done only in the field with trading parties. At Zanzibar, the regular Mullams supersede them.

No objection would be made to teaching the natives of the country to read their own languages in the Roman character. No Arab has ever attempted to teach them the Arabic-Koran, they are called ***guma***, hard, or difficult as to religion. This is not wonderful, since the Koran is never translated, and a very extraordinary desire for knowledge would be required to sustain a man in committing to memory pages and chapters of, to him, unmeaning gibberish. One only of all the native chiefs, Monyumgo, has sent his children to Zanzibar to be taught to read and write the Koran; and he is said to possess an unusual admiration of such civilization as he has seen among the Arabs. To the natives, the chief attention of the Mission should be directed. It would not be desirable, or advisable, to refuse explanation to others; but I have avoided giving offence to intelligent Arabs, who have pressed me, asking if I believed in Mohamad by saying, "No I do not: I am a child of Jesus bin Miriam," avoiding anything offensive in my tone, and often adding that Mohamad found their forefathers bowing down to trees and stones, and did good to them by forbidding idolatry, and teaching the worship of the only One God. This, they all know, and it pleases them to have it recognised.

It might be good policy to hire a respectable Arab to engage free porters, and conduct the Mission to the country chosen, and obtain permission from the chief to build temporary houses. If this Arab were well paid, it might pave the way for employing others to bring supplies of goods and stores not produced in the country, as tea, coffee, sugar. The first porters had better all go back, save a couple or so, who have behaved especially well. Trust to the people among whom you live for general services, as bringing wood, water, cultivation, reaping, smith's work, carpenter's work, pottery, baskets, &c. Educated free blacks from a distance are to be avoided: they are expensive, and are too much of gentlemen for your work. You may in a few months raise natives who will teach reading to others better than they can, and teach you also much that the liberated never know. A cloth and some beads occasionally will satisfy them, while neither the food, the wages, nor the work will please those who, being brought from a distance, naturally consider themselves missionaries. Slaves also have undergone a process which has spoiled them for life; though liberated young, everything of childhood and opening life possesses an indescribable charm. It is so with our own offspring, and nothing effaces the fairy scenes then printed on the memory. Some of my liberados eagerly bought green calabashes and tasteless squash, with fine fat beef, because this trash was their early food; and an ounce of meat never entered their mouths. It seems indispensable that each Mission should raise its own native agency. A couple of Europeans beginning, and carrying on a Mission without a staff of foreign attendants, implies coarse country fare, it is true, but this would be nothing to those who, at home amuse themselves with fastings, vigils, &c. A great deal of power is thus lost in the Church. Fastings and vigils, without a special object in view, are time run to waste. They are made to minister to a sort of self-gratification, instead of being turned to account for the good of others. They are like groaning in sickness. Some people amuse themselves when ill with continuous moaning. The forty days of Lent might be annually spent in visiting adjacent tribes, and bearing unavoidable hunger and thirst with a good grace. Considering the greatness of the object to be attained, men might go without sugar, coffee, tea, &c. I went from September 1866 to December 1868 without either. A trader, at Casembe's, gave me a dish cooked with honey, and it nauseated from its horrible sweetness, but at 100 miles inland, supplies could be easily obtained.

The expenses need not be large. Intelligent Arabs inform me that, in going from Zanzibar to Casembe's, only 3000 dollars' worth are required by a trader, say between 600 *l.* or 700 *l.*, and he may be away three or more years; paying his way, giving presents to the chiefs, and filling 200 or 300 mouths. He has paid for, say fifty muskets, ammunition, flints, and may return with 4000 lbs. of ivory, and a number of slaves for sale; all at an outlay of 600 *l.* or 700 *l.* With the experience I have gained now, I could do all I shall do in this expedition for a like sum, or at least for 1000 *l.* less than it will actually cost me.

12th July, 1872. --Two men come from Syde bin Habib report fighting as going on at discreet distances against Mirambo.

Sheikh But, son of Mohamad bin Saleh, is found guilty of stealing a tusk of 2-1/2 frasilahs from the Lewale. He has gone in disgrace to fight Mirambo: his father is disconsolate, naturally. Lewale has been merciful.

When endeavouring to give some account of the slave-trade of East Africa, it was necessary to keep far within the truth, in order not to be thought guilty of exaggeration; but in sober seriousness the subject does not admit of exaggeration. To overdraw its evils is a simple impossibility. The sights I have seen, though common incidents of the traffic, are so nauseous that I always strive to drive them from memory. In the case of most disagreeable recollections I can succeed, in time, in consigning them to oblivion, but the slaving scenes come back unbidden, and make me start up at dead of night horrified by their vividness. To some this may appear weak and unphilosophical, since it is alleged that the whole human race has passed through the process of development. We may compare cannibalism to the stone age, and the times of slavery to the iron and bronze epochs--slavery is as natural a step in human development as from bronze to iron.

Whilst speaking of the stone age I may add that in Africa I have never been fortunate enough to find one flint arrowhead or any other flint implement, though I had my eyes about me as diligently as any of my neighbours. No roads are made; no lands levelled; no drains digged; no quarries worked, nor any of the changes made on the earth's surface that might reveal fragments of the primitive manufacture of stone. Yet but little could be inferred from the negative evidence, were it not accompanied by the fact that flint does not exist in any part south of the equator. Quartz might have been used, but no remains exist, except the half-worn millstones, and stones about the size of oranges, used for chipping and making rough the nether millstone. Glazed pipes and earthenware used in smelting iron, show that iron was smelted in the remotest ages in Africa. These earthenware vessels, and fragments of others of a finer texture, were found in the delta of the Zambesi and in other parts in close association with fossil bones, which, on being touched by the tongue, showed as complete an absence of animal matter as the most ancient fossils known in Europe. They were the bones of animals, as hippopotami, water hogs, antelopes, crocodiles, identical with those now living in the country. These were the primitive fauna of Africa, and if vitrified iron from the prodigious number of broken smelting furnaces all over the country was known from the remotest times, the Africans seem to have had a start in the race, at a time when our progenitors were grubbing up flints to save a miserable existence by the game they might kill. Slave-trading seems to have been coeval with the knowledge of iron. The monuments of Egypt show that this curse has venerable antiquity. Some people say, "If so ancient, why try to stop an old established usage now?" Well, some believe that the affliction that befel the most ancient of all the patriarchs, Job, was small-pox. Why then stop the ravages of this venerable disease in London and New York by vaccination?

But no one expects any benevolent efforts from those who cavil and carp at efforts made by governments and peoples to heal the enormous open sore of the world. Some profess that they would rather give "their mite" for the degraded of our own countrymen than to "niggers"! Verily it is "a mite," and they most often forget, and make a gift of it to themselves. It is almost an axiom that those who do most for the heathen abroad are most liberal for the heathen at home. It is to this class we turn with hope. With others arguments are useless, and the only answer I care to give is the remark of an English sailor, who, on seeing slave-traders actually at their occupation, said to his companion, "Shiver my timbers, mate, if the devil don't catch these fellows, we might as well have no devil at all."

In conversing with a prince at Johanna, one of the Comoro islands lying off the north end of Madagascar, he took occasion to extol the wisdom of the Arabs in keeping strict watch over their wives. On suggesting that their extreme jealousy made them more like jailers than friends of their wives, or, indeed, that they thus reduced themselves to the level of the inferior animals, and each was like the bull of a herd and not like a reasonable man--"fuguswa"--and that they gave themselves a vast deal of trouble for very small profit; he asserted that the jealousy was reasonable because all women were bad, they could not avoid going astray. And on remarking that this might be the case with Arab women, but certainly did not apply to English women, for though a number were untrustworthy, the majority deserved all the confidence their husbands could place in them, he reiterated that women were universally bad. He did not believe that women ever would be good; and the English allowing their wives to gad about with faces uncovered, only showed their weakness, ignorance, and unwisdom.

The tendency and spirit of the age are more and more towards the undertaking of industrial enterprises of such magnitude and skill as to require the capital of the world for their support and execution--as the Pacific Railroad, Suez Canal, Mont Cenis Tunnel, and railways in India and Western Asia, Euphrates Railroad, &c. The extension and use of railroads, steamships, telegraphs, break down nationalities and bring peoples geographically remote into close connection commercially and politically. They make the world one, and capital, like water, tends to a common level.

[Geologists will be glad to find that the Doctor took pains to arrange his observations at this time in the following form.]

A really enormous area of South Central Africa is covered with volcanic rocks, in which are imbedded angular fragments of older strata, possibly sandstone, converted into schist, which, though carried along in the molten mass, still retain impressions of plants of a low order, probably the lowest--Silurian--and distinct ripple marks and raindrops in which no animal markings have yet been observed. The fewness of the organic remains observed is owing to the fact that here no quarries are worked, no roads are made, and as we advance north the rank vegetation covers up everything. The only stone buildings in the country north of the Cape colony are the church and mission houses at Kuruman. In the walls there the fragments, with impressions of fossil leaves, have been broken through in the matrix, once a molten mass of lava. The area which this basalt covers extends from near the Vaal River in the south, to a point some sixty miles beyond the Victoria Falls, and the average breadth is about 150 miles. The space is at least 100,000 square miles. Sandstone rocks stand up in it at various points like islands, but all are metamorphosed, and branches have flowed off from the igneous sea into valleys and defiles, and one can easily trace the hardening process of the fire as less and less, till at the outer end of the stream the rocks are merely hardened. These branches equal in size all the rocks and hills that stand like islands, so that we are justified in assuming the area as at least 100,000 square miles of this basaltic sea.

The molten mass seems to have flowed over in successive waves, and the top of each wave was covered with a dark vitreous scum carrying scoriae with angular fragments. This scum marks each successive overflow, as a stratum from twelve to eighteen inches or more in thickness. In one part sixty-two strata are revealed, but at the Victoria Falls (which are simply a rent) the basaltic rock is stratified as far as our eyes could see down the depth of 310 feet. This extensive sea of lava was probably sub-aerial, because bubbles often appear as coming out of the rock into the vitreous scum on the surface of each wave: in some cases they have broken and left circular rings with raised edges, peculiar to any boiling viscous fluid. In many cases they have cooled as round pustules, as if a bullet were enclosed; on breaking them the internal surface is covered with a crop of beautiful crystals of silver with their heads all directed to the centre of the bubble, which otherwise is empty.

These bubbles in stone may be observed in the bed of the Kuruman River, eight or ten miles north of the village; and the mountain called "Amhan," west-north-west of the village, has all the appearance of having been an orifice through which the basalt boiled up as water or mud does in a geyser.

The black basaltic mountains on the east of the Bamangwato, formerly called the Bakaa, furnish further evidence of the igneous eruptions being sub-aerial, for the basalt itself is columnar at many points, and at other points the tops of the huge crystals appear in groups, and the apices not flattened, as would have been the case had they been developed under the enormous pressure of an ocean. A few miles on their south a hot salt fountain boils forth and tells of interior heat. Another, far to the south-east, and of fresh water, tells the same tale.

Subsequently to the period of gigantic volcanic action, the outflow of fresh lime-water from the bowels of the earth seems to have been extremely large. The land now so dry that one might wander in various directions (especially westwards, to the Kalahari), and perish for lack of the precious fluid as certainly as if he were in the interior of Australia, was once bisected in all directions by flowing streams and great rivers, whose course was mainly to the south. These river beds are still called by the natives "*melapo*" in the south, but in the north "*wadys*," both words meaning the same thing, "river beds in which no water ever now flows." To feed these a vast number of gushing fountains poured forth for ages a perennial supply. When the eye of the fountain is seen it is an oval or oblong orifice, the lower portion distinctly water worn, and there, by diminished size, showing that as ages elapsed the smaller water supply had a manifestly lesser erosive power. In the sides of the mountain Amhan, already mentioned, good specimens of these water-worn orifices still exist, and are inhabited by swarms of bees, whose hives are quite protected from robbers by the hardness of the basaltic rocks. The points on which the streams of water fell are hollowed by its action, and the space around which the water splashed is covered by calcareous tufa, deposited there by the evaporation of the sun.

Another good specimen of the ancient fountains is in a cave near Kolobeng, called "***Lepelole***," a word by which the natives there sometimes designate the sea. The wearing power of the primeval waters is here easily traced in two branches--the upper or more ancient ending in the characteristic oval orifice, in which I deposited a Father Mathew's leaden temperance token: the lower branch is much the largest, as that by which the greatest amount of water flowed for a much longer period than the other. The cave Lepelole was believed to be haunted, and no one dared to enter till I explored it as a relief from more serious labour. The entrance is some eight or more feet high, and five or six wide, in reddish grey sandstone rock, containing in its substance banks of well rounded shingle. The whole range, with many of the adjacent hills on the south, bear evidence of the scorching to which the contiguity of the lava subjected them. In the hardening process the silica was sometimes sweated out of this rock, and it exists now as pretty efflorescences of well-shaped crystals. But not only does this range, which stands eight or ten miles north of Kolobeng, exhibit the effects of igneous action, it shows on its eastern slope the effects of flowing water, in a large pot-hole called Loee, which has the reputation of having given exit to all the animals in South Africa, and also to the first progenitors of the whole Bechuana race. Their footsteps attest the truth of this belief. I was profane enough to be sceptical, because the large footstep of the first man Matsieng was directed as if going into instead of out of this famous pot-hole. Other huge pot-holes are met with all over the country, and at heights on the slopes of the mountains far above the levels of the ancient rivers.

Many fountains rose in the courses of the ancient river beds, and the outflow was always in the direction of the current of the parent stream. Many of these ancient fountains still contain water, and form the stages on a journey, but the primitive waters seem generally to have been laden with lime in solution: this lime was deposited in vast lakes, which are now covered with calcareous tufa. One enormous fresh-water lake, in which probably sported the Dyconodon, was let off when the remarkable rent was made in the basalt which now constitutes the Victoria Falls. Another seems to have gone to the sea when a similar fissure was made at the falls of the Orange River. It is in this calcareous tufa alone that fossil animal remains have yet been found. There are no marine limestones except in friths which the elevation of the west and east coasts have placed far inland in the Coanza and Somauli country, and these contain the same shells as now live in the adjacent seas.

Antecedently to the river system, which seems to have been a great southern Nile flowing from the sources of the Zambesi away south to the Orange River, there existed a state of fluvial action of greater activity than any we see now: it produced prodigious beds of well-rounded shingle and gravel. It is impossible to form an idea of their extent. The Loangwa flows through the bed of an ancient lake, whose banks are sixty feet thick, of well-rounded shingle. The Zambesi flows above the Kebrabasa, through great beds of the same formation, and generally they are of hard crystalline rocks; and it is impossible to conjecture what the condition of the country was when the large pot-holes were formed up the hillsides, and the prodigious attrition that rounded the shingle was going on. The land does not seem to have been submerged, because marine limestones (save in the exceptional cases noted) are wanting; and torrents cutting across the ancient river beds reveal fresh-water shells identical with those that now inhabit its fresh waters. The calcareous tufa seems to be the most recent rock formed. At the point of junction of the great southern prehistoric Nile with an ancient fresh-water lake near Buchap, and a few miles from Likatlong, a mound was formed in an eddy caused by some conical lias towards the east bank of this rent within its bed, and the dead animals were floated into the eddy and sank; their bones crop out of the white tufa, and they are so well preserved that even the black tartar on buffalo and zebra's teeth remain: they are of the present species of animals that now inhabit Africa. This is the only case of fossils of these animals being found *in situ*. In 1855 I observed similar fossils in banks of gravel in transitu all down the Zambesi above Kebrabasa; and about 1862 a bed of gravel was found in the delta with many of the same fossils that had come to rest in the great deposit of that river, but where the Zambesi digs them out is not known. In its course below the Victoria Falls I observed tufaceous rocks: these must contain the bones, for were they carried away from the great tufa Lake bottom of Sesheke, down the Victoria Falls, they would all be ground into fine silt. The bones in the river and in the delta were all associated with pieces of coarse pottery, exactly the same as the natives make and use at the present day: with it we found fragments of a fine grain, only occasionally seen among Africans, and closely resembling ancient cinerary urns: none were better baked than is customary in the country now. The most ancient relics are deeply worn granite, mica-schist, and sandstone millstones; the balls used for chipping and roughing them, of about the shape and size of an orange, are found lying near them. No stone weapons or tools ever met my eyes, though I was anxious to find them, and looked carefully over every ancient village we came to for many years. There is no flint to make celts, but quartz and rocks having a slaty cleavage are abundant. It is only for the finer work that they use iron tongs, hammers, and anvils and with these they turn out work which makes English blacksmiths declare Africans never did. They are very careful of their tools: indeed, the very opposites to the flint implement men, who seem sometimes to have made celts just for the pleasure of throwing them away: even the Romans did not seem to know the value of their money.

The ancient Africans seem to have been at least as early as the Asiatics in the art of taming elephants. The Egyptian monuments show them bringing tame elephants and lions into Egypt; and very ancient sculptures show the real African species, which the artist must have seen. They refused to sell elephants, which cost them months of hard labour to catch and tame, to a Greek commander of Egyptian troops for a few brass pots: they were quite right. Two or three tons of fine fat butcher-meat were far better than the price, seeing their wives could make any number of cooking pots for nothing.

15th July, 1872. --Reported to-day that twenty wounded men have been brought into M'futu from the field of fighting. About 2000 are said to be engaged on the Arab side, and the side of Mirambo would seem to be strong, but the assailants have the disadvantage of firing against a stockade, and are unprotected, except by ant-hills, bushes, and ditches in the field. I saw the first kites to-day: one had spots of white feathers on the body below, as if it were a young one--probably come from the north.

17th July, 1872. --Went over to Sultan bin Ali yesterday. Very kind, as usual; he gave me guavas and a melon--called "matanga." It is reported that one of Mirambo's chief men, Sorura, set sharp sticks in concealed holes, which acted like Bruce's "craw-taes" at Bannockburn, and wounded several, probably the twenty reported. This has induced the Arabs to send for a cannon they have, with which to batter Mirambo at a distance. The gun is borne past us this morning: a brass 7-pounder, dated 1679. Carried by the Portuguese Commander-in-Chief to China 1679, or 193 years ago--and now to beat Mirambo, by Arabs who have very little interest in the war.

Some of his people, out prowling two days ago, killed a slave. The war is not so near an end as many hoped.

* * * * *

[Mtesa's people on their way back to Uganda were stuck fast at Unyanyembe the whole of this time: it does not appear at all who the missionary was to whom he refers.]

* * * * *

Lewale sends off the Baganda in a great hurry, after detaining them for six months or more till the war ended, and he now gets pagazi of Banyamwezi for them. This haste (though war is not ended) is probably because Lewale has heard of a missionary through me.

Mirambo fires now from inside the stockade alone.

19th July, 1872.--Visited Salim bin Seff, and was very hospitably entertained. He was disappointed that I could not eat largely. They live very comfortably: grow wheat, whilst flour and fruits grace their board. Salim says that goat's flesh at Zanzibar is better than beef, but here beef is better than goat's flesh. He is a stout, jolly fellow.

20th July, 1872.--High cold winds prevail. Temperature, 6 A.M., 57 deg.; noon, on the ground, 122 deg.. It may be higher, but I am afraid to risk the thermometer, which is graduated to 140 deg. only.

21st July, 1872.--Bought two milch cows (from a Motusi), which, with their calves, were 17 dotis or 34 fathoms. The Baganda are packing up to leave for home. They take a good deal of brandy and gin for Mtesa from the Moslems. Temperature at noon, 96 deg..

Another nest of wagtails flown. They eat bread crumbs. The whydahs are busy pairing. Lewale returns to-day from M'futu on his own private business at Kwikuru. The success of the war is a minor consideration with all. I wish my men would come, and let me off from this weary waiting.

Some philosophising is curious. It represents our Maker forming the machine of the universe: setting it a-going, and able to do nothing more outside certain of His own laws. He, as it were, laid the egg of the whole, and, like an ostrich, left it to be hatched by the sun. We can control laws, but He cannot! A fire set to this house would consume it, but we can throw on water and consume the fire. We control the elements, fire and water: is He debarred from doing the same, and more, who has infinite wisdom and knowledge? He surely is greater than His own laws. Civilization is only what has been done with natural laws. Some foolish speculations in morals resemble the idea of a Muganda, who said last night, that if Mtesa didn't kill people now and then, his subjects would suppose that he was dead!

23rd July, 1872. --The departure of the Baganda is countermanded, for fear of Mirambo capturing their gunpowder.

Lewale interdicts them from going; he says, "You may go, but leave all the gunpowder here, because Mirambo will follow and take it all to fight with us." This is an afterthought, for he hurried them to go off. A few will go and take the news and some goods to Mtesa, and probably a lot of Lewale's goods to trade at Karagwe.

The Baganda are angry, for now their cattle and much of their property are expended here; but they say, "We are strangers, and what can we do but submit?" The Banyamwesi carriers would all have run away on the least appearance of danger. No troops are sent by Seyed Burghash, though they were confidently reported long ago. All trade is at a standstill.

24th July, 1872. --The Bagohe retire from the war. This month is unlucky. I visited Lewale and Nkasiwa, putting a blister on the latter, for paralytic arm, to please him. Lewale says that a general flight from the war has taken place. The excuse is hunger.

He confirms the great damage done by a cyclone at Zanzibar to shipping, houses, cocoa-nut palms, mango-trees, and clove-trees, also houses and dhows, five days after Burghash returned. Sofeu volunteers to go with us, because Mohamad Bogharib never gave him anything, and Bwana Mohinna has asked him to go with him. I have accepted his offer, and will explain to Mohamad, when I see him, that this is what he promised me in the way of giving men, but never performed.

27th July, 1872. --At dawn a loud rumbling in the east as if of thunder, possibly a slight earthquake; no thunder-clouds visible.

Bin Nassib came last night and visited me before going home to his own house; a tall, brown, polite Arab. He says that he lately received a packet for Mr. Stanley from the American Consul, sealed in tin, and sent it back: this is the eleventh that came to Stanley. A party of native traders who went with the Baganda were attacked by Mirambo's people, and driven back with the loss of all their goods and one killed. The fugitives returned this morning sorely downcast. A party of twenty-three loads left for Karagwe a few days ago, and the leader alone has returned; he does not know more than that one was killed. Another was slain on this side of M'futu by Mirambo's people yesterday, the country thus is still in a terribly disturbed state. Sheikh bin Nassib says that the Arabs have rooted out fifty-two headmen who were Mirambo's allies.

28th July, 1872. --To Nkasiwa; blistered him, as the first relieved the pain and pleased him greatly; hope he may derive benefit.

Cold east winds, and clouded thickly over all the sky.

29th July, 1872. --Making flour of rice for the journey. Visited Sheikh bin Nassib, who has a severe attack of fever; he cannot avoid going to the war. He bought a donkey with the tusk he stole from Lewale, and it died yesterday; now Lewale says, "Give me back my tusk;" and the Arab replies, "Give me back my donkey." The father must pay, but his son's character is lost as well as the donkey. Bin Nassib gave me a present of wheaten bread and cakes.

30th July, 1872. --Weary waiting this, and the best time for travelling passes over unused. High winds from the east every day bring cold, and, to the thinly-clad Arabs, fever. Bin Omari called: goes to Katanga with another man's goods to trade there.

31st July, 1872. --We heard yesterday from Sahib bin Nassib that the caravan of his brother Kisessa was at a spot in Ugogo, twelve days off. My party had gone by another route. Thankful for even this in my wearisome waiting.

CHAPTER IX.

Short years in Baganda. Boys' playthings in Africa. Reflections. Arrival of the men. Fervent thankfulness. An end of the weary waiting. Jacob Wainwright takes service under the Doctor. Preparations for the journey. Flagging and illness. Great heat. Approaches Lake Tanganyika. The borders of Fipa. Lepidosirens and vultures. Capes and islands of Lake Tanganyika. Higher mountains. Large bay.

1st August, 1872. --A large party of Baganda have come to see what is stopping the way to Mtesa, about ten headmen and their followers; but they were told by an Arab in Usui that the war with Mirambo was over. About seventy of them come on here to-morrow, only to be despatched back to fetch all the Baganda in Usui, to aid in fighting Mirambo. It is proposed to take a stockade near the central one, and therein build a battery for the cannon, which seems a wise measure. These arrivals are a poor, slave-looking people, clad in bark-cloth, "Mbuzu," and having shields with a boss in the centre, round, and about the size of the ancient Highlanders' targe, but made of reeds. The Baganda already here said that most of the new-comers were slaves, and would be sold for cloths. Extolling the size of Mtesa's country, they say it would take a year to go across it. When I joked them about it, they explained that a year meant five months, three of rain, two of dry, then rain again. Went over to apply medicine to Nkasiwa's neck to heal the outside; the inside is benefited somewhat, but the power will probably remain incomplete, as it now is.

3rd August, 1872. --Visited Salem bin Seff, who is ill of fever. They are hospitable men. Called on Sultan bin Ali and home. It is he who effected the flight of all the Baganda pagazi, by giving ten strings of beads to Motusi to go and spread a panic among them by night; all bolted.

4th August, 1872.--Wearisome waiting, and the sun is now rainy at mid-day, and will become hotter right on to the hot season in November, but this delay may be all for the best.

5th August, 1872.--Visited Nkasiwa, and recommended shampooing the disabled limbs with oil or flour. He says that the pain is removed. More Baganda have come to Kwihara, and will be used for the Mirambo war.

In many parts one is struck by the fact of the children having so few games. Life is a serious business, and amusement is derived from imitating the vocations of the parents--hut building, making little gardens, bows and arrows, shields and spears. Elsewhere boys are very ingenious little fellows, and have several games; they also shoot birds with bows, and teach captured linnets to sing. They are expert in making guns and traps for small birds, and in making and using bird-lime. They make play guns of reed, which go off with a trigger and spring, with a cloud of ashes for smoke. Sometimes they make double-barrelled guns of clay, and have cotton-fluff as smoke. The boys shoot locusts with small toy guns very cleverly. A couple of rufous, brown-headed, and dirty speckle-breasted swallows appeared to-day for the first time this season, and lighted on the ground. This is the kind that builds here in houses, and as far south as Shupanga, on the Zambesi, and at Kuraman. Sun-birds visit a mass of spiders' web to-day; they pick out the young spiders. Nectar is but part of their food. The insects in or at the nectar could not be separated, and hence have been made an essential part of their diet. On closer inspection, however, I see that whilst seeming to pick out young spiders--and they probably do so--they end in detaching the outer coating of spiders' web from the inner stiff paper web, in order to make a nest between the two. The outer part is a thin coating of loose threads: the inner is tough paper, impervious web, just like that which forms the wasps' hive, but stronger. The hen brings fine fibres and places them round a hole 1-1/2 inch in diameter, then works herself in between the two webs and brings cotton to line the inside formed by her body.

--What is the atonement of Christ? It is Himself: it is the inherent and everlasting mercy of God made apparent to human eyes and ears. The everlasting love was disclosed by our Lord's life and death. It showed that God forgives, because He loves to forgive. He works by smiles if possible, if not by frowns; pain is only a means of enforcing love.

If we speak of strength, lo! He is strong. The Almighty; the Over Power; the Mind of the Universe. The heart thrills at the idea of His greatness.

--All the great among men have been remarkable at once for the grasp and minuteness of their knowledge. Great astronomers seem to know every iota of the Knowable. The Great Duke, when at the head of armies, could give all the particulars to be observed in a cavalry charge, and took care to have food ready for all his troops. Men think that greatness consists in lofty indifference to all trivial things. The Grand Llama, sitting in immovable contemplation of nothing, is a good example of what a human mind would regard as majesty; but the Gospels reveal Jesus, the manifestation of the blessed God over all as minute in His care of all. He exercises a vigilance more constant, complete, and comprehensive, every hour and every minute, over each of His people than their utmost selflove could ever attain. His tender love is more exquisite than a mother's heart can feel.

6th August, 1872. --Wagtails begin to discard their young, which feed themselves. I can think of nothing but "when will these men come?" Sixty days was the period named, now it is eighty-four. It may be all for the best, in the good Providence of the Most High.

9th August, 1872. --I do most devoutly thank the Lord for His goodness in bringing my men near to this. Three came to-day, and how thankful I am I cannot express. It is well--the men who went with Mr. Stanley came again to me. "Bless the Lord, my soul, and all that is within me, bless His holy name." Amen.

10th August, 1872. --Sent back the three men who came from the Safari, with 4 dotis and 3 lbs. of powder. Called on the Lewale to give the news as a bit of politeness; found that the old chief Nksiwa had been bumped by an ox, and a bruise on the ribs may be serious at his age: this is another delay from the war. It is only half-heartedly that anyone goes.

[At last this trying suspense was put an end to by the arrival of a troop of fifty-seven men and boys, made up of porters hired by Mr. Stanley on the coast, and some more Nassick pupils sent from Bombay to join Lieut. Dawson. We find the names of John and Jacob Wainwright amongst the latter on Mr. Stanley's list.

Before we incorporate these new recruits on the muster-roll of Dr. Livingstone's servants, it seems right to point to five names which alone represented at this time the list of his original followers; these were Susi, Chuma, and Amoda, who joined him in 1864 on the Zambesi, that is eight years previously, and Mabruki and Gardner, Nassick boys hired in 1866. We shall see that the new comers by degrees became accustomed to the hardships of travel, and shared with the old servants all the danger of the last heroic march home. Nor must we forget that it was to the intelligence and superior education of Jacob Wainwright (whom we now meet with for the first time) that we were indebted for the earliest account of the eventful eighteen months during which he was attached to the party.

And now all is pounding, packing, bargaining, weighing, and disputing amongst the porters. Amidst the inseparable difficulties of an African start, one thankful heart gathers, comfort and courage:--]

15th August, 1872. --The men came yesterday (14th), having been seventy-four days from Bagamoio. Most thankful to the Giver of all good I am. I have to give them a rest of a few days, and then start.

16th August, 1872. --An earthquake--"Kiti-ki-sha!"--about 7.0 P.M. shook me in my katanda with quick vibrations. They gradually became fainter: it lasted some 50 seconds, and was observed by many.

17th August, 1872. --Preparing things.

18th August, 1872. --Fando to be avoided as extortionate. Went to bid adieu to Sultan bin Ali, and left goods with him for the return journey, and many cartridges full and empty, nails for boat, two iron pillars, &c[23].

19th August, 1872. --Waiting for pagazi. Sultan bin Ali called; is going off to M'futu. ***20th August, 1872.*** --Weighed all the loads again, and gave an equal load of 50 lbs. to each, and half loads to the Nassickers. Mabruki Speke is left at Taborah

---

23 Without entering into the merits of a disputed point as to whether the men on their return journey would have been brought to a standstill at Unyanyembe but for the opportune presence of Lieutenant Cameron and his party, it will be seen nevertheless that this entry fully bears out the assertion of the men that they had cloth laid by in store here for the journey to the coast.

It seems that by an unfortunate mistake a box of desiccated milk, of which the Doctor was subsequently in great need, was left behind amongst these goods. The last words written by him will remind one of the circumstance. On their return the unlucky box was the first thing that met Susi's eye!--ED.

with Sultan bin Ali. He has long been sick, and is unable to go with us.

21st August, 1872. --Gave people an ox, and to a discarded wife a cloth, to avoid exposure by her husband stripping her. She is somebody's child!

22nd August, 1872. --Sunday. All ready, but ten pagazi lacking.

23rd August, 1872. --Cannot get pagasi. Most are sent off to the war.

[At last the start took place. It is necessary to mention that Dr. Livingstone's plan in all his travels was to make one short stage the first day, and generally late in the afternoon. This, although nothing in point of distance, acted like the drill-sergeant's "Attention!" The next morning everyone was ready for the road, clear of the town, unencumbered with parting words, and by those parting pipes, of terrible memory to all hurrying Englishmen in Africa!]

25th August, 1872. --Started and went one hour to village of Manga or Yuba by a granite ridge; the weather clear, and a fine breeze from the east refreshes. It is important to give short marches at first. Marched 1-1/4 hour.

26th August, 1872. --Two Nassickers lost a cow out of ten head of cattle. Marched to Borna of Mayonda. Sent back five men to look after the cow. Cow not found: she was our best milker.

27th August, 1872. --Started for Ebulua and Kasekera of Mamba. Cross torrent, now dry, and through forest to village of Ebulua; thence to village of Kasekera, 3-1/2 hours. Direction, S. by W.

28th August, 1872. --Reached Mayole village in 2 hours and rested; S. and by W. Water is scarce in front. Through flat forest to a marshy-looking piece of water, where we camp, after a march of 1-1/2 hour; still S. by W.

29th August, 1872. --On through level forest without water. Trees present a dry, wintry aspect; grass dry, but some flowers shoot out, and fresh grass where the old growth has been burnt off.

30th August, 1872. --The two Nassickers lost all the cows yesterday, from sheer laziness. They were found a long way off, and one cow missing. Susi gave them ten cuts each with a switch. Engaging pagazi and rest.

31st August, 1872. --The Baganda boy Kassa was followed to Gunda, and I delivered him to his countrymen. He escaped from Mayole village this morning, and came at 3 P.M., his clothes in rags by running through the forest eleven hours, say twenty-two miles, and is determined not to leave us. Pass Kisari's village, one and a half mile distant, and on to Penta or Phinta to sleep, through perfectly flat forest. 3 hours S. by W.

1st September, 1872. --The same flat forest to Chikulu, S. and by W., 4 hours 25 m. Manyara called, and is going with us to-morrow. Jangiange presented a leg of Kongolo or Taghetse, having a bunch of white hair beneath the orbital sinus. Bought food and served out rations to the men for ten days, as water is scarce, and but little food can be obtained at the villages. The country is very dry and wintry-looking, but flowers shoot out. First clouds all over to-day. It is hot now. A flock of small swallows now appears: they seem tailless and with white bellies.

2nd September, 1872. --The people are preparing their ten days' food. Two pagazi ran away with 24 dotis of the men's calico. Sent after them, but with small hopes of capturing them.

3rd September, 1872. --Unsuccessful search.

4th September, 1872. --Leave Chikulu's, and pass a large puff-adder in the way. A single blow on the head killed it, so that it did not stir. About 3 feet long, and as thick as a man's arm, a short tail, and flat broad head. The men say this is a very good sign for our journey, though it would have been a bad sign, and suffering and death, had one trodden on it. Come to Liwane; large tree and waters. S.S.W. 4-1/2 hours.

5th September, 1872. --A long hot tramp to Manyara's. He is a kind old man. Many of the men very tired and sick. S.S.W. 5-3/4 hours.

6th September, 1872. --Rest the caravan, as we shall have to make forced marches on account of tsetse fly.

7th September, 1872. --Obliged to remain, as several are ill with fever.

8th September, 1872. --On to N'gombo nullah. Very hot and people ill. Tsetse. A poor woman of Ujiji followed one of Stanley's men to the coast. He cast her off here, and she was taken by another; but her temper seems too excitable. She set fire to her hut by accident, and in the excitement quarrelled all round; she is a somebody's bairn nevertheless, a tall, strapping young woman, she must have been the pride of her parents.

9th September, 1872. --Telekeza[24] at broad part of the nullah, then went on

---
24 Midday halt.

two hours and passed the night in the forest.

10th September, 1872. --On to Mweras, and spent one night there by a pool in the forest. Village two miles off.

11th September, 1872. --On 8-1/2 hours to Telekeza. Sun very hot, and marching fatiguing to all.

Majwara has an insect in the aqueous chamber of his eye. It moves about and is painful.

We found that an old path from Mwaro has water, and must go early to-morrow morning, and so avoid the roundabout by Morefu. We shall thus save two days, which in this hot weather is much for us. We hear that Simba has gone to fight with Fipa. Two Banyamwezi volunteer. ***12th September, 1872.*** --We went by this water till 2 P.M., then made a march, and to-morrow get to villages. Got a buffalo and remain overnight. Water is in haematite. I engaged four pagazi here, named Motepatonze, Nsakusi, Muanamazungu, and Mayombo.

15th September, 1872. --On to near range of hills. Much large game here. Ill.

16th September, 1872. --Climbed over range about 200 feet high; then on westward to stockaded villages of Kamirambo. His land begins at the M'toni.

17th September, 1872. --To Metambo River: 1-1/4 broad, and marshy. Here begins the land of Merera. Through forest with many strychnus trees, 3-1/4 hours, and arrive at Merera's.

18th September, 1872. --Remain at Merera's to prepare food.

[There is a significant entry here: the old enemy was upon him. It would seem that his peculiar liability during these travels to one prostrating form of disease was now redoubled. The men speak of few periods of even comparative health from this date.]

19th September, 1872. --Ditto, ditto, because I am ill with bowels, having eaten nothing for eight days. Simba wants us to pass by his village, and not by the straight path.

20th September, 1872. --Went to Simba's; 3-1/2 hours. About north-west. Simba sent a handsome present of food, a goat, eggs, and a fowl, beans, split rice, dura, and sesame. I gave him three dotis of superior cloth.

21st September, 1872. --Rest here, as the complaint does not yield to medicine or time; but I begin to eat now, which is a favourable symptom. Under a lofty tree at Simba's, a kite, the common brown one, had two pure white eggs in its nest, larger than a fowl's, and very spherical. The Banyamwesi women are in general very coarse, not a beautiful woman amongst them, as is so common among the Batusi; squat, thick-set figures, and features too; a race of pagazi. On coming inland from sea-coast, the tradition says, they cut the end of a cone shell, so as to make it a little of the half-moon shape; this is their chief ornament. They are generally respectful in deportment, but not very generous; they have learned the Arab adage, "Nothing for nothing," and are keen slave-traders. The gingerbread palm of Speke is the *Hyphene*; the Borassus has a large seed, very like the Coco-de-mer of the Seychelle Islands, in being double, but it is very small compared to it.

22nd September, 1872.--Preparing food, and one man pretends inability to walk; send for some pagazi to carry loads of those who carry him. Simba sends copious libations of pombe.

23rd September, 1872.--The pagazi, after demanding enormous pay, walked off. We went on along rocky banks of a stream, and, crossing it, camped, because the next water is far off.

24th September, 1872.--Recovering and thankful, but weak; cross broad sedgy stream, and so on to Boma Misonghi, W. and by S.

25th September, 1872.--Got a buffalo and M'jure, and remain to eat them. I am getting better slowly. The M'jure, or water hog, was all eaten by hyaenas during night; but the buffalo is safe.

26th September, 1872.--Through forest, along the side of a sedgy valley. Cross its head water, which has rust of iron in it, then W. and by S. The forest has very much tsetse. Zebras calling loudly, and Senegal long claw in our camp at dawn, with its cry, "O-o-o-o-o-o-o-o-o-o."

27th September, 1872.--On at dawn. No water expected, but we crossed three abundant supplies before we came to hill of our camp. Much game about here. Getting well again--thanks. About W. 3-3/4 hours. No people, or marks of them. Flowers sprouting in expectation of rains; much land burned off, but grass short yet.

28th September, 1872.--At two hills with mushroom-topped trees on west side. Crossed a good stream 12 feet broad and knee deep.

Buffaloes grazing. Many of the men sick. Whilst camping, a large musk cat broke forth among us and was killed. (Ya bude--musk). Musk cat (N'gawa), black with white stripes; from point of nose to tip of tail, 4 feet; height at withers, 1 foot 6 inches.

29th September, 1872.--Through much bamboo and low hills to M'pokwa ruins and river. The latter in a deep rent in alluvial soil. Very hot, and many sick in consequence. Sombala fish abundant. Course W.

30th September, 1872.--Away among low tree-covered hills of granite and sandstone. Found that Bangala had assaulted the village to which we went a few days ago, and all were fugitives. Our people found plenty of Batatas[25] in the deserted gardens. A great help, for all were hungry.

1st October, 1872, Friday--On through much deserted cultivation in rich damp soil. Surrounded with low tree-covered ranges. We saw a few people, but all are in terror.

2nd October, 1872.--Obtained M'tama in abundance for brass wire, and remained to grind it. The people have been without any for some days, and now rejoice in plenty. A slight shower fell at 5 A.M., but not enough to lay the dust.

3rd October, 1872.--Southwards, and down a steep descent into a rich valley with much green maize in ear; people friendly; but it was but one hour's march, so we went on through hilly country S.W. Men firing off ammunition, had to be punished. We crossed the Katuma River in the bottom of a valley; it is 12 feet broad, and knee deep; camped in a forest. Farjella shot a fine buffalo. The weather disagreeably hot and sultry.

4th October, 1872.--Over the same hilly country; the grass is burnt off, but the stalks are disagreeable. Came to a fine valley with a large herd of zebras feeding quietly; pretty animals. We went only an hour and a half to-day, as one sick man is carried, and it is hot and trying for all. I feel it much internally, and am glad to more slowly.

5th October, 1872.--Up and down mountains, very sore on legs and lungs. Trying to save donkey's strength I climbed and descended, and as soon as I mounted, off he set as hard as he could run, and he felt not the bridle; the saddle was loose, but I stuck on till we reached water in a bamboo hollow with spring.

6th October, 1872.--A long bamboo valley with giraffes in it. Range on our

---

25 Sweet potatoes.

right stretches away from us, and that on the left dwindled down; all covered with bamboos, in tufts like other grasses; elephants eat them. Travelled W. and by S. 2-3/4 hours. Short marches on account of carrying one sick man.

7th October, 1872. --Over fine park-like country, with large belts of bamboo and fine broad shady trees. Went westwards to the end of the left-hand range. Went four hours over a level forest with much haematite. Trees large and open. Large game evidently abounds, and waters generally are not far apart. Our neighbour got a zebra, a rhinoceros, and two young elephants.

8th October, 1872. --Came on early as sun is hot, and in two hours saw the Tanganyika from a gentle hill. The land is rough, with angular fragments of quartz; the rocks of mica schist are tilted up as if away from the Lake's longer axis. Some are upright, and some have basalt melted into the layers, and crystallized in irregular polygons. All are very tired, and in coming to a stockade we were refused admittance, because Malongwana had attacked them lately, and we might seize them when in this stronghold. Very true; so we sit ontside in the shade of a single palm (Borassus).

9th October, 1872. --Rest, because all are tired, and several sick. This heat makes me useless, and constrains me to lie like a log. Inwardly I feel tired too. Jangeange leaves us to-morrow, having found canoes going to Ujiji.

10th October, 1872. --People very tired, and it being moreover Sunday we rest. Gave each a keta of beads. Usowa chief Ponda.

11th October, 1872. --Reach Kalema district after 2-3/4 hours over black mud all deeply cracked, and many deep torrents now dry. Kalema is a stockade. We see Tanganyika, but a range of low hills intervenes. A rumour of war to-morrow.

12th October, 1872. --We wait till 2 P.M., and then make a forced march towards Fipa. The people cultivate but little, for fear of enemies; so we can buy few provisions. We left a broad valley with a sand river in it, where we have been two days, and climbed a range of hills parallel to Tanganyika, of mica schist and gneiss, tilted away from the Lake. We met a buffalo on the top of one ridge, it was shot into and lay down, but we lost it. Course S.W. to brink of Tanganyika water.

13th October, 1872. --Our course went along the top of a range of hills lying parallel with the Lake. A great part of yesterday was on the same range. It is a thousand feet above the water, and is covered with trees rather scraggy. At sunset the red glare on the surface made the water look like a sea of reddish gold; it seemed so near that many went off to drink, but were three or four hours in doing so. One cannot see the other side on account of the smokes in the air, but this morning three capes jut out, and the last bearing S.E. from our camp seems to go near the other side. Very hot weather. To the town of Fipa to-morrow. Course about S. Though we suffer much from the heat by travelling at this season, we escape a vast number of running and often muddy rills, also muddy paths which would soon knock the donkey up. A milk-and-water sky portends rain. Tipo Tipo is reported to be carrying it with a high hand in Nsama's country, Itawa, insisting that all the ivory must be brought as his tribute--the conqueror of Nsama. Our drum is the greatest object of curiosity we have to the Banyamwezi. A very great deal of cotton is cultivated all along the shores of Lake Tanganyika; it is the Pernambuco kind, with the seeds clinging together, but of good and long fibre, and the trees are left standing all the year to enable them to become large; grain and ground-nuts are cultivated between them. The cotton is manufactured into coarse cloth, which is the general clothing of all.

14th October, 1872. --Crossed two deep gullies with sluggish water in them, and one surrounding an old stockade. Camp on a knoll, overlooking modern stockade and Tanganyika very pleasantly. Saw two beautiful sultanas with azure blue necks. We might have come here yesterday, but were too tired. Mukembe land is ruled by chief Kariaria; village, Mokaria. Mount M'Pumbwe goes into the Lake. N'Tambwe Mount; village, Kafumfwe. Kapufi is the chief of Fipa.

Noon, and about fifty feet above Lake; clouded over. Temperature 91 deg. noon; 94 deg. 3 P.M.

15th October, 1872. --Rest, and kill an ox. The dry heat is distressing, and all feel it sorely. I am right glad of the rest, but keep on as constantly as I can. By giving dura and maize to the donkeys, and riding on alternate days, they hold on; but I feel the sun more than if walking. The chief Kariaria is civil.

16th October, 1872. --Leave Mokaia and go south. We crossed several bays of Tanganyika, the path winding considerably. The people set fire to our camp as soon as we started.

17th October, 1872. --Leave a bay of Tanganyika, and go on to Mpimbwe; two lions growled savagely as we passed. Game is swarming here, but my men cannot shoot except to make a noise. We found many lepidosirens in a muddy pool, which a group of vultures were catching and eating. The men speared one of them, which had scales on; its tail had been bitten off by a cannibal brother: in length it was about two feet: there were curious roe-like portions near its backbone, yellow in colour; the flesh was good. We climbed up a pass at the east end of Mpimbwe mountain, and at a rounded mass of it found water.

18th October, 1872.--Went on about south among mountains all day till we came down, by a little westing, to the Lake again, where there were some large villages, well stockaded, with a deep gully half round them. Ill with my old complaint again. Bubwe is the chief here. Food dear, because Simba made a raid lately. The country is Kilando.

19th October, 1872.--Remained to prepare food and rest the people. Two islets, Nkoma and Kalenge, are here, the latter in front of us.

20th October, 1872.--We got a water-buck and a large buffalo, and remained during the forenoon to cut up the meat, and started at 2 P.M.

Went on and passed a large arm of Tanganyika, having a bar of hills on its outer border. Country swarming with large game. Passed two bomas, and spent the night near one of them. Course east and then south.

21st October, 1872.--Mokassa, a Moganda boy, has a swelling of the ankle, which prevents his walking. We went one hour to find wood to make a litter for him. The bomas round the villages are plastered with mud, so as to intercept balls or arrows. The trees are all cut down for these stockades, and the flats are cut up with deep gullies. A great deal of cotton is cultivated, of which the people make their cloth. There is an arm of Tanganyika here called Kafungia.

I sent a doti to the headman of the village, where we made the litter, to ask for a guide to take us straight south instead of going east to Fipa, which is four days off and out of our course. Tipo Tipo is said to be at Morero, west of Tanganyika.

22nd October, 1872.--Turned back westwards, and went through the hills down to some large islets in the Lake, and camped in villages destroyed by Simba. A great deal of cotton is cultivated here, about thirty feet above the Lake.

23rd October, 1872.--First east, and then passed two deep bays, at one of which we put up, as they had food to sell. The sides of the Tanganyika Lake are a succession of rounded bays, answering to the valleys which trend down to the shore between the numerous ranges of hills. In Lake Nyassa they seem made by the prevailing winds. We only get about one hour and a half south and by east. Rain probably fell last night, for the opposite shore is visible to-day. The mountain range of Banda slopes down as it goes south. This is the district of Motoshi. Wherever buffaloes are to be caught, falling traps are suspended over the path in the trees near the water.

24th October, 1872.--There are many rounded bays in mountainous Fipa. We rested two hours in a deep shady dell, and then came along a very slippery mountain-side to a village in a stockade. It is very hot to-day, and the first thunderstorm away in the east. The name of this village is Linde.

25th October, 1872.--The coast runs south-south-east to a cape. We went up south-east, then over a high steep hill to turn to south again, then down into a valley of Tanganyika, over another stony side, and down to a dell with a village in it. The west coast is very plain to-day; rain must have fallen there.

26th October, 1872.--Over hills and mountains again, past two deep bays, and on to a large bay with a prominent islet on the south side of it, called Kitanda, from the chiefs name. There is also a rivulet of fine water of the same name here.

27th October, 1872.--Remained to buy food, which is very dear. We slaughtered a tired cow to exchange for provisions.

28th October, 1872.--Left Kitanda, and came round the cape, going south. The cape furthest north bore north-north-west. We came to three villages and some large spreading trees, where we were invited by the headman to remain, as the next stage along the shore is long. Morilo islet is on the other or western side, at the crossing-place. The people brought in a leopard in great triumph. Its mouth and all its claws were bound with grass and bands of bark, as if to make it quite safe, and its tail was curled round: drumming and lullilooing in plenty.

The chief Mosirwa, or Kasamane, paid us a visit, and is preparing a present of food. One of his men was bitten by the leopard in the arm before he killed it. Molilo or Morilo islet is the crossing-place of Banyamwezi when bound for Casembe's country, and is near to the Lofuko River, on the western shore of the Lake. The Lake is about twelve or fifteen miles broad, at latitude 7 deg. 52' south. Tipo Tipo is ruling in Itawa, and bound a chief in chains, but loosed him on being requested to do so by Syde bin Ali. It takes about three hours to cross at Morilo.

29th October, 1872. --Crossed the Thembwa Rivulet, twenty feet broad and knee deep, and sleep on its eastern bank. Fine cold water over stony bottom. The mountains now close in on Tanganyika, so there is no path but one, over which luggage cannot be carried. The stage after this is six hours up hill before we come to water. This forced me to stop after only a short crooked march of two and a quarter hours. We are now on the confines of Fipa. The next march takes us into Burungu.

30th October, 1872. --The highest parts of the mountains are from 500 feet to 700 feet higher than the passes, say from 1300 feet to 1500 feet above the Lake. A very rough march to-day; one cow fell, and was disabled. The stones are collected in little heaps and rows, which shows that all these rough mountains were cultivated. We arrive at a village on the Lake shore. Kirila islet is about a quarter of a mile from the shore. The Megunda people cultivated these hills in former times. Thunder all the morning, and a few drops of rain fell. It will ease the men's feet when it does fall. They call out earnestly for it, "Come, come with hail!" and prepare their huts for it.

31st October, 1872. --Through a long pass after we had climbed over Winelao. Came to an islet one and a half mile long, called Kapessa, and then into a long pass. The population of Megunda must have been prodigious, for all the stones have been cleared, and every available inch of soil cultivated.

The population are said to have been all swept away by the Matuta.

Going south we came to a very large arm of the Lake, with a village at the end of it in a stockade. This arm is seven or eight miles long and about two broad. We killed a cow to-day, and found peculiar flat worms in the substance of the liver, and some that were rounded.

CHAPTER X.

False guides. Very difficult travelling. Donkey dies of tsetse bites. The Kasonso family. A hospitable chief. The River Lofu. The nutmeg tree. Famine. Ill. Arrives at Chama's town. A difficulty. An immense snake. Account of Casembe's death. The flowers of the Babisa country. Reaches the River Lopoposi. Arrives at Chitunkue's. Terrible marching. The Doctor is borne through the flooded country.

1st November, 1872. --We hear that an eruption of Babemba, on the Baulungu, destroyed all the food. We tried to buy food here, but everything is hidden in the mountains, so we have to wait to-day till they fetch it. If in time, we shall make an afternoon's march. Raining to-day. The Eiver Mulu from Chingolao gave us much trouble in crossing from being filled with vegetation: it goes into Tanganyika. Our course south and east.

2nd November, 1872. --Deceived by a guide, who probably feared his countrymen in front. Went round a stony cape, and then to a land-locked harbour, three miles long by two broad. Here was a stockade, where our guide absconded. They told us that if we continued our march we should not get water for four hours, so we rested, having marched four and a quarter hours.

3rd November, 1872. --We marched this morning to a village where food was reported. I had to punish two useless men for calling out, "Posho! posho! posho!" (rations) as soon as I came near. One is a confirmed bange-smoker[26]; the blows were given slightly, but I promised that the next should be severe. The people of Liemba village having a cow or two, and some sheep and goats, eagerly advised us to go on to the next village, as being just behind a hill, and well provisioned. Four very rough

---

26 Bange or hemp in time produces partial idiotcy if smoked in excess. It is used amongst all the Interior tribes.

hills were the penalty of our credulity, taking four hours of incessant toil in these mountain fastnesses. They hide their food, and the paths are the most difficult that can be found, in order to wear out their enemies. To-day we got to the River Luazi, having marched five and a half hours, and sighting Tanganyika near us twice.

4th November, 1872. --All very tired. We tried to get food, but it is very dear, and difficult to bargain for. Goods are probably brought from Fipa. A rest will be beneficial to us.

5th November, 1872. --We went up a high mountain, but found that one of the cows could not climb up, so I sent back and ordered it to be slaughtered, waiting on the top of the mountain whilst the people went down for water.

6th November, 1872. --Pass a deep narrow bay and climb a steep mountain. Too much for the best donkey. After a few hours' climb we look down on the Lake, with its many bays. A sleepy glare floats over it. Further on we came on a ledge of rocks, and looked sheer down 500 feet or 600 feet into its dark green waters. We saw three zebras and a young python here, and fine flowers.

7th November, 1872, Sunday. --Remained, but the headman forbade his people to sell us food. We keep quiet except to invite him to a parley, which he refuses, and makes loud lullilooing in defiance, as if he were inclined to fighting. At last, seeing that we took no notice of him, he sent us a present; I returned three times its value.

8th November, 1872. --The large donkey is very ill, and unable to climb the high mountain in our front. I left men to coax him on, and they did it well. I then sent some to find a path out from the Lake mountains, for they will kill us all; others were despatched to buy food, but the Lake folks are poor except in fish.

Swifts in flocks were found on the Lake when we came to it, and there are small migrations of swallows ever since. Though this is the very hottest time of year, and all the plants are burnt off or quite dried, the flowers persist in bursting out of the hot dry surface, generally without leaves. A purple ginger, with two yellow patches inside, is very lovely to behold, and it is alternated with one of a bright canary yellow; many trees, too, put on their blossoms. The sun makes the soil so hot that the radiation is as if it came from a furnace. It burns the feet of the people, and knocks them up. Subcutaneous inflammation is frequent in the legs, and makes some of my most hardy men useless. We have been compelled to slowness very much against my will. I too was ill, and became better only by marching on foot. Riding exposes one to the bad influence of the sun, while by walking the perspiration modifies beneficially the excessive heat. It is like the difference in effect of cold if one is in activity or sitting, and falling asleep on a stage-coach. I know ten hot fountains north of the Orange River; the further north the more hot and numerous they become.

[Just here we find a note, which does not bear reference to anything that occurred at this time. Men, in the midst of their hard earnest toil, perceive great truths with a sharpness of outline and a depth of conviction which is denied to the mere idle theorist: he says:--]

The spirit of Missions is the spirit of our Master: the very genius of His religion. A diffusive philanthropy is Christianity itself. It requires perpetual propagation to attest its genuineness.

9th November, 1872. --We got very little food, and kill a calf to fill our mouths a little. A path east seems to lead out from these mountains of Tanganyika. We went on east this morning in highland open forest, then descended by a long slope to a valley in which there is water. Many Milenga gardens, but the people keep out of sight. The highlands are of a purple colour from the new leaves coming out. The donkey began to eat to my great joy. Men sent off to search for a village return empty-handed, and we must halt. I am ill and losing much blood.

10th November, 1872. --Out from the Lake mountains, and along high ridges of sandstone and dolomite. Our guide volunteered to take the men on to a place where food can be bought--a very acceptable offer. The donkey is recovering; it was distinctly the effects of tsetse, for the eyes and all the mouth and nostrils swelled. Another died at Kwihara with every symptom of tsetse poison fully developed.

[The above remarks on the susceptibility of the donkey to the bite of the tsetse fly are exceedingly important. Hitherto Dr. Livingstone had always maintained, as the result of his own observations, that this animal, at all events, could be taken through districts in which horses, mules, dogs, and oxen would perish to a certainty. With the keen perception and perseverance of one who was exploring Africa with a view to open it up for Europeans, he laid great stress on these experiments, and there is no doubt that the distinct result which he here arrived at must have a very significant bearing on the question of travel and transport.

Still passing through the same desolate country, we see that he makes a note on the forsaken fields and the watch-towers in them. Cucumbers are cultivated in large quantities by the natives of Inner Africa, and the reader will no doubt call to mind the simile adopted by Isaiah some 2500 years ago, as he pictured the coming desolation of Zion, likening her to a "lodge in a garden of cucumbers."[27]]

11th November, 1872. --Over gently undulating country, with many old gardens and watch-houses, some of great height, we reached the River Kalambo, which I know as falling into Tanganyika. A branch joins it at the village of Mosapasi; it is deep, and has to be crossed by a bridge, whilst the Kalambo is shallow, and say twenty yards wide, but it spreads out a good deal.

[Their journey of the **12th** and **13th** led them over low ranges of sandstone and haematite, and past several strongly stockaded villages. The weather was cloudy and showery--a relief, no doubt, after the burning heat of the last few weeks. They struck the Halocheche River, a rapid stream fifteen yards wide and thigh deep, on its way to the Lake, and arrived at Zombe's town, which is built in such a manner that the river runs through it, whilst a stiff palisade surrounds it. He says:--]

It was entirely surrounded by M'toka's camp, and a constant fight maintained at the point where the line of stakes was weakened by the river running through. He killed four of the enemy, and then Chitimbwa and Kasonso coming to help him, the siege was raised.

M'toka compelled some Malongwana to join him, and plundered many villages; he has been a great scourge. He also seems to have made an attack upon an Arab caravan, plundering it of six bales of cloth and one load of beads, telling them that if they wanted to get their things back they must come and help him conquer Zombe. The siege lasted three months, till the two brothers of Zombe, before-mentioned, came, and then a complete rout ensued. M'toka left nearly all his guns behind him; his allies, the Malongwana, had previously made their escape. It is two months since this rout, so we have been prevented by a kind Providence from coming soon enough. He was impudent and extortionate before, and much more now that he has been emboldened by success in plundering.

16th November, 1872. --After waiting some time for the men I sent men back yesterday to look after the sick donkey, they arrived, but the donkey died this morning. Its death was evidently caused by tsetse bite and bad usage by one of the

---

27 Isaiah i. 8.

men, who kept it forty-eight hours without water. The rain, no doubt, helped to a fatal end; it is a great loss to me.

17th November, 1872. --We went on along the bottom of a high ridge that flanks the Lake on the west, and then turned up south-east to a village hung on the edge of a deep chasm in which flows the Aeezy.

18th November, 1872. --We were soon overwhelmed in a pouring rain, and had to climb up the slippery red path which is parallel and near to Mbette's. One of the men picked up a little girl who had been deserted by her mother. As she was benumbed by cold and wet he carried her; but when I came up he threw her into the grass. I ordered a man to carry her, and we gave her to one of the childless women; she is about four years old, and not at all negro-looking. Our march took us about S.W. to Kampamba's, the son of Kasonso, who is dead.

19th November, 1872. --I visited Kampamba. He is still as agreeable as he was before when he went with us to Liemba. I gave him two cloths as a present. He has a good-sized village. There are heavy rains now and then every day.

20th, 21st, and 23rd November, 1872. --The men turn to stringing beads for future use, and to all except defaulters I give a present of 2 dotis, and a handful of beads each. I have diminished the loads considerably, which pleases them much. We have now 3-1/2 loads of calico, and 120 bags of beads. Several go idle, but have to do any odd work, such as helping the sick or anything they are ordered to do. I gave the two Nassickers who lost the cow and calf only 1 doti, they were worth 14 dotis. One of our men is behind, sick with dysentery. I am obliged to leave him, but have sent for him twice, and have given him cloth and beads.

24th November, 1872. --Left Kampamba's to-day, and cross a meadow S.E. of the village in which the River Muanani rises. It flows into the Kapondosi and so on to the Lake. We made good way with Kiteneka as our guide, who formerly accompanied Kampamba and ourselves to Liemba. We went over a flat country once covered with trees, but now these have all been cut down, say 4 to 5 feet from the ground, most likely for clearing, as the reddish soil is very fertile. Long lines of hills of denudation are in the distance, all directed to the Lake.

We came at last to Kasonso's successor's village on the River Molulwe, which is, say, thirty yards wide, and thigh deep. It goes to the Lofu. The chief here gave a sheep--a welcome present, for I was out of flesh for four days. Kampamba is stingy as compared with his father.

25th November, 1872.--We came in an hour's march to a rivulet called the Casembe--the departed Kasonso lived here. The stream is very deep, and flows slowly to the Lofu. Our path lay through much pollarded forest, troublesome to walk in, as the stumps send out leafy shoots.

26th November, 1872.--Started at daybreak. The grass was loaded with dew, and a heavy mist hung over everything. Passed two villages of people come out to cultivate this very fertile soil, which they manure by burning branches of trees. The Rivulet Loela flows here, and is also a tributary of the Lofu.

27th November, 1872.--As it is Sunday we stay here at N'dari's village, for we shall be in an uninhabited track to-morrow, beyond the Lofu. The headman cooked six messes for us and begged us to remain for more food, which we buy. He gave us a handsome present of flour and a fowl, for which I return him a present of a doti. Very heavy rain and high gusts of wind, which wet us all.

28th November, 1872.--We came to the River Lofu in a mile. It is sixty feet across and very deep. We made a bridge, and cut the banks down, so that the donkey and cattle could pass over. It took us two hours, during which time we hauled them all across with a rope. We were here misled by our guide, who took us across a marsh covered with tufts of grass, but with deep water between that never dries; there is a path which goes round it. We came to another village with a river which must be crossed--no stockade here, and the chief allowed us to camp in his town. There are long low lines of hills all about. A man came to the bridge to ask for toll-fee: as it was composed of one stick only, and unfit for our use because rotten, I agreed to pay provided he made it fit for our large company; but if I re-made and enlarged it, I said he ought to give me a goat for the labour. He slunk away, and we laid large trees across, where previously there was but one rotten pole.

29th November, 1872.--Crossed the Loozi in two branches, and climbed up the gentle ascent of Malembe to the village of Chiwe, whom I formerly called Chibwe, being misled by the Yao tongue. Ilamba is the name of the rill at his place. The Loozi's two branches were waist deep. The first was crossed by a natural bridge of a fig-tree growing across. It runs into the Lofu, which river rises in Isunga country at a mountain called Kwitette. The Chambeze rises east of this, and at the same place as Louzua.

Chiwe presented a small goat with crooked legs and some millet flour, but he grumbled at the size of the fathom cloth I gave. I offered another fathom, and a bundle of needles, but he grumbled at this too, and sent it back. On this I returned his goat and marched.

[The road lay through the same country among low hills, for several miles, till they came on the **1st December** to a rivulet called Lovu Katanta, where curiously enough they found a nutmeg-tree in full bearing. A wild species is found at Angola on the West Coast and it was probably of this description, and not the same species as that which is cultivated in the East. In two places he says:--]

Who planted the nutmeg-tree on the Katanta?

[Passing on with heavy rain pouring down, they now found themselves in the Wemba country, the low tree-covered hills exhibiting here and there "fine-grained schist and igneous rocks of red, white, and green colour."]

3rd December, 1872.--No food to be got on account of M'toka's and Tipo Tipo's raids.

A stupid or perverse guide took us away to-day N.W. or W.N.W. The villagers refused to lead us to Chipwite's, where food was to be had; he is S.W. 1-1/2 day off. The guide had us at his mercy, for he said, "If you go S.W. you will be five days without food or people." We crossed the Kanomba, fifteen yards wide, and knee deep. Here our guide disappeared, and so did the path. We crossed the Lampussi twice; it is forty yards wide, and knee deep; our course is W.N.W. for about 4-1/2 hours to-day. We camped and sent men to search for a village that has food. My third barometer (aneroid) is incurably injured by a fall, the man who carried it slipped upon a clayey path.

4th December, 1872.--Waiting for the return of our men in a green wooded valley on the Lampussi River. Those who were sent yesterday return without anything; they were directed falsely by the country people, where nought could be bought. The people themselves are living on grubs, roots, and fruits. The young plasterer Sphex is very fat on coming out of its clay house, and a good relish for food. A man came to us demanding his wife and child; they are probably in hiding; the slaves of Tipo Tipo have been capturing people. One sinner destroyeth much good!

5th December, 1872.--The people eat mushrooms and leaves. My men returned about 5 P.M. with two of Kafimbe's men bringing a present of food to me. A little was bought, and we go on to-morrow to sleep two nights on the way, and so to Kafimbe, who is a brother of Nsama's, and fights him.

6th December, 1872. --We cross the Lampussi again, and up to a mountain along which we go, and then down to some ruins. This took us five hours, and then with 2-1/4 more hours we reach Sintila. We hasten along as fast as hungry men (four of them sick) can go to get food.

1th December, 1872. --Off at 6.15 A.M. A leopard broke in upon us last night and bit a woman. She screamed, and so did the donkey, and it ran off. Our course lay along between two ranges of low hills, then, where they ended, we went by a good-sized stream thirty yards or so across, and then down into a valley to Kafimbe's.

8th December, 1872. --Very heavy rains. I visited Kafimbe. He is an intelligent and pleasant young man, who has been attacked several times by Kitandula, the successor of Nsama of Itawa, and compelled to shift from Motononga to this rivulet Motosi, which flows into the Kisi and thence into Lake Moero.

9th December, 1872. --Send off men to a distance for food, and wait of course. Here there is none for either love or money. To-day a man came from the Arab party at Kumba-Kumba's with a present of M'chele and a goat. He reports that they have killed Casembe, whose people concealed from him the approach of the enemy till they were quite near. Having no stockade, he fell an easy prey to them. The conquerors put his head and all his ornaments on poles. His pretty wife escaped over Mofwe, and the slaves of the Arabs ran riot everywhere. We sent a return present of two dotis of cloth, one jorah of Kanike, one doti of coloured cloth, three pounds of beads, and a paper of needles.

10th December, 1872. --Left Kafimbe's. He gave us three men to take us into Chama's village, and came a mile along the road with us. Our road took us by a winding course from one little deserted village to another.

11th December, 1872. --Being far from water we went two hours across a plain dotted with villages to a muddy rivulet called the Mukubwe (it runs to Moero), where we found the village of a nephew of Nsama. This young fellow was very liberal in gifts of food, and in return I gave him two cloths. An Arab, Juma bin Seff, sent a goat to-day. They have been riding it roughshod over all the inhabitants, and confess it.

12th December, 1872.--Marenza sent a present of dura flour and a fowl, and asked for a little butter as a charm. He seems unwilling to give us a guide, though told by Kafimbe to do so. Many Garaganza about: they trade in leglets, ivory, and slaves. We went on half-an-hour to the River Mokoe, which is thirty yards wide, and carries off much water into Malunda, and so to Lake Moero.

When palm-oil palms are cut down for toddy, they are allowed to lie three days, then the top shoot is cut off smoothly, and the toddy begins to flow; and it flows for a month, or a month and a half or so, lying on the soil.

[The note made on the following day is written with a feeble hand, and scarce one pencilled word tallies with its neighbour in form or distinctness--in fact, it is seen at a glance what exertion it cost him to write at all. He says no more than "Ill" in one place, but this is the evident explanation; yet with the same painstaking determination of old, the three rivers which they crossed have their names recorded, and the hours of marching and the direction are all entered in his pocket book.]

13th December, 1872.--Westward about by south, and crossed a river, Mokobwe, thirty-five yards. Ill, and after going S.W. camped in a deserted village, S.W. travelling five hours. River Mekanda 2nd. Menomba 3, where we camp.

14th December, 1872.--Guides turned N.W. to take us to a son of Nsama, and so play the usual present into his hands. I objected when I saw their direction, but they said, "The path turns round in front." After going a mile along the bank of the Menomba, which has much water, Susi broke through and ran south, till he got a S. by W. path, which we followed, and came to a village having plenty of food. As we have now camped in village, we sent the men off to recall the fugitive women, who took us for Komba-Komba's men. Crossed the Lupere, which runs into the Makobwe.

A leech crawling towards me in the village this morning elicited the Bemba idea that they fall from the clouds or sky--"mulu." It is called here "Mosunda a maluze," or leech of the rivers; "Luba" is the Zanzibar name. In one place I counted nineteen leeches in our path, in about a mile; rain had fallen, and their appearance out of their hiding-places suddenly after heavy rain may have given rise to the idea of their fall with it as fishes do, and the thunder frog is supposed to do. Always too cloudy and rainy for observations of stars.

15th December, 1872.--The country is now level, covered with trees pollarded for clothing, and to make ashes of for manure. There are many deserted villages, few birds. Cross the Eiver Lithabo, thirty yards wide and thigh deep, running fast to the S.W., joined by a small one near. Reached village of Chipala, on the Rivulet Chikatula, which goes to Moipanza. The Lithabo goes to Kalongwesi by a S.W. course.

16th December, 1872.--Off at 6 A.M. across the Chikatula, and in three-quarters of an hour crossed the Lopanza, twelve yards wide and waist deep, being now in flood. The Lolela was before us in half-an-hour, eight yards wide and thigh deep, both streams perennial and embowered in tall umbrageous trees that love wet; both flow to the Kalongwesi.

We came to quite a group of villages having food, and remain, as we got only driblets in the last two camps. Met two Banyamwezi carrying salt to Lobemba, of Moambu. They went to Kabuire for it, and now retail it on the way back.

At noon we got to the village of Kasiane, which is close to two rivulets, named Lopanza and Lolela. The headman, a relative of Nsama, brought me a large present of flour of dura, and I gave him two fathoms of calico.

Floods by these sporadic rainfalls have discoloured waters, as seen in Lopanza and Lolela to-day. The grass is all springing up quickly, and the Maleza growing fast. The trees generally in full foliage. Different shades of green, the dark prevailing; especially along rivulets, and the hills in the distance are covered with dark blue haze. Here, in Lobemba, they are gentle slopes of about 200 or 300 feet, and sandstone crops out over their tops. In some parts clay schists appear, which look as if they had been fused or were baked by intense heat.

The pugnacious spirit is one of the necessities of life. When people have little or none of it, they are subjected to indignity and loss. My own men walk into houses where we pass the nights without asking any leave, and steal cassava without shame. I have to threaten and thrash to keep them honest, while if we are at a village where the natives are a little pugnacious they are as meek as sucking doves. The peace plan involves indignity and wrong. I give little presents to the headmen, and to some extent heal their hurt sensibilities. This is indeed much appreciated, and produces profound hand-clapping.

17th December, 1872.--It looked rainy, but we waited half-an-hour, and then went on one hour and a half, when it set in and forced us to seek shelter in a village.

The head of it was very civil, and gave us two baskets of cassava, and one of dura. I gave a small present first. The district is called Kisinga, and flanks the Kalongweze.

18th December, 1872. --Over same flat pollarded forest until we reached the Kalongwese Kiver on the right bank, and about a quarter of a mile east of the confluence of the Luena or Kisaka. This side of the river is called Kisinga, the other is Chama's and Kisinga too. The Luena comes from Jange in Casembe's land, or W.S.W. of this. The Kalongwese comes from the S.E. of this, and goes away N.W. The donkey sends a foot every now and then through the roof of cavities made apparently by ants, and sinks down 18 inches or more and nearly falls. These covered hollows are right in the paths.

19th December, 1872. --So cloudy and wet that no observations can be taken for latitude and longitude at this real geographical point. The Kalongwese is sixty or eighty yards wide and four yards deep, about a mile above the confluence of the Luena. We crossed it in very small canoes, and swamped one twice, but no one was lost. Marched S. about 1-1/4 hour.

20th December, 1872. --Shut in by heavy clouds. Wait to see if it will clear up. Went on at 7.15, drizzling as we came near the Mozumba or chiefs stockade. A son of Chama tried to mislead us by setting out west, but the path being grass-covered I objected, and soon came on to the large clear path. The guide ran off to report to the son, but we kept on our course, and he and the son followed us. We were met by a party, one of whom tried to regale us by vociferous singing and trumpeting on an antelope's horn, but I declined the deafening honour. Had we suffered the misleading we should have come here to-morrow afternoon.

A wet bed last night, for it was in the canoe that was upset. It was so rainy that there was no drying it.

21st December, 1872. --Arrived at Chama's. Heavy clouds drifting past, and falling drizzle. Chama's brother tried to mislead us yesterday, in hopes of making us wander hopelessly and helplessly. Failing in this, from my refusal to follow a grass-covered path, he ran before us to the chief's stockade, and made all the women flee, which they did, leaving their chickens damless. We gave him two handsome cloths, one for himself and one for Chama, and said we wanted food only, and would buy it. They are accustomed to the bullying of half-castes, who take what they like for nothing. They are alarmed at our behaviour to-day, so we took quiet possession of the stockade, as the place that they put us in was on the open defenceless plain. Seventeen human skulls ornament the stockade. They left their fowls, and pigeons. There was no bullying. Our women went in to grind food, and came out without any noise. This flight seems to be caused by the foolish brother of the chief, and it is difficult to prevent stealing by my horde. The brother came drunk, and was taking off a large sheaf of arrows, when we scolded and prevented him.

22nd December, 1872. --We crossed a rivulet at Chama's village ten yards wide and thigh deep, and afterwards in an hour and a half came to a sedgy stream which we could barely cross. We hauled a cow across bodily. Went on mainly south, and through much bracken.

23rd December, 1872. --Off at 6 A.M. in a mist, and in an hour and a quarter came to three large villages by three rills called Misangwa, and much sponge; went on to other villages south, and a stockade.

24th December, 1872. --Cloud in sky with drifting clouds from S. and S.W. Very wet and drizzling. Sent back Chama's arrows, as his foolish brother cannot use them against us now; there are 215 in the bundle. Passed the Lopopussi running west to the Lofubu about seven yards wide, it flows fast over rocks with heavy aquatic plants. The people are not afraid of us here as they were so distressingly elsewhere: we hope to buy food here.

25th December, 1872, Christmas Day. --I thank the good Lord for the good gift of His Son Christ Jesus our Lord. Slaughtered an ox, and gave a fundo and a half to each of the party. This is our great day, so we rest. It is cold and wet, day and night. The headman is gracious and generous, which is very pleasant compared with awe, awe, and refusing to sell, or stop to speak, or show the way.

The White Nile carrying forward its large quasi-tidal wave presents a mass of water to the Blue Nile, which acts as a buffer to its rapid flood. The White Nile being at a considerable height when the Blue rushes down its steep slopes, presents its brother Nile with a soft cushion into which it plunges, and is restrained by the *vis inertiae* of the more slowly moving river, and, both united, pass on to form the great inundation of the year in Lower Egypt. The Blue River brings down the heavier portion of the Nile deposit, while the White River comes down with the black finely divided matter from thousands of square miles of forest in Manyuema, which probably gave the Nile its name, and is in fact the real fertilizing ingredient in the mud that is annually left. Some of the rivers in Manyuema, as the Luia and Machila, are of inky blackness, and make the whole main stream of a very Nilotic hue. An acquaintance with these dark flowing rivers, and scores of rills of water tinged as dark as strong tea, was all my reward for plunging through the terrible Manyuema mud or "glaur."

26th December, 1872.--Along among the usual low tree-covered hills of red and yellow and green schists--paths wet and slippery. Came to the Lofubu, fifteen yards broad and very deep, water clear, flowing north-west to join Luena or Kisaka, as the Lopopussi goes west too into Lofubu it becomes large as we saw. We crossed by a bridge, and the donkey swam with men on each side of him. We came to three villages on the other side with many iron furnaces. Wet and drizzling weather made us stop soon. A herd of buffaloes, scared by our party, rushed off and broke the trees in their hurry, otherwise there is no game or marks of game visible.

27th December, 1872.--Leave the villages on the Lofubu. A cascade comes down on our left. The country undulating deeply, the hills, rising at times 300 to 400 feet, are covered with stunted wood. There is much of the common bracken fern and hart's-tongue. We cross one rivulet running to the Lofubu, and camp by a blacksmith's rill in the jungle. No rain fell to-day for a wonder, but the lower tier of clouds still drifts past from N.W.

I killed a Naia Hadje snake seven feet long here, he reared up before me and turned to fight. The under north-west stratum of clouds is composed of fluffy cottony masses, the edges spread out as if on an electrical machine--the upper or southeast is of broad fields like striated cat's hair. The N.W. flies quickly, the S.E. slowly away where the others come from. No observations have been possible through most of this month. People assert that the new moon will bring drier weather, and the clouds are preparing to change the N.W. lower stratum into S.E., ditto, ditto, and the N.W. will be the upper tier.

A man, ill and unable to come on, was left all night in the rain, without fire. We sent men back to carry him. Wet and cold. We are evidently ascending as we come near the Chambeze. The N.E. clouds came up this morning to meet the N.W. and thence the S.E. came across as if combating the N.W. So as the new moon comes soon, it may be a real change to drier weather.

4 P.M.--The man carried in here is very ill; we must carry him to-morrow.

29th December, 1872. --Our man Chipangawazi died last night and was buried this morning. He was a quiet good man, his disease began at Kampamba's. New moon last night.

29th, or 1st January, 1873. --I am wrong two days.

29th December, 1872. --After the burial and planting four branches of Moringa at the corners of the grave we went on southwards 3-1/4 hours to a river, the Luongo, running strongly west and south to the Luapula, then after one hour crossed it, twelve yards wide and waist deep. We met a man with four of his kindred stripping off bark to make bark-cloth: he gives me the above information about the Luongo.

1st January, 1873. (30th.)--Came on at 6 A.M. very cold. The rains have ceased for a time. Arrive at the village of the man who met us yesterday. As we have been unable to buy food, through the illness and death of Chipangawazi, I camp here.

2nd January, 1873. --Thursday--Wednesday was the 1st, I was two days wrong.

3rd January, 1873. --The villagers very anxious to take us to the west to Chikumbi's, but I refused to follow them, and we made our course to the Luongo. Went into the forest south without a path for 1-1/2 hour, then through a flat forest, much fern and no game. We camped in the forest at the Situngula Rivulet. A little quiet rain through the night. A damp climate this--lichens on all the trees, even on those of 2 inches diameter. Our last cow died of injuries received in crossing the Lofubu. People buy it for food, so it is not an entire loss.

4th January, 1873. --March south one hour to the Lopoposi or Lopopozi stream of 25 or 30 feet, and now breast deep, flowing fast southwards to join the Chambeze. Camped at Ketebe's at 2 P.M. on the Rivulet Kizima after very heavy rain.

5th January, 1873. --A woman of our party is very ill; she will require to be carried to-morrow.

6th January, 1873. --Ketebe or Kapesha very civil and generous. He sent three men to guide us to his elder brother Chungu. The men drum and sing harshly for him continually. I gave him half-a-pound of powder, and he lay on his back rolling and clapping his hands, and all his men lulliloed; then he turned on his front, and did the same. The men are very timid--no wonder, the Arab slaves do as they choose with them. The women burst out through, the stockade in terror when my men broke into a chorus as they were pitching my tent. Cold, cloudy, and drizzling. Much cultivation far from the stockades.

The sponges here are now full and overflowing, from the continuous and heavy rains. Crops of mileza, maize, cassava, dura, tobacco, beans, ground-nuts, are growing finely. A border is made round each patch, manured by burning the hedge, and castor-oil plants, pumpkins, calabashes, are planted in it to spread out over the grass.

7th January, 1873. --A cold rainy day keeps us in a poor village very unwillingly. 3 P.M. Fair, after rain all the morning--on to the Rivulet Kamalopa, which runs to Kamolozzi and into Kapopozi.

8th January, 1873. --Detained by heavy continuous rains in the village Moenje. We are near Lake Bangweolo and in a damp region. Got off in the afternoon in a drizzle; crossed a rill six feet wide, but now very deep, and with large running sponges on each side; it is called the Kamalopa, then one hour beyond came to a sponge, and a sluggish rivulet 100 yards broad with broad sponges on either bank waist deep, and many leeches. Came on through flat forest as usual S.W. and S.

[We may here call attention to the alteration of the face of the country and the prominent notice of "sponges." His men speak of the march from this point as one continual plunge in and out of morass, and through rivers which were only distinguishable from the surrounding waters by their deep currents and the necessity for using canoes. To a man reduced in strength and chronically affected with dysenteric symptoms ever likely to be aggravated by exposure, the effect may be well conceived! It is probable that had Dr. Livingstone been at the head of a hundred picked Europeans, every man would have been down within the next fortnight. As it is, we cannot help thinking of his company of followers, who must have been well led and under the most thorough control to endure these marches at all, for nothing cows the African so much as rain. The next day's journey may be taken as a specimen of the hardships every one had to endure:--]

9th January, 1873. --Mosumba of Chungu. After an hour we crossed the rivulet and sponge of Nkulumuna, 100 feet of rivulet and 200 yards of flood, besides some 200 yards of sponge full and running off; we then, after another hour, crossed the large rivulet Lopopozi by a bridge which was 45 feet long, and showed the deep water; then 100 yards of flood thigh deep, and 200 or 300 yards of sponge. After this we crossed two rills called Linkanda and their sponges, the rills in flood 10 or 12 feet broad and thigh deep. After crossing the last we came near the Mosumba, and received a message to build our sheds in the forest, which we did.

Chungu knows what a nuisance a Safari (caravan) makes itself. Cloudy day, and at noon heavy rain from N.W. The headman on receiving two cloths said he would converse about our food and show it to-morrow. No observations can be made, from clouds and rain.

10th January, 1873. --Mosumba of Chungu. Rest to-day and get an insight into the ford: cold rainy weather. When we prepared to visit Chungu, we received a message that he had gone to his plantations to get millet. He then sent for us at 1 P.M. to come, but on reaching the stockade we heard a great Kelele, or uproar, and found it being shut from terror. We spoke to the inmates but in vain, so we returned. Chungu says that we should put his head on a pole like Casembe's! We shall go on without him to-morrow. The terror guns have inspired is extreme.

11th January, 1873. --Chungu sent a goat and big basket of flour, and excused his fears because guns had routed Casembe and his head was put on a pole; it was his young men that raised the noise. We remain to buy food, as there is scarcity at Mombo, in front. Cold and rainy weather, never saw the like; but this is among the sponges of the Nile and near the northern shores of Bangweolo.

12th January, 1873. --A dry day enabled us to move forward an hour to a rivulet and sponge, but by ascending it we came to its head and walked over dry-shod, then one hour to another broad rivulet--Pinda, sluggish, and having 100 yards of sponge on each side. This had a stockaded village, and the men in terror shut the gates. Our men climbed over and opened them, but I gave the order to move forward through flat forest till we came to a running rivulet of about twenty feet, but with 100 yards of sponge on each side. The white sand had come out as usual and formed the bottom. Here we entered a village to pass the night. We passed mines of fine black iron ore ("motapo"); it is magnetic.

13th January, 1873. --Storm-stayed by rain and cold at the village on the Rivulet Kalambosi, near the Chambeze. Never was in such a spell of cold rainy weather except in going to Loanda in 1853. Sent back for food.

14th January, 1873. --Went on dry S.E. and then S. two hours to River Mozinga, and marched parallel to it till we came to the confluence of Kasie. Mosinga, 25 feet, waist deep, with 150 yards of sponge on right bank and about 50 yards on left. There are many plots of cassava, maize, millet, dura, ground-nuts, voandzeia, in the forest, all surrounded with strong high hedges skilfully built, and manured with wood ashes. The villagers are much afraid of us. After 4-1/2 hours we were brought up by the deep rivulet Mpanda, to be crossed to-morrow in canoes. There are many flowers in the forest: marigolds, a white jonquil-looking flower without smell, many orchids, white, yellow, and pink Asclepias, with bunches of French-white flowers, clematis--**Methonica gloriosa**, gladiolus, and blue and deep purple polygalas, grasses with white starry seed-vessels, and spikelets of brownish red and yellow. Besides these there are beautiful blue flowering bulbs, and new flowers of pretty delicate form and but little scent. To this list may be added balsams, compositae of blood-red colour and of purple; other flowers of liver colour, bright canary yellow, pink orchids on spikes thickly covered all round, and of three inches in length; spiderworts of fine blue or yellow or even pink. Different coloured asclepedials; beautiful yellow and red umbelliferous flowering plants; dill and wild parsnips; pretty flowery aloes, yellow and red, in one whorl of blossoms; peas, and many other flowering plants which I do not know. Very few birds or any kind of game. The people are Babisa, who have fled from the west and are busy catching fish in basket traps.

15th January, 1873. --Found that Chungu had let us go astray towards the Lake, and into an angle formed by the Mpande and Lopopussi, and the Lake-full of rivulets which are crossed with canoes. Chisupa, a headman on the other side of the Mpanda, sent a present and denounced Chungu for heartlessness. We explained to one man our change of route and went first N.E., then E. to the Monsinga, which we forded again at a deep place full of holes and rust-of-iron water, in which we floundered over 300 yards. We crossed a sponge thigh deep before we came to the Mosinga, then on in flat forest to a stockaded village; the whole march about east for six hours.

16th January, 1873. --Away north-east and north to get out of the many rivulets near the Lake back to the River Lopopussi, which now looms large, and must be crossed in canoes. We have to wait in a village till these are brought, and have only got 1-3/4 hour nearly north.

We were treated scurvily by Chungu. He knew that we were near the Chambeze, but hid the knowledge and himself too. It is terror of guns.

17th January, 1873. --We are troubled for want of canoes, but have to treat gently with the owners, otherwise they would all run away, as they have around Chungu's, in the belief that we should return to punish their silly headman. By waiting patiently yesterday, we drew about twenty canoes towards us this morning, but all too small for the donkey, so we had to turn away back north-west to the bridge above Chungu's. If we had tried to swim the donkey across alongside a canoe it would have been terribly strained, as the Lopopussi is here quite two miles wide and full of rushes, except in the main stream. It is all deep, and the country being very level as the rivulets come near to the Lake, they become very broad. Crossed two sponges with rivulets in their centre.

Much cultivation in the forest. In the second year the mileza and maize are sickly and yellow white; in the first year, with fresh wood ashes, they are dark green and strong. Very much of the forest falls for manure. The people seem very eager cultivators. Possibly mounds have the potash brought up in forming.

18th January, 1873. --We lost a week by going to Chungu (a worthless terrified headman), and came back to the ford of Lopopussi, which we crossed, only from believing him to be an influential man who would explain the country to us. We came up the Lopopussi three hours yesterday, after spending two hours in going down to examine the canoes. We hear that Sayde bin Ali is returning from Katanga with much ivory.

19th January, 1873. --After prayers we went on to a fine village, and on from it to the Mononse, which, though only ten feet of deep stream flowing S., had some 400 yards of most fatiguing, plunging, deep sponge, which lay in a mass of dark-coloured rushes, that looked as if burnt off: many leeches plagued us. We were now two hours out. We went on two miles to another sponge and village, but went round its head dryshod, then two hours more to sponge Lovu. Flat forest as usual.

20th January, 1873. --Tried to observe lunars in vain; clouded over all, thick and muggy. Came on disappointed and along the Lovu 1-1/2 mile. Crossed it by a felled tree lying over it. It is about six feet deep, with 150 yards of sponge. Marched about 2-1/2 hours: very unsatisfactory progress.

[In answer to a question as to whether Dr. Livingstone could possibly manage to wade so much, Susi says that he was carried across these sponges and the rivulets on the shoulders of Chowpere or Chumah.]

21st January, 1873. --Fundi lost himself yesterday, and we looked out for him. He came at noon, having wandered in the eager pursuit of two herds of eland; having seen no game for a long time, he lost himself in the eager hope of getting one. We went on 2-1/2 hours, and were brought up by the River Malalanzi, which is about 15 feet wide, waist deep, and has 300 yards or more of sponge. Guides refused to come as Chitunkue, their headman, did not own them. We started alone: a man came after us and tried to mislead us in vain.

22nd January, 1873. --We pushed on through many deserted gardens and villages, the man evidently sent to lead us astray from our S.E. course; he turned back when he saw that we refused his artifice. Crossed another rivulet, possibly the Lofu, now broad and deep, and then came to another of several deep streams but sponge, not more than fifty feet in all. Here we remained, having travelled in fine drizzling rain all the morning. Population all gone from the war of Chitoka with this Chitunkue.

No astronomical observations worth naming during December and January; impossible to take any, owing to clouds and rain.

It is trying beyond measure to be baffled by the natives lying and misleading us wherever they can. They fear us very, greatly, and with a terror that would gratify an anthropologist's heart. Their unfriendliness is made more trying by our being totally unable to observe for our position. It is either densely clouded, or continually raining day and night. The country is covered with brackens, and rivulets occur at least one every hour of the march. These are now deep, and have a broad selvage of sponge. The lower stratum of clouds moves quickly from the N.W.; the upper move slowly from S.E., and tell of rain near.

23rd January, 1873. --We have to send back to villages of Chitunkue to buy food. It was not reported to me that the country in front was depopulated for three days, so I send a day back. I don't know where we are, and the people are deceitful in their statements; unaccountably so, though we deal fairly and kindly. Rain, rain, rain as if it never tired on this watershed. The showers show little in the gauge, but keep everything and every place wet and sloppy.

Our people return with a wretched present from Chitunkue; bad flour and a fowl, evidently meant to be rejected. He sent also an exorbitant demand for gunpowder, and payment of guides. I refused his present, and must plod on without guides, and this is very difficult from the numerous streams.

24th January, 1873. --Went on E. and N.E. to avoid the deep part of a large river, which requires two canoes, but the men sent by the chief would certainly hide them. Went 1-3/4 hour's journey to a large stream through drizzling rain, at least 300 yards of deep water, amongst sedges and sponges of 100 yards. One part was neck deep for fifty yards, and the water cold. We plunged in elephants' footprints 1-1/2 hour, then came on one hour to a small rivulet ten feet broad, but waist deep, bridge covered and broken down. Carrying me across one of the broad deep sedgy rivers is really a very difficult task. One we crossed was at least 2000 feet broad, or more than 300 yards. The first part, the main stream, came up to Susi's mouth, and wetted my seat and legs. One held up my pistol behind, then one after another took a turn, and when he sank into a deep elephant's foot-print, he required two to lift him, so as to gain a footing on the level, which was over waist deep. Others went on, and bent down the grass, to insure some footing on the side of the elephants' path. Every ten or twelve paces brought us to a clear stream, flowing fast in its own channel, while over all a strong current came bodily through all the rushes and aquatic plants. Susi had the first spell, then Farijala, then a tall, stout, Arab-looking man, then Amoda, then Chanda, then Wade Sale, and each time I was lifted off bodily, and put on another pair of stout willing shoulders, and fifty yards put them out of breath: no wonder! It was sore on the women folk of our party. It took us full an hour and a half for all to cross over, and several came over turn to help me and their friends. The water was cold, and so was the wind, but no leeches plagued us. We had to hasten on the building of sheds after crossing the second rivulet, as rain threatened us. After 4 P.M. it came on a pouring cold rain, when we were all under cover. We are anxious about food. The Lake is near, but we are not sure of provisions, as there have been changes of population. Our progress is distressingly slow. Wet, wet, wet; sloppy weather, truly, and no observations, except that the land near the Lake being very level, the rivers spread out into broad friths and sponges. The streams are so numerous that there has been a scarcity of names. Here we have Loon and Luena. We had two Loous before, and another Luena.

25th January, 1873. --Kept in by rain. A man from Unyanyembe joined us this morning. He says that he was left sick. Rivulets and sponges again, and through flat forest, where, as usual, we can see the slope of the land by the leaves being washed into heaps in the direction which the water in the paths wished to take. One and a half hours more, and then to the River Loou, a large stream with bridge destroyed. Sent to make repairs before we go over it, and then passed. The river is deep, and flows fast to the S.W., having about 200 yards of safe flood flowing in long grass--clear water. The men built their huts, and had their camp ready by 3 P.M. A good day's work, not hindered by rain. The country all depopulated, so we can buy nothing. Elephants and antelopes have been here lately.

26th January, 1873. --I arranged to go to our next River Luena, and ascend it till we found it small enough for crossing, as it has much "Tinga-tinga," or yielding spongy soil; but another plan was formed by night, and we were requested to go down the Loou. Not wishing to appear overbearing, I consented until we were, after two hours' southing, brought up by several miles of Tinga-tinga. The people in a fishing village ran away from us, and we had to wait for some sick ones. The women are collecting mushrooms. A man came near us, but positively refused to guide us to Matipa, or anywhere else.

The sick people compelled us to make an early halt.

27th January, 1873. --On again through streams, over sponges and rivulets thigh deep. There are marks of gnu and buffalo. I lose much blood, but it is a safety-valve for me, and I have no fever or other ailments.

28th January, 1873. --A dreary wet morning, and no food that we know of near. It is drop, drop, drop, and drizzling from the north-west. We killed our last calf but one last night to give each a mouthful. At 9.30 we were allowed by the rain to leave our camp, and march S.E. for two hours to a strong deep rivulet ten feet broad only, but waist deep, and 150 yards of flood all deep too. Sponge about forty yards in all, and running fast out. Camped by a broad prairie or Bouga.

29th January, 1873. --No rain in the night, for a wonder. We tramped 1-1/4 hour to a broad sponge, having at least 300 yards of flood, and clear water flowing S.W., but no usual stream. All was stream flowing through the rushes, knee and thigh deep. On still with the same, repeated again and again, till we came to broad branching sponges, at which I resolved to send out scouts S., S.E., and S.W. The music of the singing birds, the music of the turtle doves, the screaming of the frankolin proclaim man to be near.

30th January, 1873. --Remain waiting for the scouts. Manuasera returned at dark, having gone about eight hours south, and seen the Lake and two islets. Smoke now appeared in the distance, so he turned, and the rest went on to buy food where the smoke was. Wet evening.

CHAPTER XI.

Entangled amongst the marshes of Bangweolo. Great privations. Obliged to return to Chitunkue's. At the chief's mercy. Agreeably surprised with the chief. Start once more. Very difficult march. Robbery exposed. Fresh attack of illness. Sends scouts out to find villages. Message to Chirubwe. An ant raid. Awaits news from Matipa. Distressing perplexity. The Bougas of Bangweolo. Constant rain above and flood below. Ill. Susi and Chuma sent as envoys to Matipa. Reach Bangweolo. Arrive at Matipa's islet. Matipa's town. The donkey suffers in transit. Tries to go on to Kabinga's. Dr. Livingstone makes a demonstration. Solution of the transport difficulty. Susi and detachment sent to Kabinga's. Extraordinary extent of flood. Reaches Kabinga's. An upset. Crosses the Chambeze. The River Muanakazi. They separate into companies by land and water. A disconsolate lion. Singular caterpillars. Observations on fish. Coasting along the southern flood of Lake Bangweolo. Dangerous state of Dr. Livingstone.

1st February, 1873.--Waiting for the scouts. They return unsuccessful--forced to do so by hunger. They saw a very large river flowing into the Lake, but did not come across a single soul. Killed our last calf, and turn back for four hard days' travel to Chitunkue's. I send men on before us to bring food back towards us.

2nd February, 1873.--March smartly back to our camp of 28th ult. The people bear their hunger well. They collect mushrooms and plants, and often get lost in this flat featureless country.

3rd February, 1873.--Return march to our bridge on the Lofu, five hours. In going we went astray, and took six hours to do the work of five. Tried lunars in vain. Either sun or moon in clouds. On the Luena.

4th February, 1873.--Return to camp on the rivulet with much ***Methonica gloriosa*** on its banks. Our camp being on its left bank of 26th. It took long to cross the next river, probably the Kwale, though the elephants' footprints are all filled up now. Camp among deserted gardens, which afford a welcome supply of cassava and sweet potatoes. The men who were sent on before us slept here last night, and have deceived us by going more slowly without loads than we who are loaded.

5th February, 1873.--Arrived at Chitunkue's, crossing two broad deep brooks, and on to the Malalenzi, now swollen, having at least 200 yards of flood and more than 300 yards of sponge. Saluted by a drizzling shower. We are now at Chitunkue's mercy.

We find the chief more civil than we expected. He said each chief had his own land and his own peculiarities. He was not responsible for others. We were told that we had been near to Matipa and other chiefs: he would give us guides if we gave him a cloth and some powder.

We returned over these forty-one miles in fifteen hours, through much deep water. Our scouts played us false both in time and beads: the headmen punished them. I got lunars, for a wonder. Visited Chitunkubwe, as his name properly is. He is a fine jolly-looking man, of a European cast of countenance, and very sensible and friendly. I gave him two cloths, for which he seemed thankful, and promised good guides to Matipa's. He showed me two of Matipa's men who had heard us firing guns to attract one of our men who had strayed; these men followed us. It seems we had been close to human habitations, but did not know it. We have lost half a month by this wandering, but it was all owing to the unfriendliness of some and the fears of all. I begged for a more northerly path, where the water is low. It is impossible to describe the amount of water near the Lake. Rivulets without number. They are so deep as to damp all ardour. I passed a very large striped spider in going to visit Chitunkubwe. The stripes were of yellowish green, and it had two most formidable reddish mandibles, the same shape as those of the redheaded white ant. It seemed to be eating a kind of ant with a light-coloured head, not seen elsewhere. A man killed it, and all the natives said that it was most dangerous. We passed gardens of dura; leaves all split up with hail, and forest leaves all punctured.

6th February, 1873.--Chitunkubwe gave a small goat and a large basket of flour as a return present. I gave him three-quarters of a pound of powder, in addition to the cloth.

7th February, 1873. --This chief showed his leanings by demanding prepayment for his guides. This being a preparatory step to their desertion I resisted, and sent men to demand what he meant by his words; he denied all, and said that his people lied, not he. We take this for what it is worth. He gives two guides to-morrow morning, and visits us this afternoon.

8th February, 1873. --The chief dawdles, although he promised great things yesterday. He places the blame on his people, who did not prepare food on account of the rain. Time is of no value to them. We have to remain over to-day. It is most trying to have to wait on frivolous pretences. I have endured such vexatious delays. The guides came at last with quantities of food, which they intend to bargain with my people on the way. A Nassicker who carried my saddle was found asleep near my camp.

9th February, 1873. --Slept in a most unwholesome, ruined village. Rank vegetation had run over all, and the soil smelled offensively. Crossed a sponge, then a rivulet, and sponge running into the Miwale Eiver, then by a rocky passage we crossed the Mofiri, or great Tinga-tinga, a water running strongly waist and breast deep, above thirty feet broad here, but very much broader below. After this we passed two more rills and the River Methonua, but we build a camp above our former one. The human ticks called "papasi" by the Suaheli, and "karapatos" by the Portuguese, made even the natives call out against their numbers and ferocity.

10th February, 1873. --Back again to our old camp on the Lovu or Lofu by the bridge. We left in a drizzle, which continued from 4 A.M. to 1 P.M. We were three hours in it, and all wetted, just on reaching camp by 200 yards, of flood mid-deep; but we have food.

11th February, 1873. --Our guides took us across country, where we saw tracks of buffaloes, and in a meadow, the head of a sponge, we saw a herd of Hartebeests. A drizzly night was followed by a morning of cold wet fog, but in three hours we reached our old camp: it took us six hours to do this distance before, and five on our return. We camped on a deep bridged stream, called the Kiachibwe.

12th February, 1873. --We crossed the Kasoso, which joins the Mokisya, a river we afterwards crossed: it flows N.W., then over the Mofungwe. The same sponges everywhere.

13th February, 1873.--In four hours we came within sight of the Luena and Lake, and saw plenty of elephants and other game, but very shy. The forest trees are larger. The guides are more at a loss than we are, as they always go in canoes in the flat rivers and rivulets. Went E., then S.E. round to S.

14th February, 1873.--Public punishment to Chirango for stealing beads, fifteen cuts; diminished his load to 40 lbs., giving him blue and white beads to be strung. The water stands so high in the paths that I cannot walk dryshod, and I found in the large bougas or prairies in front, that it lay knee deep, so I sent on two men to go to the first villages of Matipa for large canoes to navigate the Lake, or give us a guide to go east to the Chambeze, to go round on foot. It was Halima who informed on Chirango, as he offered her beads for a cloth of a kind which she knew had not hitherto been taken out of the baggage. This was so far faithful in her, but she has an outrageous tongue. I remain because of an excessive haemorrhagic discharge.

[We cannot but believe Livingstone saw great danger in these constant recurrences of his old disorder: we find a trace of it in the solemn reflections which he wrote in his pocket-book, immediately under the above words:--]

If the good Lord gives me favour, and permits me to finish my work, I shall thank and bless Him, though it has cost me untold toil, pain, and travel; this trip has made my hair all grey.

15th February, 1873, Sunday.--Service. Killed our last goat while waiting for messengers to return from Matipa's. Evening: the messenger came back, having been foiled by deep tinga-tinga and bouga. He fired his gun three times, but no answer came, so as he had slept one night away he turned, but found some men hunting, whom he brought with him. They say that Matipa is on Chirube islet, a good man too, but far off from this.

16th February, 1873.--Sent men by the hunter's canoe to Chirube, with a request to Matipa to convey us west if he has canoes, but, if not, to tell us truly, and we will go east and cross the Chambeze where it is small. Chitunkubwe's men ran away, refusing to wait till we had communicated with Matipa. Here the water stands underground about eighteen inches from the surface. The guides played us false, and this is why they escaped.

17th February, 1873.--The men will return to-morrow, but they have to go all the way out to the islet of Chirube to Matipa's.

Suffered a furious attack at midnight from the red Sirafu or Driver ants. Our cook fled first at their onset. I lighted a candle, and remembering Dr. Van der Kemp's idea that no animal will attack man unprovoked, I lay still. The first came on my foot quietly, then some began to bite between the toes, then the larger ones swarmed over the foot and bit furiously, and made the blood start out. I then went out of the tent, and my whole person was instantly covered as close as small-pox (not confluent) on a patient. Grass fires were lighted, and my men picked some off my limbs and tried to save me. After battling for an hour or two they took me into a hut not yet invaded, and I rested till they came, the pests, and routed me out there too! Then came on a steady pour of rain, which held on till noon, as if trying to make us miserable. At 9 A.M. I got back into my tent. The large Sirafu have mandibles curved like reaping-sickles, and very sharp--as fine at the point as the finest needle or a bee's sting. Their office is to remove all animal refuse, cockroaches, &c., and they took all my fat. Their appearance sets every cockroach in a flurry, and all ants, white and black, get into a panic. On man they insert the sharp curved mandibles, and then with six legs push their bodies round so as to force the points by lever power. They collect in masses in their runs and stand with mandibles extended, as if defying attack. The large ones stand thus at bay whilst the youngsters hollow out a run half an inch wide, and about an inch deep. They remained with us till late in the afternoon, and we put hot ashes on the defiant hordes. They retire to enjoy the fruits of their raid, and come out fresh another day.

18th February, 1873.--We wait hungry and cold for the return of the men who have gone to Matipa, and hope the good Lord will grant us influence with this man.

Our men have returned to-day, having obeyed the native who told them to sleep instead of going to Matipa. They bought food, and then believed that the islet Chirube was too far off, and returned with a most lame story. We shall make the best of it by going N.W., to be near the islets and buy food, till we can communicate with Matipa. If he fails us by fair means, we must seize canoes and go by force. The men say fear of me makes them act very cowardly. I have gone amongst the whole population kindly and fairly, but I fear I must now act rigidly, for when they hear that we have submitted to injustice, they at once conclude that we are fair game for all, and they go to lengths in dealing falsely that they would never otherwise attempt. It is, I can declare, not my nature, nor has it been my practice, to go as if "my back were up."

19th February, 1873. --A cold wet morning keeps us in this uncomfortable spot. When it clears up we go to an old stockade, to be near an islet to buy food. The people, knowing our need, are extortionate. We went on at 9 A.M. over an extensive water-covered plain. I was carried three miles to a canoe, and then in it we went westward, in branches of the Luena, very deep and flowing W. for three hours. I was carried three miles to a canoe, and we were then near enough to hear Bangweolo bellowing. The water on the plain is four, five, and seven feet deep. There are rushes, ferns, papyrus, and two lotuses, in abundance. Many dark grey caterpillars clung to the grass and were knocked off as we paddled or poled. Camped in an old village of Matipa's, where, in the west, we see the Luena enter Lake Bangweolo; but all is flat prairie or buga, filled with fast-flowing water, save a few islets covered with palms and trees. Rain continued sprinkling us from the N.W. all the morning. Elephants had run riot over the ruins, eating a species of grass now in seed. It resembles millet, and the donkey is fond of it. I have only seen this and one other species of grass in seed eaten by the African elephant. Trees, bulbs, and fruits are his dainties, although ants, whose hills he overturns, are relished. A large party in canoes came with food as soon as we reached our new quarters: they had heard that we were in search of Matipa. All are eager for calico, though they have only raw cassava to offer. They are clothed in bark-cloth and skins. Without canoes no movement can be made in any direction, for it is water everywhere, water above and water below.

20th February, 1873. --I sent a request to a friendly man to give me men, and a large canoe to go myself to Matipa; he says that he will let me know to-day if he can. Heavy rain by night and drizzling by day. No definite answer yet, but we are getting food, and Matipa will soon hear of us as he did when we came and returned back for food. I engaged another man to send a canoe to Matipa, and I showed him his payment, but retain it here till he comes back.

21st February, 1873. --The men engaged refuse to go to Matipa's, they have no honour. It is so wet we can do nothing. Another man spoken to about going, says that they run the risk of being killed by some hostile people on another island between this and Matipa's.

22nd February, 1873. --A wet morning. I was ill all yesterday, but escape fever by haemorrhage. A heavy mantle of N.W. clouds came floating over us daily. No astronomical observation can possibly be taken. I was never in such misty cloudy weather in Africa. A man turned up at 9 A.M. to carry our message to Matipa; Susi and Chumah went with him. The good Lord go with them, and lend me influence and grant me help.

23rd February, 1873, Sunday. --Service. Rainy.

24th February, 1873. --Tried hard for a lunar, but the moon was lost in the glare of the sun.

25th February, 1873. --For a wonder it did not rain till 4 P.M. The people bring food, but hold out for cloth, which is inconvenient.

Susi and Chumah not appearing may mean that the men are preparing canoes and food to transport us.

25th February, 1873. --Susi returned this morning with good news from Matipa, who declares his willingness to carry us to Kabende for the five bundles of brass wire I offered. It is not on Chirube, but amid the swamps of the mainland on the Lake's north side. Immense swampy plains all around except at Kabende. Matipa is at variance with his brothers on the subject of the lordship of the lands and the produce of the elephants, which are very numerous. I am devoutly thankful to the Giver of all for favouring me so far, and hope that He may continue His kind aid.

No mosquitoes here, though Speke, at the Victoria Nyanza, said they covered the bushes and grass in myriads, and struck against the hands and face most disagreeably.

27th February, 1873. --Waiting for other canoes to be sent by Matipa. His men say that there is but one large river on the south of Lake Bangweolo, and called Luomba. They know the mountains on the south-east as I do, and on the west, but say they don't know any on the middle of the watershed. They plead their youth as an excuse for knowing so little.

Matipa's men proposed to take half our men, but I refused to divide our force; they say that Matipa is truthful.

28th February, 1873. --No night rain after 8 P.M., for a wonder. Baker had 1500 men in health on 15th June, 1870, at lat. 9 deg. 26' N., and 160 on sick list;

many dead. Liberated 305 slaves. His fleet was thirty-two vessels; wife and he well. I wish that I met him. Matipa's men not having come, it is said they are employed bringing the carcase of an elephant to him. I propose to go near to him to-morrow, some in canoes and some on foot. The good Lord help me. New moon this evening.

1st March, 1873.--Embarked women and goods in canoes, and went three hours S.E. to Bangweolo. Stopped on an island where people were drying fish over fires. Heavy rain wetted us all as we came near the islet, the drops were as large as half-crowns by the marks they made. We went over flooded prairie four feet deep, and covered with rushes, and two varieties of lotus or sacred lily; both are eaten, and so are papyrus. The buffaloes are at a loss in the water. Three canoes are behind. The men are great cowards. I took possession of all the paddles and punting poles, as the men showed an inclination to move off from our islet. The water in the country is prodigiously large: plains extending further than the eye can reach have four or five feet of clear water, and the Lake and adjacent lands for twenty or thirty miles are level. We are on a miserable dirty fishy island called Motovinza; all are damp. We are surrounded by scores of miles of rushes, an open sward, and many lotus plants, but no mosquitoes.

2nd March, 1873.--It took us 7-1/2 hours' punting to bring us to an island, and then the miserable weather rained constantly on our landing into the Boma (stockade), which is well peopled. The prairie is ten hours long, or about thirty miles by punting. Matipa is on an island too, with four bomas on it. A river, the Molonga, runs past it, and is a protection[28].

The men wear a curious head-dress of skin or hair, and large upright ears.

3rd March, 1873.--Matipa paid off the men who brought us here. He says that five Sangos or coils (which brought us here) will do to take us to Kabende, and I sincerely hope that they will. His canoes are off, bringing the meat of an elephant.

---

28   It will be observed that these islets were in reality slight eminences standing above water on the flooded plains which border on Lake Bangweolo. The men say that the actual deep-water Lake lay away to their right, and on being asked why Dr. Livingstone did not make a short cut across to the southern shore, they explain that the canoes could not live for an hour on the Lake, but were merely suited for punting about over the flooded land.--Ed.

There are many dogs in the village, which they use in hunting to bring elephants to bay. I visited Matipa at noon. He is an old man, slow of tongue, and self-possessed; he recommended our crossing to the south bank of the Lake to his brother, who has plenty of cattle, and to goalong that side where there are few rivers and plenty to eat. Kabende's land was lately overrun by Banyamwezi, who now inhabit that country, but as yet have no food to sell. Moanzabamba was the founder of the Babisa tribe, and used the curious plaits of hair which form such a singular head-dress here like large ears. I am rather in a difficulty, as I fear I must give the five coils for a much shorter task; but it is best not to appear unfair, although I will be the loser. He sent a man to catch a Sampa for me, it is the largest fish in the Lake, and he promised to have men ready to take my men over to-morrow. Matipa never heard from any of the elders of his people that any of his forefathers ever saw a European. He knew perfectly about Pereira, Lacerda, and Monteiro, going to Casembe, and my coming to the islet Mpabala. No trace seems to exist of Captain Singleton's march[29]. The native name of Pereira is "Moenda Mondo:" of Lacerda, "Charlie:" of Monteiro's party, "Makabalwe," or the donkey men, but no other name is heard. The following is a small snatch of Babisa lore. It was told by an old man who came to try for some beads, and seemed much interested about printing. He was asked if there were any marks made on the rocks in any part of the country, and this led to his story. Lukerenga came from the west a long time ago to the River Lualaba. He had with him a little dog. When he wanted to pass over he threw his mat on the water, and this served as a raft, and they crossed the stream. When he reached the other side there were rocks at the landing place, and the mark is still to be seen on the stone, not only of his foot, but of a stick which he cut with his hatchet, and of his dog's feet; the name of the place is Uchewa.

4th March, 1873. --Sent canoes off to bring our men over tothe island of Matipa. They brought ten, but the donkey could not come as far through the "tinga-tinga" as they, so they took it back for fear that it should perish. I spoke to Matipa this morning to send more canoes, and he consented. We move outside, as the town swarms with mice, and is very closely built and disagreeable. I found mosquitoes in the town.

---

29 Defoe's book, 'Adventures of Captain Singleton,' is alluded to.
It would almost appear as if Defoe must have come across some unknown African traveller who gave him materials for this work.--Ed.

5th March, 1873.--Time runs on quickly. The real name of this island is Masumbo, and the position may be probably long. 31 deg. 3'; lat. 10 deg. 11' S. Men not arrived yet. Matipa very slow.

6th March, 1873.--Building a camp outside the town for quiet and cleanliness, and no mice to run over us at night. This islet is some twenty or thirty feet above the general flat country and adjacent water.

At 3 P.M. we moved up to the highest part of the island where we can see around us and have the fresh breeze from the Lake. Rainy as we went up, as usual.

7th March, 1873.--We expect our men to-day. I tremble for the donkey! Camp sweet and clean, but it, too, has mosquitoes, from which a curtain protects me completely--a great luxury, but unknown to the Arabs, to whom I have spoken about it. Abed was overjoyed by one I made for him; others are used to their bites, as was the man who said that he would get used to a nail through the heel of his shoe. The men came at 3 P.M., but eight had to remain, the canoes being too small. The donkey had to be tied down, as he rolled about on his legs and would have forced his way out. He bit Mabruki Speke's lame hand, and came in stiff from lying tied all day. We had him shampooed all over, but he could not eat dura--he feels sore. Susi did well under the circumstances, and we had plenty of flour ready for all. Chanza is near Kabinga, and this last chief is coming to visit me in a day or two.

8th March, 1873.--I press Matipa to get a fleet of canoes equal to our number, but he complains of their being stolen by rebel subjects. He tells me his brother Kabinga would have been here some days ago but for having lost a son, who was killed by an elephant: he is mourning for him but will come soon. Kabinga is on the other side of the Chambeze. A party of male and female drummers and dancers is sure to turn up at every village; the first here had a leader that used such violent antics perspiration ran off his whole frame. I gave a few strings of beads, and the performance is repeated to-day by another lot, but I rebel and allow them to dance unheeded. We got a sheep for a wonder for a doti; fowls and fish alone could be bought, but Kabinga has plenty of cattle.

There is a species of carp with red ventral fin, which is caught and used in very large quantities: it is called "pumbo." The people dry it over fires as preserved provisions. Sampa is the largest fish in the Lake, it is caught by a hook. The Luena goes into Bangweolo at Molandangao. A male Msobe had faint white stripes across the

Dr. Livingstone's Mosquito Curtain.

back and one well-marked yellow stripe along the spine. The hip had a few faint white spots, which showed by having longer hair than the rest; a kid of the same species had a white belly.

The eight men came from Motovinza this afternoon, and now all our party is united. The donkey shows many sores inflicted by the careless people, who think that force alone can be used to inferior animals.

11th March, 1873. --Matipa says "Wait; Kabinga is coming, and he has canoes." Time is of no value to him. His wife is making him pombe, and will drown all his cares, but mine increase and plague me. Matipa and his wife each sent me a huge calabash of pombe; I wanted only a little to make bread with.

By putting leaven in a bottle and keeping it from one baking to another (or three days) good bread is made, and the dough being surrounded by banana leaves or maize leaves (or even forest leaves of hard texture and no taste, or simply by broad leafy grass), is preserved from burning in an iron pot. The inside of the pot is greased, then the leaves put in all round, and the dough poured in to stand and rise in the sun.

Better news comes: the son of Kabinga is to be here to-night, and we shall concoct plans together.

12th March, 1873. --The news was false, no one came from Kabinga. The men strung beads to-day, and I wrote part of my despatch for Earl Granville.

13th March, 1873. --- I went to Matipa, and proposed to begin the embarkation of my men at once, as they are many, and the canoes are only sufficient to take a few at a time. He has sent off a big canoe to reap his millet, when it returns he will send us over to see for ourselves where we can go. I explained the danger of setting my men astray.

14th March, 1873. --Rains have ceased for a few days. Went down to Matipa and tried to take his likeness for the sake of the curious hat he wears.

15th March, 1873. --Finish my despatch so far.

16th March, 1873, Sunday. --Service. I spoke sharply to Matipa for his duplicity. He promises everything and does nothing: he has in fact no power over his people. Matipa says that a large canoe will come to-morrow, and next day men will go to Kabinga to reconnoitre. There may be a hitch there which we did not take

Matipa and his Wife.

into account; Kabinga's son, killed by an elephant, may have raised complications: blame may be attached to Matipa, and in their dark minds it may appear all important to settle the affair before having communication with him. Ill all day with my old complaint.

17th March, 1873.--The delay is most trying. So many detentions have occurred they ought to have made me of a patient spirit.

As I thought, Matipa told us to-day that it is reported he has some Arabs with him who will attack all the Lake people forthwith, and he is anxious that we shall go over to show them that we are peaceful.

18th March, 1873.--Sent off men to reconnoitre at Kabinga's and to make a camp there. Rain began again after nine days' dry weather, N.W. wind, but in the morning fleecy clouds came from S.E. in patches. Matipa is acting the villain, and my men are afraid of him: they are all cowards, and say that they are afraid of me, but this is only an excuse for their cowardice.

19th March, 1873.--Thanks to the Almighty Preserver of men for sparing me thus far on the journey of life. Can I hope for ultimate success? So many obstacles have arisen. Let not Satan prevail over me, Oh! my good Lord Jesus[30].

8 A.M. Got about twenty people off to canoes. Matipa not friendly. They go over to Kabinga on S.W. side of the Chambeze, and thence we go overland. 9 A.M. Men came back and reported Matipa false again; only one canoe had come. I made a demonstration by taking quiet possession of his village and house; fired a pistol through the roof and called my men, ten being left to guard the camp; Matipa fled to another village. The people sent off at once and brought three canoes, so at 11 A.M. my men embarked quietly. They go across the Chambeze and build a camp on its left bank. All Kabinga's cattle are kept on an island called Kalilo, near the mouth of the Chambeze, and are perfectly wild: they are driven into the water like buffaloes, and pursued when one is wanted for meat. No milk is ever obtained of course.

20th March, 1873.--Cold N.W. weather, but the rainfall is small, as the S.E. stratum comes down below the N.W. by day. Matipa sent two large baskets of flour (cassava), a sheep, and a cock. He hoped that we should remain with him till the water of the over-flood dried, and help him to fight his enemies, but I explained our delays, and our desire to complete our work and meet Baker.

---

30   This was written on his last birthday.--ED.

21st March, 1873.--Very heavy N.W. rain and thunder by night, and by morning. I gave Matipa a coil of thick brass wire, and his wife a string of large neck beads, and explained my hurry to be off. He is now all fair, and promises largely: he has been much frightened by our warlike demonstration. I am glad I had to do nothing but make a show of force.

22nd March, 1873.--Susi not returned from Kabinga. I hope that he is getting canoes, and men also, to transport us all at one voyage. It is flood as far as the eye can reach; flood four and six feet deep, and more, with three species of rushes, two kinds of lotus, or sacred lily, papyrus, arum, &c. One does not know where land ends, and Lake begins: the presence of land-grass proves that this is not always overflowed.

23rd March, 1873.--Men returned at noon. Kabinga is mourning for his son killed by an elephant, and keeps in seclusion. The camp is formed on the left bank of the Chambeze.

24th March.--The people took the canoes away, but in fear sent for them. I got four, and started with all our goods, first giving a present that no blame should follow me. We punted six hours to a little islet without a tree, and no sooner did we land than a pitiless pelting rain came on. We turned up a canoe to get shelter. We shall reach the Chambeze to-morrow. The wind tore the tent out of our hands, and damaged it too; the loads are all soaked, and with the cold it is bitterly uncomfortable. A man put my bed into the bilge, and never said "Bale out," so I was for a wet night, but it turned out better than I expected. No grass, but we made a bed of the loads, and a blanket fortunately put into a bag.

25th March, 1873.--Nothing earthly will make me give up my work in despair. I encourage myself in the Lord my God, and go forward.

We got off from our miserably small islet of ten yards at 7 A.M., a grassy sea on all sides, with a few islets in the far distance. Four varieties of rushes around us, triangular and fluted, rise from eighteen inches to two feet above the water. The caterpillars seem to eat each other, and a web is made round others; the numerous spiders may have been the workmen of the nest. The wind on the rushes makes a sound like the waves of the sea. The flood extends out in slightly depressed arms of the Lake for twenty or thirty miles, and far too broad to be seen across; fish abound, and ant-hills alone lift up their heads; they have trees on them. Lukutu flows from

E. to W. to the Chambeze, as does the Lubanseusi also. After another six hours' punting, over the same wearisome prairie or Bouga, we heard the merry voices of children. It was a large village, on a flat, which seems flooded at times, but much cassava is planted on mounds, made to protect the plants from the water, which stood in places in the village, but we got a dry spot for the tent. The people offered us huts. We had as usual a smart shower on the way to Kasenga, where we slept. We passed the Islet Luangwa.

26th March, 1873. --We started at 7.30, and got into a large stream out of the Chambeze, called Mabziwa. One canoe sank in it, and we lost a slave girl of Amoda. Fished up three boxes, and two guns, but the boxes being full of cartridges were much injured; we lost the donkey's saddle too. After this mishap we crossed the Lubanseusi, near its confluence with the Chambeze, 300 yards wide and three fathoms deep, and a slow current. We crossed the Chambeze. It is about 400 yards wide, with a quick clear current of two knots, and three fathoms deep, like the Lubanseuse; but that was slow in current, but clear also. There is one great lock after another, with thick mats of hedges, formed of aquatic plants between. The volume of water is enormous. We punted five hours, and then camped.

27th March, 1873. --I sent canoes and men back to Matipa's to bring all the men that remained, telling them to ship them at once on arriving, and not to make any talk about it. Kabinga keeps his distance from us, and food is scarce; at noon he sent a man to salute me in his name.

28th March, 1873. --Making a pad for a donkey, to serve instead of a saddle. Kabinga attempts to sell a sheep at an exorbitant price, and says that he is weeping over his dead child. Mabruki Speke's hut caught fire at night, and his cartridge box was burned.

29th March, 1873. --I bought a sheep for 100 strings of beads. I wished to begin the exchange by being generous, and told his messenger so; then a small quantity of maize was brought, and I grumbled at the meanness of the present: there is no use in being bashful, as they are not ashamed to grumble too. The man said that Kabinga would send more when he had collected it.

30th March, 1873, Sunday. --A lion roars mightily. The fish-hawk utters his weird voice in the morning, as if he lifted up to a friend at a great distance, in a sort of falsetto key.

5 P.M. Men returned, but the large canoe having been broken by the donkey, we have to go back and pay for it, and take away about twenty men now left. Matipa kept all the payment from his own people, and so left us in the lurch; thus another five days is lost.

31st March, 1873. --I sent the men back to Matipa's for all our party. I give two dotis to repair the canoe. Islanders are always troublesome, from a sense of security in their fastnesses. Made stirrups of thick brass wire four-fold; they promise to do well. Sent Kabinga a cloth, and a message, but he is evidently a niggard, like Matipa: we must take him as we find him, there is no use in growling. Seven of our men returned, having got a canoe from one of Matipa's men. Kabinga, it seems, was pleased with the cloth, and says that he will ask for maize from his people, and buy it for me; he has rice growing. He will send a canoe to carry me over the next river.

3rd April, 1873. --Very heavy rain last night. Six inches fell in a short time. The men at last have come from Matipa's.

4th April, 1873. --Sent over to Kabinga to buy a cow, and got a fat one for 2-1/2 dotis, to give the party a feast ere we start. The kambari fish of the Chambeze is three feet three inches in length.

Two others, the "polwe" and "lopatakwao," all go up the Chambeze to spawn when the rains begin. Casembe's people make caviare of the spawn of the "pumbo."

[The next entry is made in a new pocket-book, numbered XVII. For the first few days pen and ink were used, afterwards a well-worn stump of pencil, stuck into a steel penholder and attached to a piece of bamboo, served his purpose.]

5th April, 1873. --March from Kabinga's on the Chambeze, our luggage in canoes, and men on land. We punted on flood six feet deep, with many ant-hills all about, covered with trees. Course S.S.E. for five miles, across the River Lobingela, sluggish, and about 300 yards wide.

6th April, 1873. --Leave in the same way, but men were sent from Kabinga to steal the canoes, which we paid his brother Mateysa handsomely for. A stupid drummer, beating the alarm in the distance, called us inland; we found the main body of our people had gone on, and so by this, our party got separated[31], and we pulled and punted six or seven hours S.W. in great difficulty, as the fishermen we saw refused to show us where the deep water lay. The whole country S. of the Lake was covered with water, thickly dotted over with lotus-leaves and rushes. It has a greenish appearance, and it might be well on a map to show the spaces annually flooded by a broad wavy band, twenty, thirty, and even, forty miles out from the permanent banks of the Lake: it might be coloured light green. The broad estuaries fifty or more miles, into which the rivers form themselves, might be coloured blue, but it is quite impossible at present to tell where land ends, and Lake begins; it is all water, water everywhere, which seems to be kept from flowing quickly off by the narrow bed of the Luapula, which has perpendicular banks, worn deep down in new red sandstone. It is the Nile apparently enacting its inundations, even at its sources. The amount of water spread out over the country constantly excites my wonder; it is prodigious. Many of the ant-hills are cultivated and covered with dura, pumpkins, beans, maize, but the waters yield food plenteously in fish and lotus-roots. A species of wild rice grows, but the people neither need it nor know it. A party of fishermen fled from us, but by coaxing we got them to show us deep water. They then showed us an islet, about thirty yards square, without wood, and desired us to sleep there. We went on, and then they decamped.

Pitiless pelting showers wetted everything; but near sunset we saw two fishermen paddling quickly off from an ant-hill, where we found a hut, plenty of fish, and some firewood. There we spent the night, and watched by turns, lest thieves should come and haul away our canoes and goods. Heavy rain. One canoe sank, wetting everything in her. The leaks in her had been stopped with clay, and a man sleeping near the stern had displaced this frail caulking. We did not touch the fish, and I cannot conjecture who has inspired fear in all the inhabitants.

7th April, 1873. --Went on S.W., and saw two men, who guided us to the River Muanakazi, which forms a connecting link between the River Lotingila and the Lolotikila, about the southern borders of the flood. Men were hunting, and we passed near large herds of antelopes, which made a rushing, plunging sound as they ran and sprang away among the waters. A lion had wandered into this world of water and ant-hills, and roared night and morning, as if very much disgusted:

---

31 Dr. Livingstone's object was to keep the land party marching parallel to him whilst he kept nearer to the Lake in a canoe.--ED.

we could sympathise with him! Near to the Muanakazi, at a broad bank in shallow water near the river, we had to unload and haul. Our guides left us, well pleased with the payment we had given them. The natives beating a drum on our east made us believe them to be our party, and some thought that they heard two shots. This misled us, and we went towards the sound through papyrus, tall rushes, arums, and grass, till tired out, and took refuge on an ant-hill for the night. Lion roaring. We were lost in stiff grassy prairies, from three to four feet deep in water, for five hours. We fired a gun in the stillness of the night, but received no answer; so on the *8th* we sent a small canoe at daybreak to ask for information and guides from the village where the drums had been beaten. Two men came, and they thought likewise that our party was south-east; but in that direction the water was about fifteen inches in spots and three feet in others, which caused constant dragging of the large canoe all day, and at last we unloaded at another branch of the Muanakazi with a village of friendly people. We slept there.

All hands at the large canoe could move her only a few feet. Putting all their strength to her, she stopped at every haul with a jerk, as if in a bank of adhesive plaister. I measured the crown of a papyrus plant or palm, it was three feet across horizontally, its stalk eight feet in height. Hundreds of a large dark-grey hairy caterpillar have nearly cleared off the rushes in spots, and now live on each other. They can make only the smallest progress by swimming or rather wriggling in the water: their motion is that of a watch-spring thrown down, dilating and contracting.

9th April, 1873. --After two hours' threading the very winding, deep channel of this southern branch of the Muanakazi, we came to where our land party had crossed it and gone on to Gandochite, a chief on the Lolotikila. My men were all done up, so I hired a man to call some of his friends to take the loads; but he was stopped by his relations in the way, saying, "You ought to have one of the traveller's own people with you." He returned, but did not tell us plainly or truly till this morning.

[The recent heavy exertions, coupled with constant exposure and extreme anxiety and annoyance, no doubt brought on the severe attack which is noticed, as we see in the words of the next few days.]

10th April, 1873. --The headman of the village explained, and we sent two of our men, who had a night's rest with the turnagain fellow of yesterday. I am pale, bloodless, and; weak from bleeding profusely ever since the 31st of March last: an artery gives off a copious stream, and takes away my strength. Oh, how I long to be permitted by the Over Power to finish my work.

12th April, 1873. --Cross the Muanakazi. It is about 100 or 130 yards broad, and deep. Great loss of **ai mua** made me so weak I could hardly walk, but tottered along nearly two hours, and then lay down quite done. Cooked coffee--our last--and went on, but in an hour I was compelled to lie down. Very unwilling to be carried, but on being pressed I allowed the men to help me along by relays to Chinama, where there is much cultivation. We camped in a garden of dura.

13th April, 1873. --Found that we had slept on the right bank of the Lolotikila, a sluggish, marshy-looking river, very winding, but here going about south-west. The country is all so very flat that the rivers down here are of necessity tortuous. Fish and other food abundant, and the people civil and reasonable. They usually partake largely of the character of the chief, and this one, Gondochite, is polite. The sky is clearing, and the S.E. wind is the lower stratum now. It is the dry season well begun. Seventy-three inches is a higher rainfall than has been observed anywhere else, even in northern Manyuema; it was lower by inches than here far south on the watershed. In fact, this is the very heaviest rainfall known in these latitudes; between fifty and sixty is the maximum.

One sees interminable grassy prairies with lines of trees, occupying quarters of miles in breadth, and these give way to bouga or prairie again. The bouga is flooded annually, but its vegetation consists of dry land grasses. Other bouga extend out from the Lake up to forty miles, and are known by aquatic vegetation, such as lotus, papyrus, arums, rushes of different species, and many kinds of purely aquatic subaqueous plants which send up their flowers only to fructify in the sun, and then sink to ripen one bunch after another. Others, with great cabbage-looking leaves, seem to remain always at the bottom. The young of fish swarm, and bob in and out from the leaves. A species of soft moss grows on most plants, and seems to be good fodder for fishes, fitted by hooked or turned-up noses to guide it into their maws.

One species of fish has the lower jaw turned down into a hook, which enables the animal to hold its mouth close to the plant, as it glides up or down, sucking in all the soft pulpy food. The superabundance of gelatinous nutriment makes these swarmers increase in bulk with extraordinary rapidity, and the food supply of the people is plenteous in consequence. The number of fish caught by weirs, baskets, and nets now, as the waters decline, is prodigious. The fish feel their element becoming insufficient for comfort, and retire from one bouga to another towards the Lake; the narrower parts are duly prepared by weirs to take advantage of their necessities; the sun heat seems to oppress them and force them to flee. With the south-east aerial current comes heat and sultriness. A blanket is scarcely needed till the early hours of the morning, and here, after the turtle doves and cocks give out their warning calls to the watchful, the fish-eagle lifts up his remarkable voice. It is pitched in a high falsetto key, very loud, and seems as if he were calling to some one in the other world. Once heard, his weird unearthly voice can never be forgotten--it sticks to one through life.

We were four hours in being ferried over the Loitikila, or Lolotikila, in four small canoes, and then two hours south-west down its left bank to another river, where our camp has been formed. I sent over a present to the headman, and a man returned with the information that he was ill at another village, but his wife would send canoes to-morrow to transport us over and set us on our way to Muanazambamba, south-west, and over Lolotikila again.

14th April, 1873.--At a branch of the Lolotikila.

15th April, 1873.--Cross Lolotikila again (where it is only fifty yards) by canoes, and went south-west an hour. I, being very weak, had to be carried part of the way. Am glad of resting; **ai mua** flow copiously last night. A woman, the wife of the chief, gave a present of a goat and maize.

16th April, 1873.--Went south-west two and a half hours, and crossed the Lombatwa River of 100 yards in width, rush deep, and flowing fast in aquatic vegetation, papyrus, &c., into the Loitikila. In all about three hours south-west.

17th April, 1873.--A tremendous rain after dark burst all our now rotten tents to shreds. Went on at 6.35 A.M. for three hours, and I, who was suffering severely all night, had to rest. We got water near the surface by digging in yellow sand. Three hills now appear in the distance. Our course, S.W. three and three-quarter hours to a village on the Kazya River. A Nyassa man declared that his father had brought the heavy rain of the 16th on us. We crossed three sponges.

18th April, 1873.--On leaving the village on the Kazya, we forded it and found it seventy yards broad, waist to breast deep all over. A large weir spanned it, and we went on the lower side of that. Much papyrus and other aquatic plants in it. Fish are returning now with the falling waters, and are guided into the rush-cones set for them. Crossed two large sponges, and I was forced to stop at a village after travelling S.W. for two hours: very ill all night, but remembered that the bleeding and most other ailments in this land are forms of fever. Took two scruple doses of quinine, and stopped it quite.

19th April, 1873.--A fine bracing S.E. breeze kept me on the donkey across a broad sponge and over flats of white sandy soil and much cultivation for an hour and a half, when we stopped at a large village on the right bank of[32], and men went over to the chief Muanzambamba to ask canoes to cross to-morrow. I am excessively weak, and but for the donkey could not move a hundred yards. It is not all pleasure this exploration. The Lavusi hills are a relief to the eye in this flat upland. Their forms show an igneous origin. The river Kazya comes from them and goes direct into the Lake. No observations now, owing to great weakness; I can scarcely hold the pencil, and my stick is a burden. Tent gone; the men build a good hut for me and the luggage. S.W. one and a half hour.

20th April, 1873, Sunday.--Service. Cross over the sponge, Moenda, for food and to be near the headman of these parts, Moanzambamba. I am excessively weak. Village on Moenda sponge, 7 A.M. Cross Lokulu in a canoe. The river is about thirty yards broad, very deep, and flowing in marshes two knots from S.S.B. to N.N.W. into Lake.

---

32 He leaves room for a name which perhaps in his exhausted state he forgot to ascertain.

CHAPTER XII.

Dr. Livingstone rapidly sinking. Last entries in his diary. Susi and Chumah's additional details. Great agony in his last illness. Carried across rivers and through flood. Inquiries for the Hill of the Four Rivers. Kalunganjovu's kindness. Crosses the Mohlamo into the district of Ilala in great pain. Arrives at Chitambo's village. Chitambo comes to visit the dying traveller. The last night. Livingstone expires in the act of praying. The account of what the men saw. Remarks on his death. Council of the men. Leaders selected. The chief discovers that his guest is dead. Noble conduct of Chitambo. A separate village built by the men wherein to prepare the body for transport. The preparation of the corpse. Honour shown by the natives to Dr. Livingstone. Additional remarks on the cause of death. Interment of the heart at Chitambo's in Ilala of the Wabisa. An inscription and memorial sign-posts left to denote spot.

[We have now arrived at the last words written in Dr. Livingstone's diary: a copy of the two pages in his pocket-book which contains them is, by the help of photography, set before the reader. It is evident that he was unable to do more than make the shortest memoranda, and to mark on the map which he was making the streams which enter the Lake as he crossed them. From the *22nd* to the *27th* April he had not strength to write down anything but the several dates. Fortunately Susi and Chumah give a very clear and circumstantial account of every incident which occurred on these days, and we shall therefore add what they say, after each of the Doctor's entries. He writes:--]

21st April, 1873. --Tried to ride, but was forced to lie down, and they carried me back to vil. exhausted.

[The men explain this entry thus:--This morning the Doctor tried if he were strong enough to ride on the donkey, but he had only gone a short distance when he fell to the ground utterly exhausted and faint. Susi immediately undid his belt and pistol, and picked up his cap which had dropped off, while Chumah threw down his gun and ran to stop the men on ahead. When he got back the Doctor said, "Chumah, I have lost so much blood, there is no more strength left in my legs: you must carry me." He was then assisted gently to his shoulders, and, holding the man's head to steady himself, was borne back to the village and placed in the hut he had so recently left. It was necessary to let the Chief Muanazawamba know what had happened, and for this purpose Dr. Livingstone despatched a messenger. He was directed to ask him to supply a guide for the next day, as he trusted then to have recovered so far as to be able to march: the answer was, "Stay as long as you wish, and when you want guides to Kalunganjovu's you shall have them."]

22nd April, 1873. --Carried on kitanda over Buga S.W. 2-1/4[33].

[His servants say that instead of rallying, they saw that his strength was becoming less and less, and in order to carry him they made a kitanda of wood, consisting of two side pieces of seven feet in length, crossed with rails three feet long, and about four inches apart, the whole lashed strongly together. This framework was covered with grass, and a blanket laid on it. Slung from a pole, and borne between two strong men, it made a tolerable palanquin, and on this the exhausted traveller was conveyed to the next village through a flooded grass plain. To render the kitanda more comfortable another blanket was suspended across the pole, so as to hang down on either side, and allow the air to pass under whilst the sun's rays were fended off fromthe sick man. The start was deferred this morning until the dew was off the heads of the long grass sufficiently to ensure his being kept tolerably dry.

The excruciating pains of his dysenteric malady caused him the greatest exhaustion as they marched, and they were glad enough to reach another village in 2-1/4 hours, having travelled S.W. from the last point. Here another hut was built. The name of the halting-place is not remembered by the men, for the villagers fled at their approach; indeed the noise made by the drums sounding the alarm had been caught by the Doctor some time before, and he exclaimed with thankfulness on hearing it, "Ah, now we are near!" Throughout this day the following men acted as bearers of the kitanda: Chowpere, Songolo, Chumah, and Adiamberi. Sowfere, too,

---

33   Two hours and a quarter in a south-westerly direction.

joined in at one time.]

23rd April, 1873. --(No entry except the date.)

[They advanced another hour and a half through the same expanse of flooded treeless waste, passing numbers of small fish-weirs set in such a manner as to catch the fish on their way back to the Lake, but seeing nothing of the owners, who had either hidden themselves or taken to flight on the approach of the caravan. Another village afforded them a night's shelter, but it seems not to be known by any particular name.]

24th April, 1873. --(No entry except the date.)

[But one hour's march was accomplished to-day, and again they halted amongst some huts--place unknown. His great prostration made progress exceedingly painful, and frequently when it was necessary to stop the bearers of the kitanda, Chumah had to support the Doctor from falling.]

25th April, 1873. --(No entry except the date.)

[In an hour's course S.W. they arrived at a village in which they found a few people. Whilst his servants were busy completing the hut for the night's encampment, the Doctor, who was lying in a shady place on the kitanda, ordered them to fetch one of the villagers. The chief of the place had disappeared, but the rest of his people seemed quite at their ease, and drew near to hear what was going to be said. They were asked whether they knew of a hill on which four rivers took their rise. The spokesman answered that they had no knowledge of it; they themselves, said he, were not travellers, and all those who used to go on trading expeditions were now dead. In former years Malenga's town, Kutchinyama, was the assembling place of the Wabisa traders, but these had been swept off by the Mazitu. Such as survived had to exist as best they could amongst the swamps and inundated districts around the Lake. Whenever an expedition was organised to go to the coast, or in any other direction, travellers met at Malenga's town to talk over the route to be taken: then would have been the time, said they, to get information about every part. Dr. Livingstone was here obliged to dismiss them, and explained that he was too ill to continue talking, but he begged them to bring as much food as they could for sale to Kalunganjovu's.]

26th April, 1873. --(No entry except the date.)

[They proceeded as far as Kalunganjovu's town, the chief himself coming to meet them on the way dressed in Arab costume and wearing a red fez. Whilst waiting here Susi was instructed to count over the bags of beads, and, on reporting that twelve still remained in stock, Dr. Livingstone told him to buy two large tusks if an opportunity occurred, as he might run short of goods by the time they got to Ujiji, and could then exchange them with the Arabs there for cloth, to spend on their way to Zanzibar.]

To-day, the *27th April, 1873,* he seems to have been almost dying. No entry at all was made in his diary after that which follows, and it must have taxed him to the utmost to write:--

"Knocked up quite, and remain--recover--sent to buy milch goats. We are on the banks of the Molilamo."

They are the last words that David Livingstone wrote.

From this point we have to trust entirely to the narrative of the men. They explain the above sentence as follows: Salimane, Amisi, Hamsani, and Laede, accompanied by a guide, were sent off to endeavour if possible to buy some milch goats on the upper part of the Molilamo[34]. They could not, however, succeed; it was always the same story--the Mazitu had taken everything. The chief, nevertheless, sent a substantial present of a kid and three baskets of ground-nuts, and the people were willing enough to exchange food for beads. Thinking he could eat some Mapira corn pounded up with ground-nuts, the Doctor gave instructions to the two women M'sozi and M'toweka, to prepare it for him, but he was not able to take it when they brought it to him.

28th April, 1873. --Men were now despatched in an opposite direction, that is to visit the villages on the right bank of the Molilamo as it flows to the Lake; unfortunately they met with no better result, and returned empty handed.

On the *29th April*, Kalunganjovu and most of his people came early to the village. The chief wished to assist his guest to the utmost, and stated that as he could not be sure that a sufficient number of canoes would be forthcoming unless he took charge of matters himself, he should accompany the caravan to the crossing place, which was about an hour's march from the spot. "Everything should be done for his friend," he said.

---

34 The name Molilamo is allowed to stand, but in Dr. Livingstone's
Map we find it Lulimala, and the men confirm, this pronunciation.--ED.

They were ready to set out. On Susi's going to the hut, Dr. Livingstone told him that he was quite unable to walk to the door to reach the kitanda, and he wished the men to break down one side of the little house, as the entrance was too narrow to admit it, and in this manner to bring it to him where he was: this was done, and he was gently placed upon it, and borne out of the village.

Their course was in the direction of the stream, and they followed it till they came to a reach where the current was uninterrupted by the numerous little islands which stood partly in the river and partly in the flood on the upper waters. Kalunganjovu was seated on a knoll, and actively superintended the embarkation, whilst Dr. Livingstone told his bearers to take him to a tree at a little distance off, that he might rest in the shade till most of the men were on the other side. A good deal of care was required, for the river, by no means a large one in ordinary times, spread its waters in all directions, so that a false step, or a stumble in any unseen hole, would have drenched the invalid and the bed also on which he was carried.

The passage occupied some time, and then came the difficult task of conveying the Doctor across, for the canoes were not wide enough to allow the kitanda to be deposited in the bottom of either of them. Hitherto, no matter how weak, Livingstone had always been able to sit in the various canoes they had used on like occasions, but now he had no power to do so. Taking his bed off the kitanda, they laid it in the bottom of the strongest canoe, and tried to lift him; but he could not bear the pain of a hand being passed under his back. Beckoning to Chumah, in a faint voice he asked him to stoop down over him as low as possible, so that he might clasp his hands together behind his head, directing him at the same how to avoid putting any pressure on the lumbar region of the back; in this way he was deposited in the bottom of the canoe, and quickly ferried across the Mulilamo by Chowpere, Susi, Farijala, and Chumah. The same precautions were used on the other side: the kitanda was brought close to the canoe, so as to prevent any unnecessary pain in disembarking.

Susi now hurried on ahead to reach Chitambo's village, and superintend the building of another house. For the first mile or two they had to carry the Doctor through swamps and plashes, glad to reach something like a dry plain at last.

It would seem that his strength was here at its very lowest ebb. Chumah, one of his bearers on these the last weary miles the great traveller was destined to accomplish, says that they were every now and then implored to stop and place their burden on the ground. So great were the pangs of his disease during this day that he could make no attempt to stand, and if lifted for a few yards a drowsiness came over him, which alarmed them all excessively. This was specially the case at one spot where a tree stood in the path. Here one of his attendants was called to him, and, on stooping down, he found him unable to speak from faintness. They replaced him in the kitanda, and made the best of their way on the journey. Some distance further on great thirst oppressed him; he asked them if they had any water, but, unfortunately for once, not a drop was to be procured. Hastening on for fear of getting too far separated from the party in advance, to their great comfort they now saw Farijala approaching with some which Susi had thoughtfully sent off from Chitambo's village.

Still wending their way on, it seemed as if they would not complete their task, for again at a clearing the sick man entreated them to place him on the ground, and to let him stay where he was. Fortunately at this moment some of the outlying huts of the village came in sight, and they tried to rally him by telling him that he would quickly be in the house that the others had gone on to build, but they were obliged as it was to allow him to remain for an hour in the native gardens outside the town.

On reaching their companions it was found that the work was not quite finished, and it became necessary therefore to lay him under the broad eaves of a native hut till things were ready.

Chitambo's village at this time was almost empty. When the crops are growing it is the custom to erect little temporary houses in the fields, and the inhabitants, leaving their more substantial huts, pass the time in watching their crops, which are scarcely more safe by day than by night; thus it was that the men found plenty of room and shelter ready to their hand. Many of the people approached the spot where he lay whose praises had reached them in previous years, and in silent wonder they stood round him resting on their bows. Slight drizzling showers were falling, and as soon as possible his house was made ready and banked round with earth.

Inside it, the bed was raised from the floor by sticks and grass, occupying a position across and near to the bay-shaped end of the hut: in the bay itself bales and boxes were deposited, one of the latter doing duty for a table, on which the medicine chest and sundry other things were placed. A fire was lighted outside, nearly opposite the door, whilst the boy Majwara slept just within to attend to his master's wants in the night.

On the **30th April, 1873,** Chitambo came early to pay a visit of courtesy, and was shown into the Doctor's presence, but he was obliged to send him away, telling him to come again on the morrow, when he hoped to have more strength to talk to him, and he was not again disturbed. In the afternoon he asked Susi to bring his watch to the bedside, and explained to him the position in which to hold his hand, that it might lie in the palm whilst he slowly turned the key.

So the hours stole on till nightfall. The men silently took to their huts, whilst others, whose duty it was to keep watch, sat round the fires, all feeling that the end could not be far off. About 11 P.M. Susi, whose hut was close by, was told to go to his master. At the time there were loud shouts in the distance, and, on entering, Dr. Livingstone said, "Are our men making that noise?" "No," replied Susi; "I can hear from the cries that the people are scaring away a buffalo from their dura fields." A few minutes afterwards he said slowly, and evidently wandering, "Is this the Luapula?" Susi told him they were in Chitambo's village, near the Mulilamo, when he was silent for a while. Again, speaking to Susi, in Suaheli this time, he said, "Sikun'gapi kuenda Luapula?" (How many days is it to the Luapula?)

"Na zani zikutatu, Bwana" (I think it is three days, master), replied Susi.

A few seconds after, as if in great pain, he half sighed, half said, "Oh dear, dear!" and then dozed off again.

It was about an hour later that Susi heard Majwara again outside the door, "Bwana wants you, Susi." On reaching the bed the Doctor told him he wished him to boil some water, and for this purpose he went to the fire outside, and soon returned with the copper kettle full. Calling him close, he asked him to bring his medicine-chest and to hold the candle near him, for the man noticed he could hardly see. With great difficulty Dr. Livingstone selected the calomel, which he told him to place by his side; then, directing him to pour a little water into a cup, and to put another empty one by it, he said in a low feeble voice, "All right; you can go out now." These were the last words he was ever heard to speak.

It must have been about 4 A.M. when Susi heard Majwara's step once more.

"Come to Bwana, I am afraid; I don't know if he is alive." The lad's evident alarm made Susi run to arouse Chumah, Chowpere, Matthew, and Muanyasere, and the six men went immediately to the hut.

Passing inside they looked towards the bed. Dr. Livingstone was not lying on it, but appeared to be engaged in prayer, and they instinctively drew backwards for the instant. Pointing to him, Majwara said, "When I lay down he was just as he is now, and it is because I find that he does not move that I fear he is dead." They asked the lad how long he had slept? Majwara said he could not tell, but he was sure that it was some considerable time: the men drew nearer.

A candle stuck by its own wax to the top of the box, shed a light sufficient for them to see his form. Dr. Livingstone was kneeling by the side of his bed, his body stretched forward, his head buried in his hands upon the pillow. For a minute they watched him: he did not stir, there was no sign of breathing; then one of them, Matthew, advanced softly to him and placed his hands to his cheeks. It was sufficient; life had been extinct some time, and the body was almost cold: Livingstone was dead.

His sad-hearted servants raised him tenderly up, and laid him full length on the bed, then, carefully covering him, they went out into the damp night air to consult together. It was not long before the cocks crew, and it is from this circumstance-- coupled with the fact that Susi spoke to him some time shortly before midnight-- that we are able to state with tolerable certainty that he expired early on the 1st of May.

It has been thought best to give the narrative of these closing hours as nearly as possible in the words of the two men who attended him constantly, both here and in the many illnesses of like character which he endured in his last six years' wanderings; in fact from the first moment of the news arriving in England, it was felt to be indispensable that they should come home to state what occurred.

* * * * *

The men have much to consider as they cower around the watch-fire, and little time for deliberation. They are at their furthest point from home and their leader has fallen at their head; we shall see presently how they faced their difficulties.

* * * * *

Several inquiries will naturally arise on reading this distressing history; the foremost, perhaps, will be with regard to the entire absence of everything like a parting word to those immediately about him, or a farewell line to his family and friends at home. It must be very evident to the reader that Livingstone entertained very grave forebodings about his health during the last two years of his life, but it is not clear that he realized the near approach of death when his malady suddenly passed into a more dangerous stage.

It may be said, "Why did he not take some precautions or give some strict injunctions to his men to preserve his note-books and maps, at all hazards, in the event of his decease? Did not his great ruling passion suggest some such precaution?"

Fair questions, but, reader, you have all--every word written, spoken, or implied.

Is there, then, no explanation? Yes; we think past experience affords it, and it is offered to you by one who remembers moreover how Livingstone himself used to point out to him in Africa the peculiar features of death by malarial poisoning.

In full recollection of eight deaths in the Zambesi and Shire districts, not a single parting word or direction in any instance can be recalled. Neither hope nor courage give way as death approaches. In most cases a comatose state of exhaustion supervenes, which, if it be not quickly arrested by active measures, passes into complete insensibility: this is almost invariably the closing scene.

In Dr. Livingstone's case we find some departure from the ordinary symptoms[35]. He, as we have seen by the entry of the 18th April was alive to the conviction that malarial poison is the basis of every disorder in Tropical Africa, and he did not doubt but that he was fully under its influence whilst suffering so severely. As we have said, a man of less endurance in all probability would have perished in the first week of the terrible approach to the Lake, through the flooded country and under the continual downpour that he describes. It tried every constitution, saturated every man with fever poison, and destroyed several, as we shall see a little further on.

---

35 The great loss of blood may have had a bearing on the case.

The greater vitality in his iron system very likely staved off for a few days the last state of coma to which we refer, but there is quite sufficient to show us that only a thin margin lay between the heavy drowsiness of the last few days before reaching Chitambo's and the final and usual symptom that brings on unconsciousness and inability to speak.

On more closely questioning the men one only elicits that they imagine he hoped to recover as he had so often done before, and if this really was the case it will in a measure account for the absence of anything like a dying statement, but still they speak again and again of his drowsiness, which in itself would take away all ability to realize vividly the seriousness of the situation. It may be that at the last a flash of conviction for a moment lit up the mind--if so, what greater consolation can those have who mourn his loss, than the account that the men give of what they saw when they entered the hut?

Livingstone had not merely turned himself, he had risen to pray; he still rested on his knees, his hands were clasped under his head: when they approached him he seemed to live. He had not fallen to right or left when he rendered up his spirit to God. Death required no change of limb or position; there was merely the gentle settling forwards of the frame unstrung by pain, for the Traveller's perfect rest had come. Will not time show that the men were scarcely wrong when they thought "he yet speaketh"--aye, perhaps far more clearly to us than he could have done by word or pen or any other means!

Is it, then, presumptuous to think that the long-used fervent prayer of the wanderer sped forth once more--that the constant supplication became more perfect in weakness, and that from his "loneliness" David Livingstone, with a dying effort, yet again besought Him for whom He laboured to break down the oppression and woe of the land?

* * * * *

Before daylight the men were quietly told in each hut what had happened, and that they were to assemble. Coming together as soon as it was light enough to see, Susi and Chumah said that they wished everybody to be present whilst the boxes were opened, so that in case money or valuables were in them, all might be responsible. Jacob Wainwright (who could write, they knew) was asked to make some notes which should serve as an inventory, and then the boxes were brought out from the hut.

Before he left England in 1865, Dr. Livingstone arranged that his travelling equipment should be as compact as possible. An old friend gave him some exceedingly well-made tin-boxes, two of which lasted out the whole of his travels. In these his papers and instruments were safe from wet and from white ants, which have to be guarded against more than anything else. Besides the articles mentioned below, a number of letters and despatches in various stages were likewise enclosed, and one can never sufficiently extol the good feeling which after his death invested all these writings with something like a sacred care in the estimation of his men. It was the Doctor's custom to carry a small metallic note-book in his pocket: a quantity of these have come to hand filled from end to end, and as the men preserved every one that they found, we have a daily entry to fall back upon. Nor was less care shown for his rifles, sextants, his Bible and Church-service, and the medicine chest.

Jacob's entry is as follows, and it was thoughtfully made at the back end of the same note-book that was in use by the Doctor when he died. It runs as follows:--

"11 o'clock night, 28th April.

"In the chest was found about a shilling and half, and in other chest his hat, 1 watch, and 2 small boxes of measuring instrument, and in each box there was one. 1 compass, 3 other kind of measuring instrument. 4 other kind of measuring instrument. And in other chest 3 drachmas and half half scrople."

A word is necessary concerning the first part of this. It will be observed that Dr. Livingstone made his last note on the 27th April. Jacob, referring to it as the only indication of the day of the month, and fancying, moreover, that it was written on the ***preceding day,*** wrote down "28th April." Had he observed that the few words opposite the 27th in the pocket-book related to the stay at Kalunganjovu's village, and not to any portion of the time at Chitambo's, the error would have been avoided. Again, with respect to the time. It was about 11 o'clock P.M. when Susi last saw his master alive, and therefore this time is noted, but both he and Chumah feel quite sure, from what Majwara said, that death did not take place till some hours after.

It was not without some alarm that the men realised their more immediate difficulties: none could see better than they what complications might arise in an hour.

They knew the superstitious horror connected with the dead to be prevalent in the tribes around them, for the departed spirits of men are universally believed to have vengeance and mischief at heart as their ruling idea in the land beyond the grave. All rites turn on this belief. The religion of the African is a weary attempt to propitiate those who show themselves to be still able to haunt and destroy, as war comes or an accident happens.

On this account it is not to be wondered at that chief and people make common cause against those who wander through their territory, and have the misfortune to lose one of their party by death. Who is to tell the consequences? Such occurrences are looked on as most serious offences, and the men regarded their position with no small apprehension.

Calling the whole party together, Susi and Chumah placed the state of affairs before them, and asked what should be done. They received a reply from those whom Mr. Stanley had engaged for Dr. Livingstone, which was hearty and unanimous. "You," said they, "are old men in travelling and in hardships; you must act as our chiefs, and we will promise to obey whatever you order us to do." From this moment we may look on Susi and Chumah as the Captains of the caravan. To their knowledge of the country, of the tribes through which they were to pass, but, above all, to the sense of discipline and cohesion which was maintained throughout, their safe return to Zanzibar at the head of their men must, under God's good guidance, be mainly attributed.

All agreed that Chitambo ought to be kept in ignorance of Dr. Livingstone's decease, or otherwise a fine so heavy would be inflicted upon them as compensation for damage done that their means would be crippled, and they could hardly expect to pay their way to the coast. It was decided that, come what might, the body ***must be borne to Zanzibar.*** It was also arranged to take it secretly, if possible, to a hut at some distance off, where the necessary preparations could be carried out, and for this purpose some men were now despatched with axes to cut wood, whilst others went to collect grass. Chumah set off to see Chitambo, and said that they wanted to build a place outside the village, if he would allow it, for they did not like living amongst the huts. His consent was willingly given.

Later on in the day two of the men went to the people to buy food, and divulged the secret: the chief was at once informed of what had happened, and started for the spot on which the new buildings were being set up. Appealing to Chumah, he said, "Why did you not tell me the truth? I know that your master died last night. You were afraid to let me know, but do not fear any longer. I, too, have travelled, and more than once have been to Bwani (the Coast), before the country on the road was destroyed by the Mazitu. I know that you have no bad motives in coming to our land, and death often happens to travellers in their journeys." Reassured by this speech, they told him of their intention to prepare the body and to take it with them. He, however, said it would be far better to bury it there, for they were undertaking an impossible task; but they held to their resolution. The corpse was conveyed to the new hut the same day on the kitanda carefully covered with cloth and a blanket.

2nd May, 1873. --The next morning Susi paid a visit to Chitambo, making him a handsome present and receiving in return a kind welcome. It is only right to add, that the men speak on all occasions with gratitude of Chitambo's conduct throughout, and say that he is a fine generous fellow. Following out his suggestion, it was agreed that all honours should be shown to the dead, and the customary mourning was arranged forthwith.

At the proper time, Chitambo, leading his people, and accompanied by his wives, came to the new settlement. He was clad in a broad red cloth, which covered the shoulders, whilst the wrapping of native cotton cloth, worn round the waist, fell as low as his ankles. All carried bows, arrows, and spears, but no guns were seen. Two drummers joined in the loud wailing lamentation, which so indelibly impresses itself on the memories of people who have heard it in the East, whilst the band of servants fired volley after volley in the air, according to the strict rule of Portuguese and Arabs on such occasions.

As yet nothing had been done to the corpse.

A separate hut was now built, about ninety feet from the principal one. It was constructed in such a manner that it should be open to the air at the top, and sufficiently strong to defy the attempts of any wild beast to break through it. Firmly driven boughs and saplings were planted side by side and bound together, so as to make a regular stockade. Close to this building the men constructed their huts, and, finally, the whole settlement had another high stockade carried completely around it.

Arrangements were made the same day to treat the corpse on the following morning. One of the men, Safene, whilst in Kalunganjovu's district, bought a large quantity of salt: this was purchased of him for sixteen strings of beads, there was besides some brandy in the Doctor's stores, and with these few materials they hoped to succeed in their object.

Farijala was appointed to the necessary task. He had picked up some knowledge of the method pursued in making ***post-mortem*** examinations, whilst a servant to a doctor at Zanzibar, and at his request, Carras, one of the Nassick boys, was told off to assist him. Previous to this, however, early on the 3rd May, a special mourner arrived. He came with the anklets which are worn on these occasions, composed of rows of hollow seed-vessels, fitted with rattling pebbles, and in low monotonous chant sang, whilst he danced, as follows:

> Lelo kwa Engerese,
> Muana sisi oa konda:
> Tu kamb' tamb' Engerese.

which translated is--

> To-day the Englishman is dead,
> Who has different hair from ours:
> Come round to see the Englishman.

His task over, the mourner and his son, who accompanied him in the ceremony, retired with a suitable present of beads.

The emaciated remains of the deceased traveller were soon afterwards taken to the place prepared. Over the heads of Farijala and Carras--Susi, Chumah, and Muanyasere held a thick blanket as a kind of screen, under which the men performed their duties. Tofike and John Wainwright were present. Jacob Wainwright had been asked to bring his Prayer Book with him, and stood apart against the wall of the enclosure.

In reading about the lingering sufferings of Dr. Livingstone as described by himself, and subsequently by these faithful fellows, one is quite prepared to understand their explanation, and to see why it was possible to defer these operations so long after death: they say that his frame was little more than skin and bone. Through an incision carefully made, the viscera were removed, and a quantity of salt was placed in the trunk. All noticed one very significant circumstance in the autopsy. A clot of coagulated blood, as large as a man's hand, lay in the left side[36], whilst Farijalapointed to the state of the lungs, which they describe as dried up, and covered with black and white patches.

The heart, with the other parts removed, were placed in a tin box, which had formerly contained flour, and decently and reverently buried in a hole dug some four feet deep on the spot where they stood. Jacob was then asked to read the Burial Service, which he did in the presence of all. The body was left to be fully exposed to the sun. No other means were taken to preserve it, beyond placing some brandy in the mouth and some on the hair; nor can one imagine for an instant that any other process would have been available either for Europeans or natives, considering the rude appliances at their disposal. The men kept watch day and night to see that no harm came to their sacred charge. Their huts surrounded the building, and had force been used to enter its strongly-barred door, the whole camp would have turned out in a moment. Once a day the position of the body was changed, but at no other time was any one allowed to approach it.

No molestation of any kind took place during the fourteen days' exposure. At the end of this period preparations were made for retracing their steps. The corpse, by this time tolerably dried, was wrapped round in some calico, the leg being bent inwards at the knees to shorten the package. The next thing was to plan something in which to carry it, and, in the absence of planking or tools, an admirable substitute was found by stripping from a Myonga tree enough of the bark in one piece to form a cylinder, and in it their master was laid. Over this case a piece of sailcloth was sewn, and the whole package was lashed securely to a pole, so as to be carried by two men.

Jacob Wainwright was asked to carve an inscription on the large Mvula tree

---

36 It has been suggested by one who attended Dr. Livingstone professionally in several dangerous illnesses in Africa, that the ultimate cause of death was acute splenitis.--ED.

which stands by the place where the body rested, stating the name of Dr. Livingstone and the date of his death, and, before leaving, the men gave strict injunctions to Chitambo to keep the grass cleared away, so as to save it from the bush-fires which annually sweep over the country and destroy so many trees. Besides this, they erected close to the spot two high thick posts, with an equally strong crosspiece, like a lintel and door-posts in form, which they painted thoroughly with the tar that was intended for the boat: this sign they think will remain for a long time from the solidity of the timber. Before parting with Chitambo, they gave him a large tin biscuit-box and some newspapers, which would serve as evidence to all future travellers that a white man had been at his village.

The chief promised to do all he could to keep both the tree and the timber signposts from being touched, but added, that he hoped the English would not be long in coming to see him, because there was always the risk of an invasion of Mazitu, when he would have to fly, and the tree might be cut down for a canoe by some one, and then all trace would be lost. All was now ready for starting.

CHAPTER XIII.

They begin the homeward march from Ilala. Illness of all the men. Deaths. Muanamazungu. The Luapula. The donkey killed by a lion. A disaster at N'Kossu's. Native surgery. Approach Chawende's town. Inhospitable reception. An encounter. They take the town. Leave Chawende's. Reach Chiwaie's. Strike the old road. Wire drawing. Arrive at Kumbakumba's. John Wainwright disappears. Unsuccessful search. Reach Tanganyika. Leave the Lake. Cross the Lambalamfipa range. Immense herds of game. News of East-Coast Search Expedition. Confirmation of news. They reach Baula. Avant-couriers sent forwards to Unyanyembe. Chumah meets Lieutenant Cameron. Start for the coast. Sad death of Dr. Dillon. Clever precautions. The body is effectually concealed. Girl killed by a snake. Arrival on the coast. Concluding remarks.

The homeward march was then begun. Throughout its length we shall content ourselves with giving the approximate number of days occupied in travelling and halting. Although the memories of both men are excellent--standing the severest test when they are tried by the light of Dr. Livingstone's journals, or "set on" at any passage of his travels--they kept no precise record of the time spent at villages where they were detained by sickness, and so the exactness of a diary can no longer be sustained.

To return to the caravan. They found on this the first day's journey that some other precautions were necessary to enable the bearers of the mournful burden to keep to their task. Sending to Chitambo's village, they brought thence the cask of tar which they had deposited with the chief, and gave a thick coating to the canvas outside. This answered all purposes; they left the remainder at the next village, with orders to send it back to head-quarters, and then continued their course through

Ilala, led by their guides in the direction of the Luapula.

A moment's inspection of the map will explain the line of country to be traversed. Susi and Chumah had travelled with Dr. Livingstone in the neighbourhood of the north-west shores of Bangweolo in previous years. The last fatal road from the north might be struck by a march in a due N.E. direction, if they could but hold out so far without any serious misfortune; but in order to do this they must first strike northwards so as to reach the Luapula, and then crossing it at some part not necessarily far from its exit from the Lake, they could at once lay their course for the south end of Tanganyika.

There were, however, serious indications amongst them. First one and then the other dropped out of the file, and by the time they reached a town belonging to Chitambo's brother--and on the third day only since they set out--half their number were *hors de combat*. It was impossible to go on. A few hours more and all seemed affected. The symptoms were intense pain in the limbs and face, great prostration, and, in the bad cases, inability to move. The men attributed it to the continual wading through water before the Doctor's death. They think that illness had been waiting for some further slight provocation, and that the previous days' tramp, which was almost entirely through plashy Bougas or swamps, turned the scale against them.

Susi was suffering very much. The disease settled in one leg, and then quickly shifted to the other. Songolo nearly died. Kaniki and Bahati, two of the women, expired in a few days, and all looked at its worst. It took them a good month to rally sufficiently to resume their journey.

Fortunately in this interval the rains entirely ceased, and the natives day by day brought an abundance of food to the sick men. From them they heard that the districts they were now in were notoriously unhealthy, and that many an Arab had fallen out from the caravan march to leave his bones in these wastes. One day five of the party made an excursion to the westward, and on their return reported a large deep river flowing into the Luapula on the left bank. Unfortunately no notice was taken of its name, for it would be of considerable geographical interest.

At last they were ready to start again, and came to one of the border villages in Ilala the same night, but the next day several fell ill for the second time, Susi being quite unable to move.

Muanamazungu, at whose place these relapses occurred, was fully aware of everything that had taken place at Chitambo's, and showed the men the greatest kindness. Not a day passed without his bringing them some present or other, but there was a great disinclination amongst the people to listen to any details connected with Dr. Livingstone's death. Some return for their kindness was made by Farijala shooting three buffaloes near the town: meat and goodwill go together all over Africa, and the liberal sportsman scores points at many a turn. A cow was purchased here for some brass bracelets and calico, and on the twentieth day all were sufficiently strong on their legs to push forwards.

The broad waters of the long-looked for Luapula soon hove in sight. Putting themselves under a guide, they were conducted to the village of Chisalamalama, who willingly offered them canoes for the passage across the next day[37].

As one listens to the report that the men give of this mighty river, he instinctively bends his eyes on a dark burden laid in the canoe! How ardently would he have scanned it whose body thus passes across these waters, and whose spirit, in its last hours' sojourn in this world, wandered in thought and imagination to its stream!

It would seem that the Luapula at this point is double the width of the Zambesi at Shupanga. This gives a breadth of fully four miles. A man could not be seen on the opposite bank: trees looked small: a gun could be heard, but no shouting would ever reach a person across the river--such is the description given by men who were well able to compare the Luapula with the Zambesi. Taking to the canoes, they were able to use the "m'phondo," or punting pole, for a distance through reeds, then came clear deep water for some four hundred yards, again a broad reedy expanse, followed by another deep part, succeeded in turn by another current not so broad as those previously paddled across, and then, as on the starting side, gradually shoaling water, abounding in reeds. Two islands lay just above the crossing-place. Using pole and paddle alternately, the passage took them fully two hours across this enormous torrent, which carries off the waters of Bangweolo towards the north.

A sad mishap befell the donkey the first night of camping beyond the Lua-

---

37 The men consider it five days' march "only carrying a gun" from the Molilamo to the bank of the Luapula--this in rough reckoning, at the rate of native travelling, would give a distance of say 120 to 150 miles.--ED.

pula, and this faithful and sorely-tried servant was doomed to end his career at this spot!

According to custom, a special stable was built for him close to the men. In the middle of the night a great disturbance, coupled with the shouting of Amoda, aroused the camp. The men rushed out and found the stable broken down and the donkey gone. Snatching, some logs, they set fire to the grass, as it was pitch dark, and by the light saw a lion close to the body of the poor animal, which was quite dead. Those who had caught up their guns on the first alarm fired a volley, and the lion made off. It was evident that the donkey had been seized by the nose, and instantly killed. At daylight the spoor showed that the guns had taken effect. The lion's blood lay in a broad track (for he was apparently injured in the back, and could only drag himself along); but the footprints of a second lion were too plain to make it advisable to track him far in the thick cover he had reached, and so the search was abandoned. The body of the donkey was left behind, but two canoes remained near the village, and it is most probable that it went to make a feast at Chisalamalama's.

Travelling through incessant swamp and water, they were fain to make their next stopping-place in a spot where an enormous ant-hill spread itself out,--a small island in the waters. A fire was lit, and by employing hoes, most of them dug something like a form to sleep in on the hard earth.

Thankful to leave such a place, their guide led them next day to the village of Kawinga, whom they describe as a tall man, of singularly light colour, and the owner of a gun, a unique weapon in these parts, but one already made useless by wear and tear. The next village, N'kossu's, was much more important. The people, called Kawende, formerly owned plenty of cattle, but now they are reduced: the Banyamwesi have put them under the harrow, and but few herds remain. We may call attention to the somewhat singular fact, that the hump quite disappears in the Lake breed; the cows would pass for respectable shorthorns[38].

A present was made to the caravan of a cow; but it seems that the rule, "first catch your hare," is in full force in N'kossu's pastures. The animals are exceedingly

---

38 This comparison was got at from the remarks made by Susi and
Chuma at an agricultural show; they pointed out the resemblance borne
by the shorthorns and by the Alderney bulls to several breeds near
Lake Bemba.--ED.

An old Servant destroyed.

wild, and a hunt has to be set on foot whenever beef is wanted; it was so in this case. Safene and Muanyasere with their guns essayed to settle the difficulty. The latter, an old hunter as we have seen, was not likely to do much harm; but Safene, firing wildly at the cow, hit one of the villagers, and smashed the bone of the poor fellow's thigh. Although it was clearly an accident, such things do not readily settle themselves down on this assumption in Africa. The chief, however, behaved very well. He told them a fine would have to be paid on the return of the wounded man's father, and it had better be handed to him, for by law the blame would fall on him, as the entertainer of the man who had brought about the injury. He admitted that he had ordered all his people to stand clear of the spot where the disaster occurred, but he supposed that in this instance his orders had not been heard. They had not sufficient goods in any case to respond to the demand; the process adopted to set the broken limb is a sample of native surgery, which must not be passed over.

First of all a hole was dug, say two feet deep and four in length, in such a manner that the patient could sit in it with his legs out before him. A large leaf was then bound round the fractured thigh, and earth thrown in, so that the patient was buried up to the chest. The next act was to cover the earth which lay over the man's legs with a thick layer of mud; then plenty of sticks and grass were collected, and a fire lit on the top directly over the fracture. To prevent the smoke smothering the sufferer, they held a tall mat as a screen before his face, and the operation went on. After some time the heat reached the limbs underground. Bellowing with fear and covered with perspiration, the man implored them to let him out. The authorities concluding that he had been under treatment a sufficient time, quickly burrowed down and lifted him from the hole. He was now held perfectly fast, whilst two strong men stretched the wounded limb with all their might! Splints, duly prepared were afterwards bound round it, and we must hope that in due time benefit accrued, but as the ball had passed through the limb, we must have our doubts on the subject. The villagers told Chuma that after the Wanyamwesi engagements they constantly treated bad gunshot-wounds in this way with perfect success.

Leaving N'kossu's, they rested one night at another village belonging to him, and then made for the territory of the Wa Ussi. Here they met with a surly welcome, and were told they must pass on. No doubt the intelligence that they were carrying their master's body had a great deal to do with it, for the news seemed to

Kawende Surgery.

spread with the greatest rapidity in all directions. Three times they camped in the forest, and for a wonder began to find some dry ground. The path lay in the direct line of Chawende's town, parallel to the north shore of the Lake, and at no great distance from it.

Some time previously a solitary Unyamwesi had attached himself to the party at Chitankooi's, where he had been left sick by a passing caravan of traders: this man now assured them the country before them was well known to him.

Approaching Chawende's, according to native etiquette, Amoda and Sabouri went on in front to inform the chief, and to ask leave to enter his town. As they did not come back, Muanyasere and Chuma set off after them to ascertain the reason of the delay. No better success seemed to attend this second venture, so shouldering their burdens, all went forward in the track of the four messengers.

In the mean time, Chuma and Muanyasere met Amoda and Sabouri coming back towards them with five men. They reported that they had entered the town, but found it a very large stockaded place; moreover, two other villages of equal size were close to it. Much pombe drinking was going on. On approaching the chief, Amoda had rested his gun against the principal hut innocently enough. Chawende's son, drunk and quarrelsome, made this a cause of offence, and swaggering up, he insolently asked them how they dared to do such a thing. Chawende interfered, and for the moment prevented further disagreeables; in fact, he himself seems to have been inclined to grant the favour which was asked: however, there was danger brewing, and the men retired.

When the main body met them returning, tired with their fruitless errand, a consultation took place. Wood there was none. To scatter about and find materials with which to build shelter for the night, would only offer a great temptation to these drunken excited people to plunder the baggage. It was resolved to make for the town.

When they reached the gate of the stockade they were flatly refused admittance, those inside telling them to go down to the river and camp on the bank. They replied that this was impossible: that they were tired, it was very late, and nothing could be found there to give them shelter. Meeting with no different answer, Safene said, "Why stand talking to them? let us get in somehow or other;" and, suiting the action to the word, they pushed the men back who stood in the gateway.

Safene got through, and Muanyasere climbed over the top of the stockade, followed by Chuma, who instantly opened the gate wide and let his companions through. Hostilities might still have been averted had better counsel prevailed.

The men began to look about for huts in which to deposit their things, when the same drunken fellow drew a bow and fired at Muanyasere. The man called out to the others to seize him, which was done in an instant. A loud cry now burst forth that the chief's son was in danger, and one of the people, hurling a spear, wounded Sabouri slightly in the thigh: this was the signal for a general scrimmage.

Chawende's men fled from the town; the drums beat the assembly in all directions, and an immense number flocked to the spot from the two neighbouring villages, armed with their bows, arrows, and spears. An assault instantly began from the outside. N'chise was shot with an arrow in the shoulder through the palisade, and N'taru in the finger. Things were becoming desperate. Putting the body of Dr. Livingstone and all their goods and chattels in one hut, they charged out of the town, and fired on the assailants, killing two and wounding several others. Fearing that they would only gather together in the other remaining villages and renew the attack at night, the men carried these quickly one by one and subsequently burnt six others which were built on the same side of the river, then crossing over, they fired on the canoes which were speeding towards the deep water of Bangweolo, through the channel of the Lopupussi, with disastrous results to the fugitive people.

Returning to the town, all was made safe for the night. By the fortunes of war, sheep, goats, fowls, and an immense quantity of food fell into their hands; and they remained for a week to recruit. Once or twice they found men approaching at night to throw fire on the roofs of the huts from outside, but with this exception they were not interfered with. On the last day but one a man approached and called to them at the top of his voice not to set fire to the chief's town (it was his that they occupied); for the bad son had brought all this upon them; he added that the old man had been overruled, and they were sorry enough for his bad conduct.

Listening to the account given of this occurrence, one cannot but lament the loss of life and the whole circumstances of the fight. Whilst on the one hand we may imagine that the loss of a cool, conciliatory, brave leader was here felt in a grave degree, we must also see that it was known far and wide that this very loss was now a great weakness to his followers. There is no surer sign of mischief in Africa than these trumpery charges of bewitching houses by placing things on them: some such over-strained accusation is generally set in the front rank when other difficulties are to come: drunkenness is pretty much the same thing in all parts of the world, and gathers misery around it as easily in an African village as in an English city. Had the cortege submitted to extortion and insult, they felt that their night by the river would have been a precarious one--even if they had been in a humour to sleep in a swamp when a town was at hand. These things gave occasion to them to resort to force. The desperate nature of their whole enterprise in starting for Zanzibar perhaps had accumulated its own stock of determination, and now it found vent under evil provocation. If there is room for any other feeling than regret, it lies in the fact that, on mature consideration and in sober moments, the people who suffered, cast the real blame on the right shoulders.

For the next three days after leaving Chawende's they were still in the same inundated fringe of Bouga, which surrounds the Lake, and on each occasion had to camp at nightfall wherever a resting-place could be found in the jungle, reaching Chama's village on the fourth day. A delay of forty-eight hours was necessary, as Susi's wife fell ill; and for the next few marches she was carried in a kitanda. They met an Unyamwesi man here, who had come from Kumbakumba's town in the Wa Ussi district. He related to them how on two occasions the Wanyamwesi had tried to carry Chawende's town by assault, but had been repulsed both times. It would seem that, with the strong footing these invaders have in the country, armed as they are besides with the much-dreaded guns, it can only be a matter of time before the whole rule, such as it is, passes into the hands of the new-comers.

The next night was spent in the open, before coming to the scattered huts of Ngumbu's, where a motley group of stragglers, for the most part Wabisa, were busy felling the trees and clearing the land for cultivation. However, the little community gave them a welcome, in spite of the widespread report of the fighting at Chawende's, and dancing and drumming were kept up till morning.

One more night was passed in the plain, and they reached a tributary of the Lopupussi River, called the M'Pamba; it is a considerable stream, and takes one up to the chest in crossing. They now drew near to Chiwaie's town, which they describe as a very strong place, fortified with a stockade and ditch. Shortly before reaching it, some villagers tried to pick a quarrel with them for carrying flags. It was their invariable custom to make the drummer-boy, Majwara, march at their head, whilst the Union Jack and the red colours of Zanzibar were carried in a foremost place in the line. Fortunately a chief of some importance came up and stopped the discussion, or there might have been more mischief, for the men were in no temper to lower their flag, knowing their own strength pretty well by this time. Making their settlement close to Chiwaie's, they met with much kindness, and were visited by crowds of the inhabitants.

Three days' journey brought them to Chiwaie's uncle's village; sleeping two nights in the jungle they made Chungu's, and in another day's march found themselves, to their great delight, at Kapesha's. They knew their road from this point, for on the southern route with Dr. Livingstone they had stopped here, and could therefore take up the path that leads to Tanganyika. Hitherto their course had been easterly, with a little northing, but now they turned their backs to the Lake, which they had held on the right-hand since crossing the Luapula, and struck almost north.

From Kapesha's to Lake Bangweolo is a three days' march as the crow flies, for a man carrying a burden. They saw a large quantity of iron and copper wire being made here by a party of Wanyamwesi. The process is as follows:--A heavy piece of iron, with a funnel-shaped hole in it, is firmly fixed in the fork of a tree. A fine rod is then thrust into it, and a line attached to the first few inches which can be coaxed through. A number of men haul on this line, singing and dancing in tune, and thus it is drawn through the first drill; it is subsequently passed through others to render it still finer, and excellent wire is the result. Leaving Kapesha they went through many of the villages already enumerated in Dr. Livingstone's Diary. Chama's people came to see them as they passed by him, and after some mutterings and growlings Casongo gave them leave to buy food at his town. Reaching Chama's head-quarters they camped outside, and received a civil message, telling them to convey his orders to the people on the banks of the Kalongwesi that the travellers must be ferried safely across. They found great fear and misery prevailing in the neighbourhood from the constant raids made by Kumbakumba's men.

Leaving the Kalangwese behind them they made for M'sama's son's town, meeting four men on the way who were going from Kumbakumba to Chama to beat up recruits for an attack on the Katanga people. The request was sure to be met with alarm and refusal, but it served very well to act the part taken by the wolf in the fable. A grievance would immediately be made of it, and Chama "eaten up" in due course for daring to gainsay the stronger man. Such is too frequently the course of native oppression. At last Kumbakumba's town came in sight. Already the large district of Itawa has tacitly allowed itself to be put under the harrow by this ruffianly Zanzibar Arab. Black-mail is levied in all directions, and the petty chiefs, although really under tribute to Nsama, are sagacious enough to keep in with the powers that be. Kumbakumba showed the men a storehouse full of elephants' tusks. A small detachment was sent off to try and gain tidings of one of the Nassick boys, John, who had mysteriously disappeared a day or two previously on the march. At the time no great apprehensions were felt, but as he did not turn up the grass was set on fire in order that he might see the smoke if he had wandered, and guns were fired. Some think he purposely went off rather than carry a load any further; whilst others fear he may have been killed. Certain it is that after a five days' search in all directions no tidings could be gained either here or at Chama's, and nothing more was heard of the poor fellow.

Numbers of slaves were collected here. On one occasion they saw five gangs bound neck to neck by chains, and working in the gardens outside the towns.

* * * * *

The talk was still about the break up of Casembe's power, for it will be recollected that Kumbakumba and Pemba Motu had killed him a short time before; but by far the most interesting news that reached them was that a party of Englishmen, headed by Dr. Livingstone's son, on their way to relieve his father, had been seen at Bagamoio some months previously.

The chief showed them every kindness during their five days' rest, and was most anxious that no mishap should by any chance occur to their principal charge. He warned them to beware of hyaenas, at night more especially, as the quarter in which they had camped had no stockade round it as yet.

Marching was now much easier, and the men quickly found they had crossed the watershed. The Lovu ran in front of them on its way to Tanganyika. The Kalongwese, we have seen, flows to Lake Moero in the opposite direction. More to their purpose it was perhaps to find the terror of Kumbakumba dying away as they travelled in a north-easterly direction, and came amongst the Mwambi. As yet no invasion had taken place. A young chief, Chungu, did all he could for them, for when the Doctor explored these regions before, Chungu had been much impressed with him: and now, throwing off all the native superstition, he looked on the arrival of the dead body as a cause of real sorrow.

Asoumani had some luck in hunting, and a fine buffalo was killed near the town. According to native game laws (which in some respects are exceedingly strict in Africa), Chungu had a right to a fore leg--had it been an elephant the tusk next the ground would have been his, past all doubt--in this instance, however, the men sent in a plea that theirs was no ordinary case, and that hunger had laws of its own; they begged to be allowed to keep the whole carcase, and Chungu not only listened to their story, but willingly waived his claim to the chief's share.

It is to be hoped that these sons of Tafuna, the head and father of the Amambwi a lungu, may hold their own. They seem a superior race, and this man is described as a worthy leader. His brothers Kasonso, Chitimbwa, Sombe, and their sister Mombo, are all notorious for their reverence for Tafuna. In their villages an abundance of coloured homespun cloth speaks for their industry; whilst from the numbers of dogs and elephant-spears no further testimony is needed to show that the character they bear as great hunters is well deserved.

The steep descent to the Lake now lay before them, and they came to Kasakalawe's. Here it was that the Doctor had passed weary months of illness on his first approach to Tanganyika in previous years. The village contained but few of its old inhabitants, but those few received them hospitably enough and mourned the loss of him who had been so well appreciated when alive. So they journeyed on day by day till the southern end of the Lake was rounded.

The previous experience of the difficult route along the heights bordering on Tanganyika made them determine to give the Lake a wide berth this time, and for this purpose they held well to the eastward, passing a number of small deserted villages, in one of which they camped nearly every night. It was necessary to go through the Fipa country, but they learnt from one man and another that the chief, Kafoofi, was very anxious that the body should not be brought near to his town--indeed, a guide was purposely thrown in their way who led them past it by a considerable detour. Kafoofi stands well with the coast Arabs. One, Ngombesassi by name, was at the time living with him, accompanied by his retinue of slaves. He had collected a very large quantity of ivory further in the interior, but dared not approach nearer at present to Unyanyembe with it to risk the chance of meeting one of Mirambo's hordes.

This road across the plain seems incomparably the best, No difficulty whatever was experienced, and one cannot but lament the toil and weariness which Dr. Livingstone endured whilst holding a course close to Tanganyika, although one must bear in mind that by no other means at the time could he complete his survey of this great inland sea, or acquaint us with its harbours, its bays, and the rivers which find their way into it on the east; these are details which will prove of value when small vessels come to navigate it in the future.

The chief feature after leaving this point was a three days' march over Lambalamfipa, an abrupt mountain range, which crosses the country east and west, and attains, it would seem, an altitude of some 4000 feet. Looking down on the plain from its highest passes a vast lake appears to stretch away in front towards the north, but on descending this resolves itself into a glittering plain, for the most part covered with saline incrustations. The path lay directly across this. The difficulties they anticipated had no real existence, for small villages were found, and water was not scarce, although brackish. The first demand for toll was made near here, but the headman allowed them to pass for fourteen strings of beads. Susi says that this plain literally swarms with herds of game of all kinds: giraffe and zebra were particularly abundant, and lions revelled in such good quarters. The settlements they came to belonged chiefly to elephant hunters. Farijala and Muanyasere did well with the buffalo, and plenty of beef came into camp.

They gained some particulars concerning a salt-water lake on their right, at no very considerable distance. It was reported to them to be smaller than Tanganyika, and goes by the name Bahari ya Muarooli--the sea of Muarooli--for such is the name of the paramount chief who lives on its shore, and if we mistake not the very Merere, or his successor, about whom Dr. Livingstone from time to time showed such interest. They now approached the Likwa River, which flows to this inland sea: they describe it as a stream running breast high, with brackish water; little satisfaction was got by drinking from it.

Just as they came to the Likwa, a long string of men was seen on the opposite side filing down to the water, and being uncertain of their intentions, precautions were quickly taken to ensure the safety of the baggage. Dividing themselves into three parties, the first detachment went across to meet the strangers, carrying the Arab flag in front. Chuma headed another band at a little distance in the rear of these, whilst Susi and a few more crouched in the jungle, with the body concealed in a roughly-made hut. Their fears, however, were needless: it turned out to be a caravan bound for Fipa to hunt elephants and buy ivory and slaves. The new arrivals told them that they had come straight through Unyanyembe from Bagamoio, on the coast, and that the Doctor's death had already been reported there by natives of Fipa.

As we notice with what rapidity the evil tidings spread (for the men found that it had preceded them in all directions), one of the great anxieties connected with African travel and exploration seems to be rather increased than diminished. It shows us that it is never wise to turn an entirely deaf ear when the report of a disaster comes to hand, because in this instance the main facts were conveyed across country, striking the great arterial caravan route at Unyanyembe, and getting at once into a channel that would ensure the intelligence reaching Zanzibar. On the other hand, false reports never lag on their journey:--how often has Livingstone been killed in former years! Nor is one's perplexity lessened by past experience, for we find the oldest and most sagacious travellers when consulted are, as a rule, no more to be depended on than the merest tyro in guessing.

With no small satisfaction, the men learnt from the outward-bound caravan that the previous story was a true one, and they were assured that Dr. Livingstone's son with two Englishmen and a quantity of goods had already reached Unyanyembe.

The country here showed all the appearance of a salt-pan: indeed a quantity of very good salt was collected by one of the men, who thought he could turn an honest bunch of beads with it at Unyanyembe.

Petty tolls were levied on them. Kampama's deputy required four dotis, and an additional tax of six was paid to the chief of the Kanongo when his town was reached.

The Lungwa River bowls away here towards Tanganyika. It is a quick tumbling stream, leaping amongst the rocks and boulders, and in its deeper pools it affords cool delight to schools of hippopotami. The men, who had hardly tasted good water since crossing Lambalamfipa, are loud in its praise. Muanyasere improved relations with the people at the next town by opportunely killing another buffalo, and all took a three days' rest. Yet another caravan met them, bound likewise for the interior, and adding further particulars about the Englishmen at Unyanyembe. This quickened the pace till they found at one stage they were melting two days of the previous outward journey into one.

Arriving at Baula, Jacob Wainwright, the scribe of the party, was commissioned to write an account of the distressing circumstances of the Doctor's death, and Chuma, taking three men with him, pressed on to deliver it to the English party in person. The rest of the cortege followed them through the jungle to Chilunda's village. On the outskirts they came across a number of Wagogo hunting elephants with dogs and spears, but although they were well treated by them, and received presents of honey and food, they thought it better to keep these men in ignorance of the fact that they were in charge of the dead body of their master.

The Manyara River was crossed on its way to Tanganyika before they got to Chikooloo, Leaving this village behind them, they advanced to the Ugunda district, now ruled by Kalimangombi, the son of Mbereke, the former chief, and so on to Kasekera, which, it will be remembered, is not far from Unyanyembe.

20th October, 1873. --We will here run on ahead with Chuma on his way to communicate with the new arrivals. He reached the Arab settlement without let or hindrance. Lieut. Cameron was quickly put in possession of the main facts of Dr. Livingstone's death by reading Jacob's letter, and Chuma was questioned concerning it in the presence of Dr. Dillon and Lieut. Murphy. It was a disappointment to find that the reported arrival of Mr. Oswell Livingstone was entirely erroneous; but Lieut. Cameron showed the wayworn men every kindness. Chuma rested one day before setting out to relieve his comrades to whom he had arranged to make his way as soon as possible. Lieut. Cameron expressed a fear that it would not be safe for him to carry the cloth he was willing to furnish them with if he had not a stronger convoy, as he himself had suffered too sorely from terrified bearers on his way thither; but the young fellows were pretty well acquainted with native marauders by this time, and set off without apprehension.

And now the greater part of their task is over. The weather-beaten company wind their way into the old well-known settlement of Kwihara. A host of Arabs and their attendant slaves meet them as they sorrowfully take their charge to the same Tembe in which the "weary waiting" was endured before, and then they submit to the systematic questioning which the native traveller is so well able to sustain.

News in abundance was offered in return. The porters of the Livingstone East-Coast Aid Expedition had plenty to relate to the porters sent by Mr. Stanley. Mirambo's war dragged on its length, and matters had changed very little since they were there before, either for better or for worse. They found the English officers extremely short of goods; but Lieut. Cameron, no doubt with the object of his Expedition full in view, very properly felt it a first duty to relieve the wants of the party that had performed this Herculean feat of bringing the body of the traveller he had been sent to relieve, together with every article belonging to him at the time of his death, as far as this main road to the coast.

In talking to the men about their intentions, Lieut. Cameron had serious doubts whether the risk of taking the body of Dr. Livingstone through the Ugogo country ought to be run. It very naturally occurred to him that Dr. Livingstone might have felt a wish during life to be buried in the same land in which the remains of his wife lay, for it will be remembered that the grave of Mrs. Livingstone is at Shupanga, on the Zambesi. All this was put before the men, but they steadily adhered to their first conviction--that it was right at all risks to attempt to bear their master home, and therefore they were no longer urged to bury him at Kwihara.

To the new comers it was of great interest to examine the boxes which the men had conveyed from Bangweolo. As we have seen, they had carefully packed up everything at Chitambo's--books, instruments, clothes, and all which would bear special interest in time to come from having been associated with Livingstone in his last hours.

It cannot be conceded for a moment that these poor fellows would have been right in forbidding this examination, when we consider the relative position in which natives and English officers must always stand to each other; but it is a source of regret to relate that the chief part of Livingstone's instruments were taken out of the packages and appropriated for future purposes. The instruments with which all his observations had been made throughout a series of discoveries extending over seven years--aneroid barometers, compasses, thermometers, the sextant and other things, have gone on a new series of travels, to incur innumerable risks of loss, whilst one only of his thermometers comes to hand.

We could well have wished these instruments safe in England with the small remnant of Livingstone's personal property, which was allowed to be shipped from Zanzibar.

The Doctor had deposited four bales of cloth as a reserve stock with the Arabs, and these were immediately forthcoming for the march down.

The termination here of the ill-fated Expedition need not be commented upon. One can only trust that Lieut. Cameron may be at liberty to pursue his separate investigations in the interior under more favourable auspices. The men seemed to anticipate his success, for he is generous and brave in the presence of the natives, and likely to win his way where others undoubtedly would have failed.

Ill-health had stuck persistently to the party, and all the officers were suffering from the various forms of fever. Lieut. Cameron gave the men to understand that it was agreed Lieut. Murphy should return to Zanzibar, and asked if they could attach his party to their march; if so, the men who acted as carriers should receive 6 dollars a man for their services. This was agreed to. Susi had arranged that they should avoid the main path of the Wagogo; inasmuch, as if difficulty was to be encountered anywhere, it would arise amongst these lawless pugnacious people.

By making a ten days' detour at "Jua Singa," and travelling by a path well known to one of their party through the jungle of Poli ya vengi, they hoped to keep out of harm's way, and to be able to make the cloth hold out with which they were supplied. At length the start was effected, and Dr. Dillon likewise quitted the Expedition to return to the coast. It was necessary to stop after the first day's march, for a long halt; for one of the women was unable to travel, they found, and progress was delayed till she, the wife of Chowpereh, could resume the journey. There seem to have been some serious misunderstandings between the leaders of Dr. Livingstone's party and Lieut. Murphy soon after setting out, which turned mainly on the subject of beginning the day's march. The former, trained in the old discipline of their master, laid stress on the necessity of very early rising to avoid the heat of the day, and perhaps pointed out more bluntly than pleasantly that if the Englishmen wanted to improve their health, they had better do so too. However, to a certain extent, this was avoided by the two companies pleasing themselves.

Making an early start, the body was carried to Kasekera, by Susi's party where, from an evident disinclination to receive it into the village, an encampment was made outside. A consultation now became necessary. There was no disguising the fact that, if they kept along the main road, intelligence would precede them concerning that in which they were engaged, stirring up certain hostility and jeopardising the most precious charge they had. A plan was quickly hit upon. Unobserved, the men removed the corpse of the deceased explorer from the package in which it had hitherto been conveyed, and buried the bark case in the hut in the thicket around the village in which they had placed it. The object now was to throw the villagers off their guard, by making believe that they had relinquished the attempt to carry the body to Zanzibar. They feigned that they had abandoned their task, having changed their minds, and that it must be sent back to Unyanyembe to be buried there. In the mean time the corpse of necessity had to be concealed in the smallest space possible, if they were actually to convey it secretly for the future; this was quickly managed.

Susi and Chuma went into the wood and stripped off a fresh length of bark from an N'gombe tree; in this the remains, conveniently prepared as to length, were placed, the whole being surrounded with calico in such a manner as to appear like an ordinary travelling bale, which was then deposited with the rest of the goods. They next proceeded to gather a faggot of mapira-stalks, cutting them in lengths of six feet or so, and swathing them round with cloth to imitate a dead body about to be buried. This done, a paper, folded so as to represent a letter, was duly placed in a cleft stick, according to the native letter-carrier's custom, and six trustworthy men were told off ostensibly to go with the corpse to Unyanyembe. With due solemnity the men set out; the villagers were only too thankful to see it, and no one suspected the ruse. It was near sundown. The bearers of the package held on their way, till fairly beyond all chance of detection, and then began to dispose of their load. The mapira-sticks were thrown one by one far away into the jungle, and when all were disposed of, the wrappings were cunningly got rid of in the same way. Going further on, first one man, and then another, sprung clear from the path into the long grass, to leave no trace of footsteps, and the whole party returned by different ways to their companions, who had been anxiously awaiting them during the night. No one could detect the real nature of the ordinary-looking bale which, henceforth, was guarded with no relaxed vigilance, and eventually disclosed the bark coffin and wrappings, containing Dr. Livingstone's body, on the arrival at Bagamoio. And now, devoid of fear, the people of Kasekera asked them all to come and take up their quarters in the town; a privilege which was denied them so long as it was known that they had the remains of the dead with them.

But a dreadful event was about to recall to their minds how many fall victims to African disease!

Dr. Dillon now came on to Kasekera suffering much from dysentery--a few hours more, and he shot himself in his tent by means of a loaded rifle.

Those who knew the brave and generous spirit in which this hard-working volunteer set out with Lieut. Cameron, fully hoping to relieve Dr. Livingstone, will feel that he ended his life by an act alien indeed to his whole nature. The malaria imbibed during their stay at Unyanyembe laid upon him the severest form of fever, accompanied by delirium, under which he at length succumbed in one of its violent paroxysms. His remains are interred at Kasekera.

We must follow Susi's troop through a not altogether eventless journey to the sea. Some days afterwards, as they wended their way through a rocky place, a little girl in their train, named Losi, met her death in a shocking way. It appears that the poor child was carrying a water-jar on her head in the file of people, when an enormous snake dashed across the path, deliberately struck her in the thigh, and made for a hole in the jungle close at hand. This work of a moment was sufficient, for the poor girl fell mortally wounded. She was carried forward, and all means at hand were applied, but in less than ten minutes the last symptom (foaming at the mouth) set in, and she ceased to breathe.

Here is a well-authenticated instance which goes far to prove the truth of an assertion made to travellers in many parts of Africa. The natives protest that one species of snake will deliberately chase and overtake his victim with lightning speed, and so dreadfully dangerous is it, both from the activity of its poison and its vicious propensities, that it is perilous to approach its quarters. Most singular to relate, an Arab came to some of the men after their arrival at Zanzibar and told them that he had just come by the Unyanyembe road, and that, whilst passing the identical spot where this disaster occurred, one of the men was attacked by the same snake, with precisely the same results; in fact, when looking for a place in which to bury him they saw the grave of Losi, and the two lie side by side.

Natal colonists will probably recognise the Mamba in this snake; it is much to be desired that specimens should be procured for purposes of comparison. In Southern Africa so great is the dread it inspires that the Kaffirs will break up a Kraal and forsake the place if a Mamba takes up his quarters in the vicinity, and, from what we have seen above, with no undue caution.

Susi, to whom this snake is known in the Shupanga tongue as "Bubu," describes it as about twelve feet long, dark in colour, of a dirty blue under the belly, with red markings like the wattles of a cock on the head. The Arabs go so far as to say that it is known to oppose the passage of a caravan at times. Twisting its tail round a branch, it will strike one man after another in the head with fatal certainty. Their remedy is to fill a pot with boiling water, which is put on the head and carried under the tree! The snake dashes his head into this and is killed--the story is given for what it is worth.

It would seem that at Ujiji the natives, as in other places, cannot bear to have snakes killed. The "Chatu," a species of python, is common, and, from being highly favoured, becomes so tame as to enter houses at night. A little meal is placed on the stool, which the uncanny visitor laps up, and then takes its departure--the men significantly say they never saw it with their own eyes. Another species utters a cry, much like the crowing of a young cock; this is well authenticated. Yet another black variety has a spine like a blackthorn at the end of the tail, and its bite is extremely deadly.

At the same time it must be added that, considering the enormous number of reptiles in Africa, it rarely occurs that anyone is bitten, and a few months' residence suffices to dispel the dread which most travellers feel at the outset.

February, 1874. --No further incident occurred worthy of special notice. At last the coast town of Bagamoio came in sight, and before many hours were over, one of Her Majesty's cruisers conveyed the Acting Consul, Captain Prideaux, from Zanzibar to the spot which the cortege had reached. Arrangements were quickly made for transporting the remains of Dr. Livingstone to the Island some thirty miles distant, and then it became perhaps rather too painfully plain to the men that their task was finished.

One word on a subject which will commend itself to most before we close this long eventful history.

We saw what a train of Indian Sepoys, Johanna men, Nassick boys, and Shupanga canoemen, accompanied Dr. Livingstone when he started from Zanzibar in 1866 to enter upon his last discoveries: of all these, five only could answer to the roll-call as they handed over the dead body of their leader to his countrymen on the shore whither they had returned, and this after eight years' desperate service.

Once more we repeat the names of these men. Susi and James Chuma have been sufficiently prominent throughout--hardly so perhaps has Amoda, their comrade ever since the Zambesi days of 1864: then we have Abram and Mabruki, each with service to show from the time he left the Nassiok College with the Doctor in 1865. Nor must we forget Ntoaeka and Halima, the two native girls of whom we have heard such a good character: they cast in their lot with the wanderers in Manyuema. It does seem strange to hear the men say that no sooner did they arrive at their journey's end than they were so far frowned out of notice, that not so much as a passage to the Island was offered them when their burden was borne away. We must hope that it is not too late--even for the sake of consistency--to put it on record that ***whoever*** assisted Livingstone, whether white or black, has not been overlooked in England. Surely those with whom he spent his last years must not pass away into Africa again unrewarded, and lost to sight.

Yes, a very great deal is owing to these five men, and we say it emphatically. If the nation has gratified a reasonable wish in learning all that concerns the last days on earth of a truly noble countryman and his wonderful enterprise, the means of doing so could never have been placed at our disposal but for the ready willingness which made Susi and Chuma determine, if possible, to render an account to some of those whom they had known as their master's old companions. If the Geographer finds before him new facts, new discoveries, new theories, as Livingstone alone could record them, it is right and proper that he should feel the part these men have played in furnishing him with such valuable matter. For we repeat that nothing but such leadership and staunchness as that which organized the march home from Ilala, and distinguished it throughout, could have brought Livingstone's bones to our land or his last notes and maps to the outer world. To none does the feat seem so marvellous as to those who know Africa and the difficulties which must have beset both the first and the last in the enterprise. Thus in his death, not less than in his life, David Livingstone bore testimony to that goodwill and kindliness which exists in the heart of the African.

THE END.

www.bookjungle.com email: sales@bookjungle.com fax: 630-214-0564 mail: Book Jungle PO Box 2226 Champaign, IL 61825

The Codes Of Hammurabi And Moses
W. W. Davies

QTY

The discovery of the Hammurabi Code is one of the greatest achievements of archaeology, and is of paramount interest, not only to the student of the Bible, but also to all those interested in ancient history...

Religion **ISBN:** *1-59462-338-4* **Pages:** 132 *MSRP $12.95*

The Theory of Moral Sentiments
Adam Smith

QTY

This work from 1749. contains original theories of conscience amd moral judgment and it is the foundation for systemof morals.

Philosophy **ISBN:** *1-59462-777-0* **Pages:** 536 *MSRP $19.95*

Jessica's First Prayer
Hesba Stretton

QTY

In a screened and secluded corner of one of the many railway-bridges which span the streets of London there could be seen a few years ago, from five o'clock every morning until half past eight, a tidily set-out coffee-stall, consisting of a trestle and board, upon which stood two large tin cans, with a small fire of charcoal burning under each so as to keep the coffee boiling during the early hours of the morning when the work-people were thronging into the city on their way to their daily toil...

Childrens **ISBN:** *1-59462-373-2* **Pages:** 84 *MSRP $9.95*

My Life and Work
Henry Ford

QTY

Henry Ford revolutionized the world with his implementation of mass production for the Model T automobile. Gain valuable business insight into his life and work with his own auto-biography... "We have only started on our development of our country we have not as yet, with all our talk of wonderful progress, done more than scratch the surface. The progress has been wonderful enough but..."

Biographies/ **ISBN:** *1-59462-198-5* **Pages:** 300 *MSRP $21.95* www.bookjungle.com *email: sales@bookjungle.com fax: 630-214-0564 mail: Book Jungle PO Box 2226 Champaign, IL 61825*

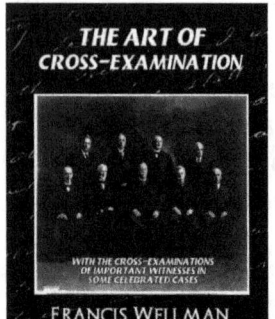

The Art of Cross-Examination
Francis Wellman

QTY

I presume it is the experience of every author, after his first book is published upon an important subject, to be almost overwhelmed with a wealth of ideas and illustrations which could readily have been included in his book, and which to his own mind, at least, seem to make a second edition inevitable. Such certainly was the case with me; and when the first edition had reached its sixth impression in five months, I rejoiced to learn that it seemed to my publishers that the book had met with a sufficiently favorable reception to justify a second and considerably enlarged edition. ..

Reference   ISBN: *1-59462-647-2*   Pages:412 MSRP *$19.95*

On the Duty of Civil Disobedience
Henry David Thoreau

QTY

Thoreau wrote his famous essay, On the Duty of Civil Disobedience, as a protest against an unjust but popular war and the immoral but popular institution of slave-owning. He did more than write—he declined to pay his taxes, and was hauled off to gaol in consequence. Who can say how much this refusal of his hastened the end of the war and of slavery ?

Law   ISBN: *1-59462-747-9*   Pages:48 MSRP *$7.45*

Dream Psychology Psychoanalysis for Beginners
Sigmund Freud

QTY

Sigmund Freud, born Sigismund Schlomo Freud (May 6, 1856 - September 23, 1939), was a Jewish-Austrian neurologist and psychiatrist who co-founded the psychoanalytic school of psychology. Freud is best known for his theories of the unconscious mind, especially involving the mechanism of repression; his redefinition of sexual desire as mobile and directed towards a wide variety of objects; and his therapeutic techniques, especially his understanding of transference in the therapeutic relationship and the presumed value of dreams as sources of insight into unconscious desires.

Psychology   ISBN: *1-59462-905-6*   Pages:196 MSRP *$15.45*

The Miracle of Right Thought
Orison Swett Marden

QTY

Believe with all of your heart that you will do what you were made to do. When the mind has once formed the habit of holding cheerful, happy, prosperous pictures, it will not be easy to form the opposite habit. It does not matter how improbable or how far away this realization may see, or how dark the prospects may be, if we visualize them as best we can, as vividly as possible, hold tenaciously to them and vigorously struggle to attain them, they will gradually become actualized, realized in the life. But a desire, a longing without endeavor, a yearning abandoned or held indifferently will vanish without realization.

Self Help   ISBN: *1-59462-644-8*   Pages:360 MSRP *$25.45*

www.bookjungle.com email: sales@bookjungle.com fax: 630-214-0564 mail: Book Jungle PO Box 2226 Champaign, IL 61825

QTY

☐ **The Rosicrucian Cosmo-Conception Mystic Christianity** *by* **Max Heindel**   ISBN: *1-59462-188-8*   **$38.95**
The Rosicrucian Cosmo-conception is not dogmatic, neither does it appeal to any other authority than the reason of the student. It is: not controversial, but is: sent forth in the, hope that it may help to clear...   *New Age/Religion Pages 646*

☐ **Abandonment To Divine Providence** *by* **Jean-Pierre de Caussade**   ISBN: *1-59462-228-0*   **$25.95**
"The Rev. Jean Pierre de Caussade was one of the most remarkable spiritual writers of the Society of Jesus in France in the 18th Century. His death took place at Toulouse in 1751. His works have gone through many editions and have been republished...   *Inspirational/Religion Pages 400*

☐ **Mental Chemistry** *by* **Charles Haanel**   ISBN: *1-59462-192-6*   **$23.95**
Mental Chemistry allows the change of material conditions by combining and appropriately utilizing the power of the mind. Much like applied chemistry creates something new and unique out of careful combinations of chemicals the mastery of mental chemistry...   *New Age Pages 354*

☐ **The Letters of Robert Browning and Elizabeth Barret Barrett 1845-1846 vol II**   ISBN: *1-59462-193-4*   **$35.95**
by **Robert Browning** and **Elizabeth Barrett**   *Biographies Pages 596*

☐ **Gleanings In Genesis (volume I)** *by* **Arthur W. Pink**   ISBN: *1-59462-130-6*   **$27.45**
Appropriately has Genesis been termed "the seed plot of the Bible" for in it we have, in germ form, almost all of the great doctrines which are afterwards fully developed in the books of Scripture which follow...   *Religion/Inspirational Pages 420*

☐ **The Master Key** *by* **L. W. de Laurence**   ISBN: *1-59462-001-6*   **$30.95**
In no branch of human knowledge has there been a more lively increase of the spirit of research during the past few years than in the study of Psychology, Concentration and Mental Discipline. The requests for authentic lessons in Thought Control, Mental Discipline and...   *New Age/Business Pages 422*

☐ **The Lesser Key Of Solomon Goetia** *by* **L. W. de Laurence**   ISBN: *1-59462-092-X*   **$9.95**
This translation of the first book of the "Lernegton" which is now for the first time made accessible to students of Talismanic Magic was done, after careful collation and edition, from numerous Ancient Manuscripts in Hebrew, Latin, and French...   *New Age/Occult Pages 92*

☐ **Rubaiyat Of Omar Khayyam** *by* **Edward Fitzgerald**   ISBN:*1-59462-332-5*   **$13.95**
Edward Fitzgerald, whom the world has already learned, in spite of his own efforts to remain within the shadow of anonymity, to look upon as one of the rarest poets of the century, was born at Bredfield, in Suffolk, on the 31st of March, 1809. He was the third son of John Purcell...   *Music Pages 172*

☐ **Ancient Law** *by* **Henry Maine**   ISBN: *1-59462-128-4*   **$29.95**
The chief object of the following pages is to indicate some of the earliest ideas of mankind, as they are reflected in Ancient Law, and to point out the relation of those ideas to modern thought.   *Religiom/History Pages 452*

☐ **Far-Away Stories** *by* **William J. Locke**   ISBN: *1-59462-129-2*   **$19.45**
"Good wine needs no bush, but a collection of mixed vintages does. And this book is just such a collection. Some of the stories I do not want to remain buried for ever in the museum files of dead magazine-numbers an author's not unpardonable vanity..."   *Fiction Pages 272*

☐ **Life of David Crockett** *by* **David Crockett**   ISBN: *1-59462-250-7*   **$27.45**
"Colonel David Crockett was one of the most remarkable men of the times in which he lived. Born in humble life, but gifted with a strong will, an indomitable courage, and unremitting perseverance...   *Biographies/New Age Pages 424*

☐ **Lip-Reading** *by* **Edward Nitchie**   ISBN: *1-59462-206-X*   **$25.95**
Edward B. Nitchie, founder of the New York School for the Hard of Hearing, now the Nitchie School of Lip-Reading, Inc, wrote "LIP-READING Principles and Practice". The development and perfecting of this meritorious work on lip-reading was an undertaking...   *How-to Pages 400*

☐ **A Handbook of Suggestive Therapeutics, Applied Hypnotism, Psychic Science**   ISBN: *1-59462-214-0*   **$24.95**
by **Henry Munro**   *Health/New Age/Health/Self-help Pages 376*

☐ **A Doll's House: and Two Other Plays** *by* **Henrik Ibsen**   ISBN: *1-59462-112-8*   **$19.95**
Henrik Ibsen created this classic when in revolutionary 1848 Rome. Introducing some striking concepts in playwriting for the realist genre, this play has been studied the world over.   *Fiction/Classics/Plays 308*

☐ **The Light of Asia** *by* **sir Edwin Arnold**   ISBN: *1-59462-204-3*   **$13.95**
In this poetic masterpiece, Edwin Arnold describes the life and teachings of Buddha. The man who was to become known as Buddha to the world was born as Prince Gautama of India but he rejected the worldly riches and abandoned the reigns of power when...   *Religion/History/Biographies Pages 170*

☐ **The Complete Works of Guy de Maupassant** *by* **Guy de Maupassant**   ISBN: *1-59462-157-8*   **$16.95**
"For days and days, nights and nights, I had dreamed of that first kiss which was to consecrate our engagement, and I knew not on what spot I should put my lips..."   *Fiction/Classics Pages 240*

☐ **The Art of Cross-Examination** *by* **Francis L. Wellman**   ISBN: *1-59462-309-0*   **$26.95**
Written by a renowned trial lawyer, Wellman imparts his experience and uses case studies to explain how to use psychology to extract desired information through questioning.   *How-to/Science/Reference Pages 408*

☐ **Answered or Unanswered?** *by* **Louisa Vaughan**   ISBN: *1-59462-248-5*   **$10.95**
Miracles of Faith in China   *Religion Pages 112*

☐ **The Edinburgh Lectures on Mental Science (1909)** *by* **Thomas**   ISBN: *1-59462-008-3*   **$11.95**
This book contains the substance of a course of lectures recently given by the writer in the Queen Street Hall, Edinburgh. Its purpose is to indicate the Natural Principles governing the relation between Mental Action and Material Conditions...   *New Age/Psychology Pages 148*

☐ **Ayesha** *by* **H. Rider Haggard**   ISBN: *1-59462-301-5*   **$24.95**
Verily and indeed it is the unexpected that happens! Probably if there was one person upon the earth from whom the Editor of this, and of a certain previous history, did not expect to hear again...   *Classics Pages 380*

☐ **Ayala's Angel** *by* **Anthony Trollope**   ISBN: *1-59462-352-X*   **$29.95**
The two girls were both pretty, but Lucy who was twenty-one who supposed to be simple and comparatively unattractive, whereas Ayala was credited, as her Bombwhat romantic name might show, with poetic charm and a taste for romance. Ayala when her father died was nineteen...   *Fiction Pages 484*

☐ **The American Commonwealth** *by* **James Bryce**   ISBN: *1-59462-286-8*   **$34.45**
An interpretation of American democratic political theory. It examines political mechanics and society from the perspective of Scotsman James Bryce   *Politics Pages 572*

☐ **Stories of the Pilgrims** *by* **Margaret P. Pumphrey**   ISBN: *1-59462-116-0*   **$17.95**
This book explores pilgrims religious oppression in England as well as their escape to Holland and eventual crossing to America on the Mayflower, and their early days in New England...   *History Pages 268*

www.bookjungle.com email: sales@bookjungle.com fax: 630-214-0564 mail: Book Jungle PO Box 2226 Champaign, IL 61825

Title	ISBN	Price	QTY
The Fasting Cure by *Sinclair Upton* — In the Cosmopolitan Magazine for May, 1910, and in the Contemporary Review (London) for April, 1910, I published an article dealing with my experiences in fasting. I have written a great many magazine articles, but never one which attracted so much attention... *New Age/Self Help/Health Pages 164*	1-59462-222-1	$13.95	
Hebrew Astrology by *Sepharial* — In these days of advanced thinking it is a matter of common observation that we have left many of the old landmarks behind and that we are now pressing forward to greater heights and to a wider horizon than that which represented the mind-content of our progenitors... *Astrology Pages 144*	1-59462-308-2	$13.45	
Thought Vibration or The Law of Attraction in the Thought World by *William Walker Atkinson* — *Psychology/Religion Pages 144*	1-59462-127-6	$12.95	
Optimism by *Helen Keller* — Helen Keller was blind, deaf, and mute since 19 months old, yet famously learned how to overcome these handicaps, communicate with the world, and spread her lectures promoting optimism. An inspiring read for everyone... *Biographies/Inspirational Pages 84*	1-59462-108-X	$15.95	
Sara Crewe by *Frances Burnett* — In the first place, Miss Minchin lived in London. Her home was a large, dull, tall one, in a large, dull square, where all the houses were alike, and all the sparrows were alike, and where all the door-knockers made the same heavy sound... *Childrens/Classic Pages 88*	1-59462-360-0	$9.45	
The Autobiography of Benjamin Franklin by *Benjamin Franklin* — The Autobiography of Benjamin Franklin has probably been more extensively read than any other American historical work, and no other book of its kind has had such ups and downs of fortune. Franklin lived for many years in England, where he was agent... *Biographies/History Pages 332*	1-59462-135-7	$24.95	

Name	
Email	
Telephone	
Address	
City, State ZIP	

☐ Credit Card   ☐ Check / Money Order

Credit Card Number	
Expiration Date	
Signature	

Please Mail to: Book Jungle
PO Box 2226
Champaign, IL 61825
or Fax to: 630-214-0564

ORDERING INFORMATION

web: *www.bookjungle.com*
email: *sales@bookjungle.com*
fax: *630-214-0564*
mail: *Book Jungle PO Box 2226 Champaign, IL 61825*
or PayPal *to sales@bookjungle.com*

Please contact us for bulk discounts

DIRECT-ORDER TERMS

20% Discount if You Order Two or More Books
Free Domestic Shipping!
Accepted: Master Card, Visa, Discover, American Express

www.ingramcontent.com/pod-product-compliance
Lightning Source LLC
Chambersburg PA
CBHW081218170426
43198CB00017B/2646